STRANGE VIRTUES

Ethics in a Multicultural World

BERNARD T. ADENEY

InterVarsity Press
Downers Grove, Illinois

InterVarsity Press® is the book-publishing division of InterVarsity Christian Fellowship®, a student movement active on campus at hundreds of universities, colleges and schools of nursing in the United States of America, and a member movement of the International Fellowship of Evangelical Students. For information about local and regional activities, write Public Relations Dept., InterVarsity Christian Fellowship, 6400 Schroeder Rd., P.O. Box 7895, Madison, WI 53707-7895.

Scripture quotations, unless otherwise noted, are from the New Revised Standard Version of the Bible, copyright 1989 by the Division of Christian Education of the National Council of the Churches of Christ in the U.S.A., and are used by permission.

ISBN 0-8308-1855-3

Printed in the United States of America ∞

Library of Congress Cataloging-in-Publication Data

Adeney, Bernard T., 1948-
    Strange virtues: ethics in a multicultural world/Bernard T.
Adeney.
      p.   cm.
    Includes bibliographical references.
    ISBN 0-8308-1855-3
    1. Christianity and culture.   2. Ethics, Comparative.
    3. Christian ethics.   I. Title.
    BR115.C8A33   1995
    241—dc20   95-6430
                                            CIP

18	17	16	15	14	13	12	11	10	9	8	7	6	5	4	3	2	1
10	09	08	07	06	05	04	03	02	01	00	99	98	97	96	95		

For
David Howard Adeney
1911-1994
tricultural teacher and father

Preface

This book does not spring from abstract academic interests. Personal experience lies behind all the issues explored in it. In fact, all my life I have grappled with issues in crosscultural ethics. My father, David H. Adeney, came from an upper-middle-class, academic English family. My mother, Ruth W. Adeney, was born to a Minnesota farming family who lost their land in the Great Depression. This unlikely couple met and married in China, where they were both missionaries. I was born in Shanghai, China, the youngest of four children.

The formation of my identity included struggles with what it means to be part of an American-English-Chinese family. As a teenager I began thinking about how culture, race and social class affect a person's values and identity. My rather rocky path to Christian faith was dominated by questions of how authentic faith could be lived in practice. Beginning in China, I grew up in England, Illinois, Hong Kong, Indiana and Taiwan. Family travels included summers in Africa, India, Europe, Japan and the Philippines.

As an undergraduate I studied East Asian philosophy, history and politics at the University of Wisconsin. In the late sixties I struggled with how Christian beliefs relate to social realities. Like many of my contemporaries, I was deeply concerned about war, racism and materialism. After a year of independent studies in France, Switzerland and Greece, my wife Frances and I moved to Singapore to study Christian theology with an Asian community. There we began to see Christian faith and the history of the Western Church through Asian eyes. While adopting our second daughter in Indonesia, we were confronted as never before with the extent of our own affluence in relation to extreme poverty.

We returned to London, where I finished a degree in Christian theology with specializations in Asian religions and ethics. From 1974 to 1991 we lived in Berkeley, California, not a bad place from which to view the world if you have three small children and can't go traveling. In Berkeley we worked with a coalition of ministries that tried to bridge the gap between the church and the counterculture, while in our marriage I was learning to see the world through the eyes of the opposite sex. After doctoral studies in ethics and international relations, I taught at New College Berkeley (NCB) and the Graduate Theological Union. At NCB I also directed the Cross-Cultural Ministries Program. Thanks to the encouragement of Bill and Grace Dyrness and David Gill, I began a serious study of crosscultural ethics. My first course in crosscultural ethics was at NCB in the summer of 1988.

During 1989-1990 NCB graciously gave me a sabbatical for research and writing on crosscultural ethics, and Frances received leave from her position as assistant professor of religion and society. This made possible a life-changing journey for our whole family to gather material for this book. For the first six months we traveled in Japan, Hong Kong, the Philippines, Indonesia, Singapore, Malaysia, Thailand, Pakistan, Egypt, Israel, Turkey, Germany and Holland. During this time I was able to interview Christian leaders from many countries who had extensive personal experience with crosscultural value conflicts. Unfortunately, there are too many to thank by name. Their stories are woven throughout the book, but usually under pseudonyms. After all the travel we were thankful to spend five months at St. Edmund's College, Cambridge University, for library research and writing.

Studying crosscultural ethics is rather dangerous. In our case it led to our resigning from New College Berkeley, which had nurtured us for so long, and accepting an invitation to help begin a graduate program in religion and society in Indonesia. NCB graciously appointed us "professors at large," and the Presbyterian Church (U.S.A.) provided sponsorship to send us on our way. Living and teaching in Central Java at Satya Wacana Christian University since 1991 has lent realism and vividness to all my thinking on crosscultural ethics. I am thankful to John Titalay, the director of the program, for his persistence in inviting us and steady encouragement ever since. Bung John, Bung Th. Sumartana and Bung Soegeng Hardiyanto, as well as our students here, have been our most gracious and rigorous teachers in the arts of crosscultural understanding.

You might hope that international experience would free you from the constricting boundaries of a specific cultural heritage. In part it does. Nevertheless, this book is definitely written from a North American, white, male, middle-class, Protestant, heterosexual and overeducated perspective. Everything I write is colored by these fundamental facts. I have often wished I could see the world through some other set of eyes and experiences. No doubt that is partly why I wrote this book—as an attempt to understand why people with different cultural backgrounds see good and evil differently. More precisely, it is an attempt to examine the ethical problems Christians face when there is a cultural clash of values.

Melba Maggay, a gifted writer from the Philippines, once said, "The problem with Westerners is that they think they know more than everyone else, whereas really they know much less. Asians know far more about Western culture and experience than Westerners know about Asia." Too true. Educated North Americans, in particular, are among the most insular of peoples. If you are reading this book, perhaps you are one of the increasing number who want to know more.

With her typical love for paradox, Melba on another occasion said, "The problem with Western-educated people is that we know too much. We have information overload." Her point was that we intellectually know far more than we can assimilate. We know so many different things that we cannot even see the truth, let alone live by it. The purpose of study is not to build up a bank account of knowledge but to gain wisdom and virtue in living. Or, to paraphrase Marx's well-known dictum, the purpose is not to understand the world but to change it. This book is a modest attempt to add to your information overload in the hope that it will not do you too much damage, but will contribute to the richness that comes when you cross over the boundary into the unknown.

Many people have read parts or all of this manuscript at different stages. Most have provided helpful comments and suggestions that I sometimes followed. If I had been able to follow up all the interesting lines of research suggested to me, this would be a better (and longer) book. I have received substantive suggestions from David Adeney, Frances Adeney, Jen Marion Adeney, William Dyrness, Grace Dyrness, Anthony Gittins and Soegeng Hardiyanto. My editor, Rodney Clapp, not only found many ways to make my ideas clearer but also contributed to the strength of my argument.

The debt of gratitude I owe my family cannot be adequately expressed in a preface. They are in a different category from mundane experience. Yet they impinge on everything that is mundane. Without them nothing would look the same. My father and mother, David and Ruth Adeney, gave me the world with my milk. They taught me to love it. Their deep faith and commitment to lifelong service of God in the real world are a continuing example to me. Joseph and Elsie Screnock gave me their daughter and made me their son. With them, I like being an American.

Our daughter Jennifer Marion reminds me to be ashamed of being a white Anglo male. With her around I feel hope for the future. Rina, our American-Indonesian daughter, has shown me what a beautiful creation can come out of the marriage of Javanese ethnicity and California culture. Rina's unique construction of her own identity makes me happy. Peter, our youngest, teaches me to laugh in the midst of struggle. His fluency in Indonesian and zest for all the experiences of life inspire me.

My closest colleague, friend and wife during the years of writing was Frances Screnock Adeney. Many of the following chapters are better because of her criticisms and encouragement. The structure of my thinking about ethics, theology and culture is indebted to her far more than I know.

This book is dedicated to David H. Adeney. Many people knew him as an inspiring preacher. Others knew him as a China expert, a missionary statesman or a leader of Christian student movements. Many Chinese knew him as a lover of China whose personality was molded by deep identification with the cultures of China, America and Britain. Some people knew him as a man of God or even thought of him as a saint. His biography refers to him as "an ordinary man with an extraordinary vision."[1] Not long ago he said to me with a laugh, "But you know better than all that." He meant that I knew his weaknesses. Perhaps. I knew him as a profoundly good man and a gifted human being. Most of all I knew him as a father. For that I am grateful.

ONE

INTRODUCTION
TO CROSSCULTURAL
ETHICS

One day during a class on crosscultural ethics in Berkeley, California, one of my students excused himself at the break to make a call to Haiti. He was facing a crisis that required an immediate decision. In the hour following the break he shared his story with the class. "James" is a fundraiser for a Christian development organization that provides financial and other resources to indigenous Christian organizations in Two-Thirds World countries.

James had organized a team of physicians, nurses and other health-care professionals to visit Haiti for several weeks and set up rural clinics. The health needs of the poverty-stricken people were extreme, and the clinics were expected to offer help that in some cases would be life-saving. The team was made up of Christians who had donated their time and expenses. Arrangements for the clinics had been made by local Haitian churches. Airline tickets for the team of twenty-five people had been purchased at a cost of thousands of dollars. They were discounted tickets and could not be refunded or changed. Thousands of dollars' worth of medical supplies had been shipped to Haiti months beforehand. The team was due to fly to Haiti that weekend.

The problem was that the medical supplies had been sitting on the dock in customs for weeks. The main Haitian organizer, a pastor, said customs officials were waiting for a bribe. Appeals had been made to higher officials, but to no avail. Time was running out. Because the stakes were so high, the pastor urged James to authorize a substantial payment immediately. Without the supplies the clinics could not be set up. So much work and so much potential good hung in the balance.

But if James authorized the bribe, how could he live with his conscience? Wouldn't his participation in corruption undermine the credibility of his organization and contradict the integrity of the Gospel? What kind of person would give, or not give, an extralegal gift to customs officials?

Others could advise him, but James had to decide within the next few hours. What should he do?

Value Clashes

How do we respond to situations where our values are incongruent with those of another culture? This book explores how the meaning of what we believe is revealed in our practices—that is, in our life. Who we are is shown by what we do. This is a book of stories, stories of real people in real situations of moral conflict, like James and the customs officials in Haiti. Stories reveal the heart of the value conflicts people face as they become submerged in another culture. When ethical dilemmas are cast in the form of stories, they are more difficult to tease out than if they are posed in abstract terms. If we ask, "Should Christians give bribes?" we may find it easier to say no than if we tell the story of James. Stories get closer to reality. Goodness and evil are real, not abstract. Abstractions lack the countless details that shape people and give form to their moral decisions.

Our cultural practices are not just personal or subjective; they are socially constituted. As Charles Taylor puts it, they are "intersubjective."[1] In other words, we never act alone. The meaning of our practices is a shared meaning that is grounded in the assumptions and practices of our culture. When James decides whether or not to pay extra money to the customs official, the meaning of his act will be determined neither by his own subjectivity (how it feels) nor by an abstract principle (is it right or wrong to pay extra money to customs officials?). The meaning of his act will be construed by his communities. This does not imply that whether he pays or not should be *determined* by his communities.

Haitian and North American culture may justify or condemn his action, but ultimately God will be his judge. This book does not advocate cultural moral relativism. But James cannot know whether paying or not paying is good unless he knows what it means in his particular time and place.

James faces a crosscultural problem. He does not fully understand the assumptions and practices of Haiti. But even if he did, the virtues expected by the Haitian pastor and organizer (wisdom, compassion and generosity in giving a gift to the customs officials?) conflict with the virtues of his culture (honesty, legality, justice?). Haitian virtues appear alien and may even undermine the values of James's Christian faith.

An exquisitely beautiful work of art, such as Michelangelo's *David*, is made up of countless small details that derive their goodness from the way they contribute to the final form of the statue. Similarly, cultural practices are considered good by their practitioners because they contribute to a vision of what is good: the vision of a virtuous person in a good community.

I once attended an African-American church where I was embarrassed to hear the pastor praise his own accomplishments, and those of various members of the church, with great emotion. The black pastor would have fit into certain Middle Eastern cultures where people, especially leaders, are expected to exaggerate their own importance. By doing so they encourage their community and give them pride. In contrast, British people and many Anglo-Americans consider it virtuous to understate their accomplishments.

An American teacher in Egypt was asked by a colleague if he played Ping-Pong. The American replied, "A little." The Egyptian stated that he himself was an excellent player, and he challenged the American to a game. When they played, the American won easily over the Egyptian, creating a deep strain in their relationship. The American felt that the Egyptian was an empty braggart, while the Egyptian felt the American had lied about his ability in order to shame him. Each had different assumptions about how the truth should be stated by a virtuous person in community.

Christians believe that what is good is determined by the will of God, not by culture. The goal of ethics is not cultural conformity but transformation into the likeness of Christ. All Christians in every culture are invited to have the mind of Christ, to humble themselves and be servants to others (Phil 2).

But how the virtues are expressed and how they are prioritized may be very different in different cultures. The self-congratulating black pastor may be far more humble than the white onlooker. For an oppressed community, humility may be a lower priority than self-confidence or even pride. The will of God is incarnated in human practices that derive their meaning from the cultural communities in which they take place. To mean the same thing in different cultures, our practices may have to change.[2]

Culture Defined

The word *culture*, like the word *religion*, is very difficult to define. In one sense every different person is from a different culture. We each have our own symbol system and ways of defining the meaning of our life. In some ways my wife and I and each of our three children are culturally quite different from each other. At the other extreme, it is common to speak of "globalization" and "the global village" as if all but remote tribal peoples shared a common culture of technological, capitalistic modernity.

The Willowbank Report of the Lausanne Committee provides the following definition of culture which conflates culture with its derivative, social structure:

Culture is an integrated system of beliefs (about God, or reality, or ultimate meaning), of values (about what is true, good, beautiful and normative), of customs (how to behave, relate to others, talk, pray, dress, work, play, trade, farm, eat, etc.), and of institutions which express these beliefs, values and customs (governments, law, courts, temples or churches, family, schools, hospitals, factories, shops, unions, clubs, etc.), which bind a society together and give it a sense of identity, dignity, security, and continuity.[3]

Cultures and subcultures overlap. The world religions create commonalties among people from very different parts of the world. Value differences and peer groups divide people within the same family. Some people claim that the language of business is universal. Certainly multinational corporations create their own multinational cultures. Yet the "culture" of one multinational may be very different from that of another just down the street. The "culture" of academia sometimes appears transnational. I may have more in common with another professor, especially in a related field, than I do with a next-door neighbor.

Clifford Geertz defines culture as a symbol system of meanings: culture is that by which we understand and give meaning to our lives. Geertz says that culture "denotes an historically transmitted pattern of meanings embodied in symbols, a system of inherited conceptions expressed in symbolic forms by means of which men communicate, perpetuate, and develop their knowledge about and attitudes toward life."[4]

Differences and similarities between cultures are often difficult to define and are more readily felt by someone from outside the group. In Indonesia, Christian Bataks and Muslim Javanese consider themselves about as culturally different as any human beings can get. Yet to me both groups appear remarkably Indonesian. Similarly, a Texas Republican and a New England Democrat may feel they have nothing in common, but to an Indonesian they appear culturally similar.

In this book I will make no attempt to sort out all the different meanings of culture. As with the word *religion,* I think you know (or can feel) what I mean by *culture.* I do not limit culture to that which is exotic or far away. All major cities and most large towns have many different cultures within them. Problems of crosscultural ethics could as easily occur in your own church as they could after a long plane ride. I have no objection to the elasticity of the concept of culture. Crosscultural ethics may even help a couple understand anything from how they squeeze the toothpaste to how they make decisions.

Nevertheless, this book focuses on differences between broadly recognizable cultural groups. This book is not on comparative ethics—how different cultures compare with each other in their values. Nor is it on the ethics of multiculturalism—how (or if) people from many different cultures can build a common society. Rather, it is on how Christians should respond to strange values—patterns of meaning that are radically different from theirs.

How can Christians distinguish between symbolic structures that are particular expressions of their own culture and those that transcend specific cultural expressions? Even Christ expressed his virtue in particular, male, Jewish cultural forms. The goodness of Jesus is "historically transmitted" and culturally defined.

In this chapter's opening story James feels loath to pay the customs official because he believes that God is just and we should be just too. James identifies payment of officials with illegality, dishonesty and subversion of justice. As we shall see in chapter five, not all cultures have the same symbol structure in relation to bribery.

Crosscultural ethics is not simply a question of distinguishing relative and absolute values. Different cultures prioritize their values differently in relation to the patterns of meaning relevant to the story of their people. Different priorities may require the understanding of "absolute" values differently in different contexts. Certain practices, for example truth-telling, may be correctly interpreted in a variety of ways in different cultures. In order to know whether the American or Egyptian Ping-Pong player told the truth about his ability, we would have to know more, both about their motives and about the cultural conventions that formed their statements.

An Indonesian student from North Sulawesi expressed his frustration that when he asked a neighbor if she could introduce them to a house helper, she answered, "Yes." When asked, "When?" she answered, "Tomorrow." As is common in Java, "tomorrow" never came. Was this a case of lying or simply an accepted form of politeness in a culture in which it is considered very rude to turn down a direct request, even if you cannot fulfill it? Just as in Latin America, where the term *mañana* is often used to refer to the indefinite future, in Java the word *besok* frequently has no literal reference to its normal meaning "tomorrow." People's intent in using the word *tomorrow* is not to deceive but to be polite.

Should Christians behave differently in different cultures? When our understanding of right and wrong conflicts with common practices in another culture, what should we do about it? "Strange virtues" may seem like vices to someone from a foreign culture. This book explores these questions through the stories of Christians facing crosscultural ethical dilemmas.

Who Needs Crosscultural Ethics?

Today many Christians live in crosscultural situations. White Christians in North America and Europe have black neighbors. Blacks contend with Chinese immigrants, Chinese with South Asians. Arabs, Africans, Japanese, Indo-Chinese, Latin Americans, Western and Eastern Europeans all crowd the cities of North America and Europe. Foreign students flock to the universities from every part of the world.

Christians in Africa, Asia, Latin America and the Middle East frequently interact with people, ideas and institutions from the United States and Europe. Major cities in every part of the world are flooded with immigrants, not only from other countries but also from different ethnic groups within their own country. We remain culturally isolated only by choice.

Most people move to a strange place for economic, educational or family reasons. People move to where there are jobs, educational opportunities or family. Some move because of hardship or persecution. Today there are millions of refugees, including many Christians. The early church spread all over the Roman Empire because of persecution. Whatever their material motivations, many

Christians move to a new cultural setting with a specific desire to serve God in that place.

Many are surprised to find that the world has moved to their doorstep. Many more either are forced or consciously choose to live in the midst of another culture. Whether they are Two-Thirds World students studying in the West, businesspeople transferred by their corporation, immigrants seeking jobs in the city, missionaries called to plant churches, a young couple who find cheap housing in a different ethnic neighborhood, development workers introducing new crop strains, teachers taking a cross-town or overseas appointment, nurses working in a multiethnic state hospital, engineer consultants overseas, students on a year abroad, anthropologists studying tribal cultures, or persons from any number of other professional categories, millions of people face problems of crosscultural ethics. *When other people or societies live by different moral norms, how should we respond?*

A serious consideration of ethics today cannot afford to ignore the cultural elements that influence our perceptions of good and evil. Thus this book is written for anyone interested in Christian ethics in a multicultural world. Most of the major themes in the field of ethics are brought into sharper focus by a crosscultural approach. The book is written from the perspective of a white, male, educated Christian who interacts with people from other cultures. However, it is also intended for people of color, both within "Western" countries and in the so-called Third World. The rapid process of globalization forces members of almost every cultural group to deal with Western, white cultural values. The institutions that control money, power and information (including the church) are structured by values that are alien to most of the world.

People of color and "non-Western" Christians usually have to reinterpret books written by white authors to make sense of them in their context. Insofar as I am white and most easily imagine the problems faced by people like me, this book will surely be no exception. Nevertheless, I hope its attention to cultural issues will make the process easier. Minority and Third World Christians often have an intense interest in the issues addressed in this book, because they are constantly faced with the pressure to adapt themselves to white Western culture in order to live in the modern world or even to be considered good Christians. Their Eurocentric education taught them that Truth, Goodness, Science and Beauty are all the products of Western, white, male civilization. Globalization and Western control of information technology reinforce these assumptions. This book rejects the absolutist claim of "modern" Western culture.[5] I hope it proves a useful tool of dialogue for ethnic and Third World Christians.

Those who are trained, commissioned and supported by the church for cross-cultural ministry are often called missionaries. This book is obviously relevant to them. Christians who cross cultural boundaries, work in "secular" jobs and are committed to the gospel are sometimes called "tentmakers." Crosscultural ethics are central to their mission as well. They have the opportunity to demonstrate the reality of what they believe by how they live in a strange setting. Those who choose a context antagonistic to Christian faith face acute pressures of cross-cultural survival.[6] This book addresses the inevitable moral challenges experienced by tentmaker Christians in a foreign culture.

Most Christians do not define themselves as either missionaries or tentmakers, but are no less bewildered by the radical cultural and ethical pluralism that is a part of "postmodern" life. They must face the challenge of discovering the many ways in which their own moral norms are reflections of their education and upbringing. As Christians they must ask, "How can I distinguish between my culture and my faith as they affect my values?" This book addresses that question.

Cultural Relativity and Biblical Absolutes

Writings on culture and values usually seem to polarize between the ethical relativists and the moral absolutists. Writings from the perspective of anthropology, psychology and sociology assume at least a methodological relativism. Sometimes they affirm absolute relativism, a contradiction in terms. For example, Pierre Casse writes in a book on crosscultural orientation,

> There is no absolute truth. It is indeed up to each individual to find out what his or her truth is. . . . What is true today will be obsolete and untrue tomorrow. What is all right for one individual is not necessarily so for another. What is effective for one situation is not automatically so for any situation. In short everything is relative.[7]

In contrast, studies in crosscultural communication from the standpoint of missions often assume an ethical absolutism. Biblical values are absolute. At most they may need to be *applied* differently in different cultures.

A choice between relativism and absolutism is too extreme. As a Christian, I have no doubt that there are absolute values, but our understanding of them is always relative. "Now we see in a mirror, dimly. . . . Now I know only in part" (1 Cor 13:12). Not only the limitations of our cultural, social and economic background but also the presence of sin in our lives prevents us from an absolute understanding of right and wrong. Inadequate or wrong theology may subvert our ethics. Lack of virtue in our practices undercuts our ability to understand truth.[8]

A book on crosscultural ethics begins with the assumption that cultures give rise to value systems that can be distinguished from each other. No one culture contains a universal system of values that is universally valid. Anthropologists such as Clyde Kluckhohn have looked for universal values that occur in all cultures and have documented a great variety of rules and values that do occur in many cultures.[9] For example, laws against incest and killing within one's own group are universal. Nevertheless, the existence of culturally unique systems of values is indubitable. Kluckhohn observes,

> There is a philosophy behind the way of life of each individual and of every relatively homogeneous group. This gives . . . some sense of coherence or unity both in cognitive and affective dimensions. Each personality gives to this philosophy an idiosyncratic coloring and creative individuals will markedly reshape it. However, the basic outlines of the fundamental values, existential propositions, and basic abstractions have only exceptionally been created out of the stuff of unique biological heredity and peculiar life experience. . . . The specific formulation is ordinarily a cultural product.[10]

For those who work in a crosscultural situation, the obvious existence of cultural values that differ from their own adds to the complexity. Crosscultural experience dramatizes the fact that our own values are culturally conditioned. Nothing that we think, say or do is exempt from the influence of our culture. Nothing we believe is exempt from the influence of our race, class, age and gender. Faith does not free us from culture, because culture is the environment in which what we believe takes shape. "There is no space which is not cultural space."[11] Not only our personal practices but also our social institutions, our economic policies and our political practices reflect and influence the beliefs of our culture.

On the other hand, biblical faith has always made universal claims. Christians believe that the Creator of the universe was incarnated in a particular time and place for the sake of the whole world. Jesus, a Jewish male from Nazareth, is recognized not only as the revelation of God but as a perfect human, a person who is a model for every woman and man who comes into the world (see Jn 1).

The Bible is full of moral instruction. While some of it may be confusing, the ethical purposes of Scripture are clear. Scripture claims to be written for the purpose of "training in righteousness" (2 Tim 3:16-17). Jesus himself challenged his followers to be perfect—not perfect according to some relative cultural scale, but perfect like God (Mt 5:48). In this book I affirm both the authority of the Bible as God's Word and the cultural conditioning of all our knowledge and action.

Civilizing the World?

Christians have not always seen the connections between culture and faith as a problem. They rightly recognized that culture is also a product of faith. They believed their culture was Christian. Nineteenth-century Western missionaries explicitly understood their calling to include both the spread of the gospel and the spread of Christian civilization. Converts were asked to accept not only new doctrines but also a new lifestyle: sanitation, modern health care, literacy, hard work, monogamy, Western clothing and (for English missionaries) tea at four. As H. Richard Niebuhr observed about American missionaries,

> Christianity, democracy, Americanism, the English language and culture, the growth of industry and science, American institutions—these are all confounded and confused. The contemplation of their own righteousness filled Americans with such lofty and enthusiastic sentiments that they readily identified it with the righteousness of God. . . . The Kingdom of the Lord . . . is in particular the destiny of the Anglo-Saxon race, which is destined to bring light to the gentiles by means of lamps manufactured in America.[12]

Both the tragic and the ludicrous results of colonialism are now widely recognized, at least in theory. Unfortunately, many Westerners still sadly ignore the degree to which their own culture pervades their ideas, their lifestyle and their ethics. Most missionaries, aware of the dangers of ethnocentrism and colonialism and sensitive to the national pride of the people with whom they work, have forsworn their "civilizing" mission. Missionaries now only want to convert individuals or groups and set up indigenous churches. These churches must work out their own authentic cultural forms. Others focus on social justice or "helping" the local people in national development. Some missionaries understand their role as culturally, socially and politically neutral agents. "Modern" values such as scientific agriculture, democracy, health care and literacy are seen as somehow culturally neutral.

In fact it is precisely such modern values that may have the greatest cultural impact, for good and evil, on another culture. Modern agriculture may change the entire way of life of a people. An American missionary to Zaire expressed to me his anguish over whether his training in agricultural development was appropriate to the tribal people with whom he worked. He realized that if they changed from their slash-and-burn agriculture to a more fixed, village-based style of life, with modern methods they might increase their food production and improve their nutrition along with their preservation of the soil. On the other hand, they would lose their nomadic lifestyle and the rich culture derived from it. Similarly, modern health care might increase life expectancy but lead to the loss of a great trove of knowledge held by traditional healers.[13]

Even literacy is no longer regarded as an unambiguous good. Increasingly it is understood that the opposite of literate is not illiterate but oral. The considerable skills, amazing abilities and cultural richness of oral cultures are inevitably lost when the people become literate.[14]

No one can (or should) escape the reality of their own cultural conditioning when they enter another culture. As soon as we enter another culture we begin to have a cultural impact. Any claim to objectivity or a purely spiritual mission may display more ignorance and arrogance than the aims of the missionaries who sought to civilize as well as evangelize. Alfred C. Krass has observed,

There can be no such thing as a missionary who enters the mission process only as a catalyst. The important thing is not to be "value-free" or to pretend to "gospel objectivity," but—in fear and trembling . . . to be conscious of what our values are, to make them explicit, and to discover as best we can what the values of Scripture are.[15]

A first step in overcoming ethnocentrism is the recognition that my own values are not necessarily the same as God's. All Christians hold many values derived from their culture. A second step is to understand that our own interpretation of Scripture comes from a particular cultural context. A third step is to see that God's values may be "enfleshed" differently in another culture from how they are in my own.

Trying to Understand Alien Values

Every person who lives in a foreign culture is confronted sooner or later with actions that seem to contradict the values of her assumed world. Whether she is asked to wear a veil to protect her modesty, give a "gift" to move goods through customs or inflate the academic grades of the relatives of high officials, she is required to fit into a social structure that operates with different rules from those of her own country. Whether he is promised work that never gets done, given directions to a place that doesn't exist or given servants to wait on his every whim, he must adjust his assumptions and values to the realities of his situation.

One scientist who could not adjust to the slow pace of life in an Indonesian university was heard to remark in disgust before returning to England, "These people would be better Christians if they learned to walk faster." While his remark was trivial, it indicated a deep inability to adjust to a different scale of values regarding time, efficiency and achievement. The very values that made him a good scientist and defined his self-identity seemed to be disregarded in that context. Like many Westerners who leave the "Two-Thirds World" depressed and defeated, he could not tolerate the moral ambiguity inherent in the possibility that his "scientific" values were not universally appreciated. He could not see that perhaps he needed to learn to walk slower.

Edward T. Hall suggests that the greatest benefits of entering another culture come not from understanding the foreign culture but from understanding our own.[16] In a crosscultural situation we are often forced to see, for the first time, that our own way of living in the world is not the only way. Our glasses are not the only glasses. By seeing that there is another way of seeing, we see our own way of seeing for the first time. Hans-Georg Gadamer makes a similar point when he says, "But we cannot successfully take a prejudice into account so long as it is simply at work; it must be somehow provoked. Now this provocation of our prejudices is precisely the fruit of a renewed encounter with a tradition."[17] Crosscultural understanding comes with the shock of recognizing ourselves as others see us. An ability to adjust my own values in order to seek goodness in another cultural framework begins with understanding "what" my own values are and "why" I hold them.

There are many reasons that it is important to understand our own and others' cultural moral values. It is vital for simple communication. The values we express, consciously or unconsciously, undergird or undermine any work we wish to accomplish. Our ability to learn from another culture often rests on our ability to understand how its values differ from ours. Our own peace of mind is deeply affected by a sense of congruence between our values and those of our crosscultural associates or friends.

Beyond all pragmatic reasons, the fundamental reason for studying ethics is to become good. Unfortunately, reading this book will not make you good. But understanding crosscultural ethics can provide the tools for making sense of your experience. Crosscultural experience is a powerful means for developing the virtues that make a person good. Living in another culture throws into stark relief the meaning of what is good. When we are newly located in a culture, we cannot rely on our intimate knowledge of cultural conventions to prop up the surface appearances of goodness.

In a foreign culture we do not know how to speak, how to act or even how to feel in a way that does not bring offense. Even these surface elements can take months or even years to master. How then can we learn the deep, substantive meanings of goodness in a new cultural context?

Sheer Goodness, Wherever You Go

Goodness has two outstanding characteristics. One is that beyond all the significant differences in cultural expressions of goodness lie qualities of character or virtue that shine with clarity across cultures. The other is that all virtues and vices are made real in cultural forms. They cannot be perceived in the abstract. You do not have to live in another culture long to recognize goodness and evil in the people you meet. Our perceptions are imperfect, and a newcomer may make serious mistakes about good and evil in cultural foreigners. But some qualities of character stand out.

Most apparent are what Paul calls the fruit of the Spirit: "love, joy, peace, patience, kindness, generosity, faithfulness, gentleness, and self-control. There is no law against such things" (Gal 5:22-23). These virtues transcend culture. They are seen in people from every race, religion and cultural group. Sometimes they may be apprehended more clearly by a stranger than by a neighbor. Familiarity may mask virtue (see Lk 4:24).

Examples of kindness and sheer goodness from total strangers spring to my mind from many countries my family and I visited: the modest courage of Chinese activists in Hong Kong; the shy warmth of neighbors who came to bring us gifts in a small town in Java; the fierce pride and integrity of a woman selling us *ikat* (hand-woven) cloth in the mountains of Flores; the gentle consideration of a Pakistani fellow traveler who took off his coat to cover my sleeping son after many hours on a cold and bumpy bus.

In ethical terms, the virtues these small acts reveal point to a *deontological* (true in itself) element of goodness. They are transcultural virtues that, as a Christian, I construe as reflecting the character and will of God. All human beings bear the image of the God of Jesus Christ. Similar virtues in every culture point beyond the varieties of cultural expression to absolute moral ideals. Some qualities of character may be more accentuated in some cultures while other virtues are accentuated in other cultures. But the reality of goodness is embodied in recognizable forms in all cultures.

What Makes an Action Good?

Cultural differences in modes of communication can lead to radical misunderstandings regarding the meaning of actions that spring from virtue or vice. In one sense a particular act may be judged on the basis of its motivation. Virtuous intentions may be misunderstood by a cultural foreigner, but the basic intentions spring from motivations that may be fundamentally good or evil. Motivations give meaning to actions in a particular cultural context. If we do not understand the motivations that lie behind a word or action, we cannot understand it. As Hans-Georg Gadamer says, "A question that we do not understand as motivated can find no answer. For the motivational background of a question first opens up the realm out of which an answer can be brought and given."[18]

In ethical terms we may say the motivations are *deontologically* good or evil. That is, they may be good or evil in themselves, regardless of their cultural effect in a given situation.

In reality, however, actions cannot be judged so abstractly. Motivations are seldom entirely pure. And they are only one part of a moral context. An ethical evaluation of the part a person plays in a situation must include consideration of the outcome. The *teleological* element in ethics requires that we consider more than the motivation and intrinsic character of an action. The impact of the act, its *telos* or end in the real world, is a constitutive element in the judgment of its goodness. In different cultures, in different contexts, the same action may be considered good or evil because its intended and actual outcome may be different.

My assumption in this book is that there is goodness that lies in and behind all the cultural forms in which it is expressed. Sometimes it is helpful to call this goodness by an abstract name, like love or justice or honesty. This approach has significant precedence in the classical Western tradition. Plato saw the ideal good as larger and more perfect than any concrete manifestation of it. Our feeble attempts at virtue are like flickering shadows of a reality that exists beyond the material world. An understanding of God as the source of all goodness fits into this Platonic (and biblical) conception

Virtue Enfleshed in Cultural Practices

My approach to crosscultural ethics does not focus on theories of moral absolutes or ethical ideals. As cultural and finite beings, we can see goodness only as it is enfleshed in real times and places and peoples. Aristotle is a better guide than Plato here. Aristotle saw goodness as constituted in *practices,* virtues formed out of the habitual actions of real people. The goodness of these practices springs not from a rigid idea but from the lived-out motivations of a virtuous person, who does the right thing at the right time and in the right way.[19] Aristotle did not make the mistake of thinking that everything rests in the motivations of a virtuous person. Good motivations must issue in right practices. Aristotle also had a category of "absolutes." Of things that are absolutely wrong he says, "It is not possible then, ever to be right with regard to them; one must always be wrong. Nor does goodness or badness with regard to such things depend on [for example] committing adultery with the right woman, at the right time, and in the right way, but simply to do any of them is to go wrong."[20]

Nevertheless, Aristotle understood that virtuous action is normally the result of a deep understanding of what is appropriate in a specific situation together with the character to respond rightly. Crosscultural ethics forces us to acknowledge that the form of goodness often lies not in an act in itself but in the cultural meaning of the act. The chapters that follow explore ways in which cultural awareness can help a crosscultural Christian become good.

Plan of the Book

Chapter two, "Practicing Theology in Crosscultural Experience," compares several Christian approaches to ethics. On the one hand there are those who focus on the Bible as the source of absolute moral instructions or laws. Others insist that the Holy Spirit is the primary source of moral guidance for Christians. Still others point out that we do not even understand what is at stake in a crosscultural situation until we thoroughly understand the context. Therefore what is right or good must be struggled with in context.

I suggest a combination of these approaches in which biblical and theological understanding is developed through experience. No book or course can teach a person goodness. Virtue is learned by practice. It is also a gift to be received. Practice cannot be separated from thankfulness for the gift, commitment and theory. The integration of acceptance, commitment, theory and practical experience is called *praxis*.

In chapter three, "Knowledge, Friendship and Wisdom," I examine the process by which we develop crosscultural virtues. In another culture the rules of social interaction are different. Learning goodness in another culture means becoming a child. Even the simplest skills for survival are difficult. A humble spirit of openness to God and the stranger may be our most valuable asset in a foreign culture. Learning takes place through dialogue and relationship. Knowledge is relational. It is not abstract memorization of facts or rules but friendship with other people and with God that makes sense of crosscultural experience.

Praxis, knowledge and friendship become fused together in what the Bible calls wisdom. Wisdom is an elusive quality that lies at the core of virtue. Chapter three concludes with some reflections on how wisdom grows from and shapes crosscultural experience.

Chapter four, "The Bible and Culture in Ethics," examines how we learn goodness from the Bible. We consider how culture affects both what is written in the Bible and how we perceive it. The Bible tells a story about the meaning of human life in a particular place and time, in relation to God. The meaning of this story and the way it is relevant to modern life are revealed in many different ways. I discuss how we can learn from the extravagant emotions expressed by biblical authors. Scriptural commandments and laws are the most obvious source of ethical teaching in the Bible. This chapter explores how we should view the law and the role of culture in its interpretation. Many Christians assume that they may discard the law in favor of moral principles abstracted from it. I argue that principles are a useful tool for understanding the law but that the foundation of ethics is not abstract but concrete. This chapter also explores the motivation and power for good that can be learned from the Bible.

A study of the use of the Bible in crosscultural ethics is best accomplished from the perspective of the problems we bring to the text, problems such as are raised through the stories in this book. Biblical interpretation in a crosscultural situation requires that the reader grapple with at least three different cultures. There is the unfamiliar world of the ancient Near East; there is our culture, through which we understand everything; and there is our host culture. The *literal* meaning of the text to someone in the host culture may be different from what it meant to the original author and from what it means to us through Western cultural glasses. The chapter suggests ways to bridge the gap between the text and our context today.

Chapter five, "Cultural Value Orientations in Contrast," provides a brief survey of crosscultural studies in relation to ethics. A rapidly growing body of literature explores the problems faced by people who enter a foreign culture. This provides a rich, untapped resource for the study of ethics. An act that carries a certain meaning in one culture may carry very different meanings in another culture.

In this chapter a case study about conflict between a Western professor and the administration of an Asian university shows the difficulties that can ensue when different cultural value orientations come into conflict. Universal moral principles seem to have limited value. In contrast, an understanding of the different ways cultures prioritize their values can yield deep insights into the crosscultural meanings of goodness.

Chapter six, "Strange Communications," considers verbal and nonverbal communication as critical to crosscultural relationships. According to Edward Hall, "culture in its entirety is a form of communication."[21] The ways we communicate our intentions, or the meaning of our relationships, vary widely from culture to culture. Our language affects what we consider real or important. Difficulty in communication makes us strangers.

When we enter another culture, whether across town or across the ocean, we enter as strangers. Even if we are racially the same as the people, culturally we are strangers. In our family, our adopted Indonesian daughter is just as much a stranger to Indonesia as the rest of us. Having first left Indonesia when she was four months old, she was raised as an American. Even after many years of living in another culture, we remain strangers. Chapter six examines dangers and riches that lie hidden in strangeness.

The giving and receiving of gifts is a complex form of communication. Chapter seven, "Ethical Theory and Bribery," examines how ethical theory can help address a pervasive problem. In interviews I conducted, the most common "crosscultural ethical problem" raised by Western Christians who live in the Third World was bribery. The case at the beginning of this chapter illustrates an unfortunately common dilemma, both for Westerners and for millions of permanent residents in the "Third World."

Chapter seven begins with story of an American who is asked by the police to pay money without a receipt. The chapter discusses different responses to this story from various parts of the world and explores how they might be categorized by ethical theory. Equally sincere Christians from different countries seem to interpret this story very differently. Are their differences rooted in their theology, culture, ethical commitment or social structure? This chapter explores the confusing territory between absolutism and relativism in relation to the experience of bribery. Resources for understanding include the Bible, ethical theory, social structural analysis and experience.

The structures that give shape to the ways men and women relate to each other are often grounded in religion. Chapter eight, "The Ethical Challenge of Other Religions," explores how non-Christian moral excellence, when contrasted with various evils associated with Christianity, threatens confidence in the unique truth of Christianity. Some Christians portray non-Christian religions as implacable enemies of Christian faith, systems spawned by demonic powers to blind people's eyes and enslave them in darkness. Other Christians see non-Christians as brothers and sisters under the skin, with ethical and spiritual practices that equal or excel our own. In a sense both views are true.

Chapter eight discusses how Christians should respond practically to the positive and negative moral challenges posed by other religions. By viewing Christian faith not only as an alternate worldview but also as a competing social project, this chapter tries to transcend the theological typology of "pluralist," "inclusivist" and "exclusivist." In place of these mutually exclusive perspectives on other religions I propose a dialectical approach informed by dialogue, humility and conviction.

Chapter nine, "Women and Men as Strangers: Gender Conflict Across Cultures," probes the volatile area of sexual relations from a crosscultural perspective. Nowhere is the clash of cultural values more vivid than where differing views of the role of women come into conflict. Sexual harassment is universal, but in a foreign culture women are especially vulnerable to stereotyping and oppression stemming from crosscultural misunderstanding. The chapter examines the ethical problems faced by women and men who enter a culture with alien conceptions of sexual behavior.

While suggesting ways to break common stereotypes, the chapter also recognizes the deep, complex structures of human relationship that govern gender relations in different cultures. The formal rule of men over women is almost universal and gives rise to appalling conditions of oppression. On the other hand, swift judgments by cultural strangers are risky. In some situations women in blatantly patriarchal societies may have more power, authority and wealth than their more "liberated" Western sisters.

Nevertheless, this chapter argues that the oppression of women is a worldwide, multicultural phenomenon. Women and men who enter the mine fields of crosscultural gender relations not only face knotty moral dilemmas but also have the opportunity to participate in an international struggle for gender justice and peace.

Chapter ten, "The Unity of Personal and Social Ethics," concludes this book with the question of how a Christian's personal life in a foreign culture has inevitable social repercussions. The personal decisions Christians make about how they will live and what they will do about the evil and suffering they see around them has a profound effect on how they (and the gospel) are perceived by the local people. It can also affect the political and social structures around them, the lives of individuals, the effectiveness of the church and even the future of an ethnic group or a country.

The chapter proceeds by means of a story about two Americans living in Africa who, against their will, become involved in a dangerous struggle to stop the secret police from torturing people. The story of this couple is treated as a model that uncovers many elements of personal moral integrity which undergird effective social action in a crosscultural situation.

The presence of strangers in a community is already a political act. Where they live, how they live, how much they know about what is going on, with whom they identify, how they respond to the evils and suffering that others take for granted, their relation to the power structures that exist and a host of other factors can change the sociopolitical realities of their new community.

Unfortunately, Christian strangers in an unfamiliar culture do not always bring peace, justice and hope. Sometimes they bring to their hosts feelings of confusion, fear and inferiority. Sometimes Christians are the forerunners of objective oppression. Sometimes strangers are unwelcome. All too often Christians return home alienated and bitter. Robert Kohls suggests to Americans, "If left to luck, your chances of having a satisfying experience living abroad would be about one in seven."[22] Fortunately, crosscultural experience need not be left to luck. Moral sensitivity to the social impact we make as strangers can change the way we are received.

This book cannot guarantee positive crosscultural relations. Monocultural relations are hard enough. The number and variety of ethical problems faced by a sojourner in another culture are limitless. Fortunately, the grace of God is also without boundaries. The pages that follow are only a sketchy map to a wild and dangerous territory. As E. M. Forster put it, "I really don't know what happens next—one so seldom does."[23]

Crosscultural experience is a great adventure and well worth the risks. It forces us to rethink and refeel how we know what is good and what is evil. That is the topic of this book.

TWO

PRACTICING THEOLOGY IN CROSSCULTURAL EXPERIENCE

Three popular views of Christian ethics contribute to the approach taken in this book. The first suggests that morality comes from obedience to rules and principles, particularly those found in the Bible. The second suggests that goodness should be seen as primarily the work of the Holy Spirit in a believer's life. Third, some Christians believe crosscultural ethics can be worked out only in experience. If Christians are to achieve their goals, they must discover firsthand what works in another culture.

Each of these approaches has some truth to it; each is inadequate by itself. I will suggest a fourth approach that combines the three in a single narrative that seeks to unite the "theory" of knowing God with the practice of life in a particular culture.

Ethics as Law

Christians in the first category sometimes emphasize Bible study as the only basis for learning ethics.[1] Morality is propositional and absolute. Christians must learn God's rules, which do not change. Applications may change in different contexts, but truth is unified and immutable. The most significant problem for ethics is biblical interpretation. Plato believed that true knowledge was the key to goodness. An oversimplified extension of Plato's search for virtue in knowledge suggests that if we only know the right rules and principles we will be good. Some evangelical and fundamentalist scholars continue this approach in a legalistic biblical direction.[2]

Ethics as knowledge of rules and principles rightly recognizes that truth and goodness are not subjective constructs. Goodness is not a human possession or a personal creation. God has spoken. God's people are called to obey. Christians from this position take Scripture very seriously and often have high moral standards. There can be something clean and healthy about a humble approach to Scripture as God's propositional revelation of the meaning of goodness. There is less room for compromise and rationalization of our own weakness. Furthermore, the Bible is filled with moral wisdom. When this wisdom takes the form of law, it should be accepted as a great gift. Moral rules and principles, understood in context, provide a broad, undergirding framework for understanding the boundaries of goodness in the real world. As the psalmist wrote,

The law of the LORD is perfect,
　reviving the soul;
the decrees of the LORD are sure,
　making wise the simple;
the precepts of the LORD are right,
　rejoicing the heart;
the commandment of the LORD is clear,
　enlightening the eyes;
the fear of the LORD is pure,
　enduring forever;
the ordinances of the LORD are true
　and righteous altogether.
More to be desired are they than gold,
　even much fine gold;
sweeter also than honey,
　and drippings of the honeycomb. (Ps 19:7-10)

On the other hand, biblical law is only a small part of the total moral teaching of the Bible. Rules and principles designate what is right or wrong in the context to which they are addressed. When our context is similar, obedience to biblical law is the way of wisdom and life. But often our context and questions are different. Law may designate helpful boundaries, but the deeper meaning of goodness in a complex world lies beyond the reach of rules. The history of salvation, centered in the life, death and resurrection of Jesus, provides a much richer account of goodness than a list of rules and principles.

Ethics that focus on legalism ignore the interpretive, contextual nature of all knowledge. Humans are assumed to have a godlike capacity to understand the mind of God for all times, places and peoples. Morality is thought to be encapsulated in propositions. A lack of self-critical awareness can lead to myopia regarding how cultural values influence the interpretation of a text. Ethics becomes fixed on answering moral questions rather than developing virtue. The command of God is divorced from the context that gives it meaning.

Since answers (that is, knowledge) are the goal, the most important questions may be ignored or trivialized. Often important questions have no fixed answer. Biblical legalism can result in a narrow and rigid ethic that is out of touch with the deepest moral problems of the human spirit. Not only fundamentalists but also some theological liberals display an approach to ethics that ignores ethical questions in favor of presupposed moral rules that are the product of a fixed ideology. Assumed rules (from any source) drown out difficult questions and the particular context that gives them birth.

During an ethics course in Salatiga, Indonesia, I gave students an assignment to write "a case study of a critical moral dilemma you are facing or have faced in your life." One student presented the following story.

Is it all right to take part in the Process of Divorce?

Mr. Diduk is 37 years old. He is divorced from his wife Mimi. It is said that this was caused by his very harsh attitude: he likes to beat his wife and has beaten her many times. One day Diduk beat his wife until she was black and blue. Mrs. Tina (a widow who is Diduk's mother) saw that Diduk's actions had already gone much too far. She saw that Diduk's wildness was extremely dangerous and threatened the lives of those who lived in the house. Mrs. Tina, along with Diduk's older sisters, Titi and Netty, fled to the home of Mr. Dodok (a Christian). Mimi and her two-year-old child fled to her parents' home (non-Christian).

Secretly Aunt Netty discussed the problem with her sister, Mimi, Mr. Dodok and Mr. Didik (a Christian). They contacted a Christian lawyer to begin a legal process that involved the police. For a short time Diduk was detained in the police detention room, and after the legal process, the suit for a divorce was accepted.

Several months later a pastor met Diduk. Diduk poured out his anger at the actions of his wife. Over and over he also let out his bitterness and rage against Mr. Dodok and Mr. Didik who played a part in the process of divorce. In his anger, several times Diduk said that if necessary he would kill Mr. Dodok and Mr. Didik. Now he is living with his child. The question [from this story] is, should a Christian go along with the process of suing for divorce?[3]

Wife abuse is tragically common in many countries all over the world. In this case the abuse was repeated and life-threatening. There are many things we do not know from this brief account. We don't know why the man beat his wife, and we don't know if there had been any attempts at counseling or reconciliation.

In many cultures men pay a substantial bride price for their wife and feel she is their possession to do with as they please. Many women feel helpless and powerless to leave a situation of abuse, because of strong community sanctions. Men may leave their wives, but wives are expected to suffer in silence.

We may assume this situation was very extreme, not only because the wife left but also because she was urged to flee by her husband's mother and older sisters. They also feared for their lives. The dangerous character of the husband is further confirmed by his murder threats toward those who helped his wife. A puzzling element in the story is that the abusive ex-husband is now living with his child.

The story ends with a moral question: May Christians go along with the process of a legal suit for divorce? There are several reasons that this is a serious ethical question.

1. Local *adat* (customary) law usually does not recognize the right of a wife to leave her husband.

2. Jesus and Paul explicitly forbid divorce in the New Testament. The only possible exception given is for adultery (Mt 5:31-32; 1 Cor 7:10-11).

3. As a result of these clear rules, most Christian denominations in Indonesia also forbid divorce.[4]

4. Paul instructs wives, "Be subject to your husbands as you are to the Lord" (Eph 5:22).

5. Paul also forbids the Corinthian Christians to take each other to court. He

says it is better to suffer injustice than to sue a fellow Christian (1 Cor 6:1-8).

Thus there are five mutually reinforcing biblical, cultural and church rules that forbid a lawsuit for divorce. In a rule-oriented approach to ethics the case is closed. The answer to the question is a simple no. In this chapter I cannot discuss the complex interpretive questions raised by these passages, let alone the broader theology of marriage and divorce. But I do suggest that the rules cited do not end the discussion. The story, in its context, raises ethical questions concerning values that are more important than adherence to specific rules.

I do not mean to imply that in extreme situations moral rules can be ignored. Rules provide an orientation to the problem and indicate serious values that will be lost if they are not followed. But in this story bigger issues than divorce rules come to the fore and assume their meaning in relation to their context. Mimi's life, health and happiness are seriously threatened, along with the health of her child and other members of the household.

We cannot know, from this brief account, if a legal divorce is the only or best solution to the tragedy related in the story. Rules against divorce indicate values that will be destroyed by divorce. But it is certainly possible that even greater values will be sacrificed if the rules are rigidly followed. Mimi and her children could end up dead.

On the one hand, greater values, such as saving a life in an emergency, outweigh lesser values. Only a fool or a knave would refuse to jaywalk (break a law) on a deserted street to help an old man who has broken his leg and fallen in the gutter. On the other hand, the very meaning and content of a moral law may be changed if applied to circumstances for which it was never intended.

When Jesus healed on the sabbath, he broke one of the Ten Commandments, according to the religious authorities (Mk 3:1-6; see also 2:23-28). Jesus understood the sabbath law as intended to protect human worship, life and health. Therefore he broke the law when he saw that by doing so he would better preserve its meaning. In a similar way Jesus' strong words on divorce were addressed to men who could divorce their wives with a simple statement. Divorced women had few rights and very limited means of self-support. Jesus' teaching on divorce was, in part, intended to *prevent* the abuse of women. To forbid divorce where it is intended to *escape* extreme abuse is to mock the original meaning of Jesus' words.

A law is a proposition that assumes a shared world of meaning. This shared world is contained in the meaning of the law. If this shared world is replaced by another shared world, the meaning of the proposition must be changed to include the new world, or it becomes irrelevant. This is a crucial insight when issues in crosscultural ethics are faced.

During an intensive seminar on crosscultural ethics I again gave students an assignment to write "a case study of a critical moral dilemma you are facing or have faced in your life." One student presented the following hypothetical story.

"Bill" was attending a Bible College in Canada, studying to be a missionary to a small tribal group in the South Pacific. The language of this group had been deciphered by an old missionary who had lived with them for many years. This missionary had published a dictionary and grammar in English. Bill could not afford to purchase the books because they were so expensive, but the library had copies.

During Bill's studies, international war broke out and his town was bombed with a nuclear weapon. Somehow, the grammar and dictionary were preserved. Because of the war, Bill wanted to leave immediately. He felt God's calling to go immediately to the Pacific Island group. His dilemma concerned copyright laws. Should he Xerox the pages he needed from the books to take with him, or should he obey copyright laws against copying major portions of a book? The books could save him years of struggling with the language. Without his witness many islanders might die without hearing about Christ.

The question weighing Bill's conscience was, "to copy or not to copy?"

The most striking thing about this story is the triviality of the question in its imaginary context. Bill constructed an extreme situation because he wanted a rule that would answer every conceivable condition. Given this purpose, it is not surprising that he concluded that he should not photocopy the vital text, even if it meant years of extra study and a hundred souls in hell. Based on his reading of Romans 13, Bill concluded that laws should be obeyed.

My point in citing this story has nothing to do with the noble virtue of obeying copyright laws. It might or might not still be a significant act to respect copyrights in a nuclear war. But surely that would not be the first thing on your mind! After a nuclear explosion in a small town, many or all the inhabitants would be dead or dying. Electricity would be gone, photocopy machines useless, hospitals overflowing, water and food supplies tainted, transportation impossible, panic widespread, air poisonous, bodies unburied and epidemics threatening.

It might be a nice thought to head for the South Pacific, but this would be hardly responsible and probably impossible. A thousand questions would confront a sincere Christian, but copyright laws would not be one of them. If Bill had the money, influence and will to travel to the Pacific in those conditions, he might best preserve the books by taking them with him. He could pay for them later or deliver them to their author. The story collapses on its own absurdity because the context changes the meaning of the question.

Suppose Bill organized a hundred uninjured people to learn first aid and help the injured. Having only one first-aid manual, he photocopied it for those able to help. Such an act would be considered heroic, not criminal. He might be decorated by the Red Cross that published the book—if he and the Red Cross survived!

Moral rules and principles are to goodness as the rules of grammar are to speech. The rules of grammar are not relative. They cannot be discarded on a whim if you wish to speak well. Practicing speech that conforms to good grammar is essential to learning any language. Learning the rules can be extremely helpful. But every language learner knows that complex linguistic constructions sometimes seem to violate the standard rules. The reason there are exceptions to the rules of grammar is that the rules are drawn from speech, not vice versa. The rules are simplifications of a complex process of communication by those who speak well. All of the realities that language addresses cannot be reduced to rules.

Moral rules and principles may also admit exceptions because they are abstract conceptions drawn from watching good people do good things. Principles are drawn from goodness, not vice versa. Even God's laws may be understood as simplifications of the perfect goodness of God. Jesus came into conflict with the Pharisees precisely because they tried to flatten out goodness into a set of unchangeable rules. Jesus better understood the language of God's goodness and consistently pointed beyond the rules to the meaning of God's goodness in a particular fallen context.

Rules and principles are important guides to moral conduct. In a foreign cultural context, rules of local practice can save you from not only embarrassment but also significant moral faults. Rules are most important at the novice stage, before a person learns the deep meanings that lie behind them. Principles can sometimes be abstracted from rules for wider application. But the deepest moral knowledge is profoundly contextual and may not be expressible in propositions.

Rules and principles from the Bible, understood in context, are basic guides to living "well." Biblical law is a comfort and a guide, a means of wisdom and life. The psalmist says,

If your law had not been my delight,
    I would have perished in my misery.
I will never forget your precepts,
    for by them you have given me life. . . .
Oh, how I love your law!
    It is my meditation all day long. . . .
How sweet are your words to my taste,
    sweeter than honey to my mouth! (Ps 119:92-93, 97, 103)

Christian life would be paralyzed without the freedom given by the rules and principles of Scripture. As Karl Barth said, the Ten Commandments are ten permissions to live without the pain and destruction that comes from ignoring them. Oliver O'Donovan observed that law provides a basic ordering for life and protects us from the chaos of facing every event in our lives as totally unique.[5] The relation between biblical law and culture will be examined further in chapter four.

Goodness as the Work of the Holy Spirit

Some Christians reject a law-oriented ethics in favor of an emphasis on being led by the Spirit of God. As Paul says, "The letter kills, but the Spirit gives life" (2 Cor 3:6). Typically, academic books on ethics give very little space to the work of the Holy Spirit. At most they speak of the Holy Spirit as empowering believers to act morally. But many Christians today experience the Holy Spirit as a primary guide to right action.

The fastest-growing segments of the church today are those that have elevated the Holy Spirit to a central place for the experience of life in Christ. Prayer is seen as a two-way communication with the living God. Most would affirm that the Spirit does not contradict the teaching of Scripture, but many believe that even the Bible is "dead letter" until the Spirit addresses us through it. Establishment churches may chide charismatics for an overspiritualized message and lack of social consciousness; but many charismatic churches are flooded with poor people and have developed effective social programs to help them escape their poverty. Charismatic churches are more frequently multiracial, multiclass congregations where women are as likely to be leaders as men.

Many would affirm Karl Barth's famous (and oversimplified) statement that the

Bible becomes the Word of God for us when God addresses us in it. The complexity of biblical teaching and the confusion of a pluralistic society where many values vie for attention leads some believers to rely on the "still small voice" through which God leads them. Many Christians claim an immediacy to their experience of God which renders other sources of guidance secondary.

In recent years some segments of the church, both Catholic and Protestant, have found moral transformation through recovering the ancient Christian practices of meditation and contemplative prayer. "Prayer without words," when centered in faith on the presence of God, can bring a person or community into vital contact with God in the Spirit. Reason and analysis appear to be a rather weak and confusing source of moral knowledge when compared with direct communion with God.[6]

The experience of God through the Spirit is a powerful force for reviving the church and creating community. Many movements for social transformation have been founded in a vigorous experience of God in the Spirit. Just as the Second Great Awakening empowered the Abolitionist movement, so many Spirit-oriented churches today lead in concrete ways of reaching out to the poor.

But as a lone criterion for judging good and evil, the leading of the Spirit is a dangerous guide. Contemplative prayer is not meant to take the place of reason or verbal prayer. Anything, from the Jonestown massacre to the robbing of a gullible TV audience, can be claimed on the basis of the leading of the Spirit. Fortunately, many Christians who have been renewed by the Spirit also love the Scriptures, respect their theological tradition and show a healthy common sense.

The dangers of subjectivism inherent in a sole emphasis on the Spirit are compounded by the rampant individualism, emotivism and relativism that characterize American and European life. Alasdair MacIntyre suggests that the dominant perception of morality in the United States is "emotivism": the belief that something is right or wrong because it *feels* right or wrong.[7] Robert N. Bellah and his associates believe that a primary moral language in the United States is the language of "expressive individualism," a language that speaks in terms of what feels good or evil *to me*.[8] Bellah finds this language common in American conservative churches. Allan Bloom averred that one of the very few common assumptions of incoming freshmen at the University of Chicago was that all values are relative.

Law and Spirit, structure and freedom, *nomos* and *chaos* can all be seen as healthy polarities in human life. In the beginning of creation was chaos, and the wind (or Spirit) of God swept over the waters. Then came the Word, which gave form and structure to creation (Gen 1:2-3). Often the work of the Spirit brings creativity and with it a kind of chaos. Things are not done the way they have always been done (law). Freedom and new experience are exhilarating. But chaos undisciplined by law can easily turn destructive. Movements of the Spirit founded on charismata must develop structures or die.

Sometimes I long for the incredible freedom and creativity of the Spirit that we experienced in the radical countercultural communities of the 1960s and 1970s. The institutionalized bureaucracy of my current church is not nearly as exciting. Nor is it as effective in the short term. The quality of creative cross-cultural ministry carried out with very few material resources in those years is astonishing. It was fueled by the Spirit of God and by burning idealism.

Yet such intensity could not last. Some people were badly burned by the experience and took years to recover. Others were simply burned out. Many, with growing families, took refuge in the stability of the very establishment churches they had once despised. Law, structure and institution all make long-term survival possible. Each day does not have to be created anew. Structures protect individuals from exploitation.

Laws and institutions can easily become dead letters and crippling prisons if not infused with life by the Spirit. Because laws and institutions are hard to kill, they provide continuity and dependability in which human communities can grow. Yet without the Spirit of God they may become the very principalities and powers that oppress and destroy the human spirit. Institutional religion has a dark side that is well attested in the history of oppression.

Some Christians interpret everything they do in the language of "God said . . .": "God told me to come and see you." "God gave me a parking place." "God is leading me to marry you." "God told me that you should come and work for our ministry." Such language gives immediacy to the experience of God's presence in our lives. But the dangers of confusing your own subjectivity with the mind of God are serious. Emotivism may simply be dressed in theological language.

Since the Enlightenment, Western thought has often dichotomized reason and emotion. Reason (law) is considered the path to truth, while emotion is a barrier that undermines clear thinking. In fact, reason and emotion are interrelated ways of knowing. Both can be twisted by sin and are limited by human finitude. Both can be vehicles of human wisdom. Without emotion, reason cannot know the significance of the truth. Without reason, emotion is limited by radical subjectivity. There is a continuum, not a dichotomy, between emotion and reason. The Holy Spirit works through both reasonable emotion and emotion-laden reason.

God does not usually communicate to us outside the limitations of our own world of meaning. To understand another culture takes hard work, contextual knowledge and practical interaction. Crosscultural experience opens the floodgates of new awareness. God's Spirit can help keep things in perspective. The fruit of the Spirit can help us adjust. The power of the Spirit can push us into new territory and give us the gifts we need to do our work. But wisdom and virtue in another culture are not usually beamed into our minds by the Holy Spirit. Nor are they confined to a neat list of biblical rules and principles. Crosscultural goodness is tempered in the crucible of direct crosscultural experience.

Ethics Defined by Context

One response to the rigidity of rules and the subjectivism of Spirit as sources of goodness is to emphasize the priority of concrete experience. Contextual ethics puts the stress on "working out your faith with fear and trembling" in specific contexts that are always unique. The importance of this emphasis is obvious in a crosscultural situation. Many of the clues to goodness must come from the specific new situations faced by a believer. The context is part of a narrative that gives meaning to virtue in a particular situation.

An American couple living in Egypt got into an argument with their landlady, who continually invaded their privacy. They were very angry, and it looked as if they might have to move. An Egyptian friend advised them to draw back, not to confront the situation, but to let it die down. In contrast, an American friend said they should frankly discuss the problem with the landlady; they should never leave a "festering sore." In spite of their preference for the American solution, they decided to try the Egyptian advice. As a result, the landlady saved face and eventually became their closest friend.

Typical American values in this situation would stress individual rights and responsibilities, personal privacy and frank, open communication. In contrast, Egyptian values stress group solidarity, guarding the other's honor and maintaining social harmony. The "right" solution to the conflict was that which was appropriate to the context. Stressing the American values probably would not have "worked" in the situation.

On the other hand, a stress on context as the primary source of ethics may easily slip into an amoral utilitarianism. The language of morality may be replaced by the language of utility.

In Manila, Philippines, I requested an interview with a young man who was a consultant to Western Christians involved in business in the Middle East. "John" is an intense, committed Christian who believes "tentmaking" is the only effective way for Christians to preach the gospel in Muslim countries. John's first impulse was to decline the interview on the basis that "crosscultural ethics is not relevant to tentmakers." He saw little value in "systems of ethics" and believed "prearranged answers to moral dilemmas" were counterproductive.

Furthermore, he felt that perhaps 80 percent of crosscultural training would be forgotten or have to be relearned in another cultural setting anyway. John suggested that the most efficient way to learn crosscultural ethics was for sincere people of good character to work things out as they went along. Someone else's answer might not work for them. During our conversation he related several stories that posed moral dilemmas in the areas of honesty, bribery and deceit. All were puzzling, and all, he believed, must be solved not by formula but by the person involved.

In one case he had a client who could not get a telephone without paying a bribe. John advised him to pay the bribe: "How could I consult him if we couldn't communicate? Telexes that were received four blocks from his office were not delivered." Nevertheless, he felt his client must make the final decision, because he would bear the consequences. One risk he saw was that the man's ministry might be undermined by a bad conscience. If his conscience was troubled by his compromise in this area, he might bear an emotional strain that would make him ineffective as a minister of the gospel. Second, John suggested, there was a danger that God might not bless his ministry because of his failure in this area. If God really did disapprove of his bribing the phone company, God's judgment might fall on the man and his work.

John felt that both of these risks were less significant than the inefficiency that might result from the lack of a telephone. The bribe could be justified to his client's conscience as a cultural convention. And surely God would not withhold blessing for such a small thing. Nevertheless, he could not prejudge his client's decision. His client had to decide on his own.

What is striking about this story is that both of the risks John foresaw were stated in terms of his client's efficiency in doing his task. One was a psychological risk, the other a supernatural risk. The right choice would not be based on morals but on which action would lead to the best results. John believed the bribe might be wrong *for his client* if it interrupted his ministry more than the lack of a telephone. His values reflected common Western business practices of maximizing efficiency, even though his goals were spiritual.

John's insistence on his client's resolving the situation himself was partly based on his awareness of the subtle dynamics of Arab bargaining styles. But unlike the ideal of the Middle East, where relationships outweigh profit, John's ultimate stated value in this situation seemed to be efficiency in the work of the Lord. John used a Christian form of what Bellah and associates call the language of utilitarian individualism:[9] "What is right is what works for me." The individual is king or queen, and ethics slips toward pragmatism. The language of biblical morality (is it right?) is replaced by the language of individualistic utility (will it work for him?).[10]

Some Indonesian pastors revealed a similar approach during a discussion of bribery. As long as the discussion remained abstract, bribery was clearly condemned. But as soon as they were asked what they would personally do if asked for a small bribe from an immigration official, they said they would pay. Why? Because it is necessary to smooth or speed the process. Their action may or may not be morally justifiable (see chapter seven). But the justification they gave was purely based on efficiency.

Like John, I am suspicious of ready-made answers that can be plugged in to any situation or culture. Like him, I believe that good and evil can be understood at deeper levels in a real situation than they can in abstract. We cannot know the answers before we understand the questions. Answers we learn before making the questions our own are easily forgotten. And the real questions are made of flesh and blood, sweat and tears. They are not just words on a page.

The deepest moral problems faced by individuals and groups in a society cannot be understood through casual observation. Moral problems are rooted not just in individual situations but in social structures that oppress certain groups. We may readily see that our neighbor is poor and do something to help, at least temporarily. But to understand the root causes of her poverty and do something that will have a long-term impact for good is far more difficult. It is not only individual sin and individual sinners that destroy people's lives. Our sisters and brothers, next door and across the world, are suffering because they never had a chance for things that many Westerners consider basic rights.

Context is central to ethics, because by understanding the social, political, religious, economic and cultural causes of suffering we can learn to effectively love our neighbor. The discipline of ethics is thus wedded to the social sciences. The struggle to understand the structural causes of injustice is often generally called social analysis. "Social analysis is the effort to obtain a more complete picture of a social situation by exploring its historical and structural relationships."[11]

The academic discipline of ethics has divided into numerous specializations, such as medical ethics, business ethics, environmental ethics, economic ethics and political ethics, each of which uses the appropriate social science to better understand the contexts and causes of ethical problems. In some ways this book may be regarded in the same light, as a Christian attempt to use the insights of the fledgling field of crosscultural studies to illuminate the source of ethical problems in a crosscultural setting.

Contextual approaches to ethics, whether individualistic as in the case of John or linked to the social sciences, should not be cut loose from other sources of ethical insight. None are without bias or unaffected by subjectivity. A contextual reliance on the Spirit of God may shade into expressive individualism. A contextual focus on effective action may fuse with utilitarian individualism or any number of "social scientific" ideologies that carry religious freight.

Just as Christian ethics cannot afford to be detached from a rigorous study of the local context, neither can it be separated from its theological commitments. Biblical teaching, the Holy Spirit, reason and tradition are all important sources of moral guidance as they interact with the realities of a particular context.[12] In the remainder of this chapter I will consider how these elements can be integrated in a crosscultural situation.

The Practice of Theology in Experience

How do we learn to live "well" (or virtuously) in another culture?[13] The simple answer is that we learn through experience. We cannot really know the good until we do it. Certainly the moral teaching of the Bible, illumined by the Spirit and understood contextually, is a foundational source of ethics. But when it comes to goodness, nothing can take the place of practice. Goodness is like playing a violin. All the musical theory, inspiration and sensitivity to local musical tastes in the world cannot make you into a musician. You have to practice.

Aristotle understood that we learn virtue not by study but by living virtuously. George MacDonald and C. S. Lewis reveal again and again in their fiction how people are formed by thousands of small, "insignificant" acts. Goodness is formed in the crucible of our lives, not primarily in our heads. We are all moving—one day at a time—toward light or darkness, toward good or evil. As Bob Dylan put it, "He who is not busy being born, is busy dying." Long before we arrive in another culture, we begin setting our direction and determining what sort of people we will be in our new context.

The following Uigur folktale from China illustrates that goodness does not consist in what we know but in how we live.

One day a poor porter sat in the bazaar with his carrying pole, looking for work. After a long hot day of waiting, a great lord came by and called, "I have bought a case of porcelain. To the man who will carry it home for me, I shall give three incontrovertible moral truths. If he can prove any of them false, I shall then pay him the worth of the porcelain."

No one volunteered for the job. Who were they to dispute with so wise a man over incontrovertible moral truth? The poor man, seeing the day was almost ended and having little to lose, picked up the case with his pole and followed the lord toward his palace.

As they walked, the poor man said, "May I hear the first truth as we walk?" "Yes," said the lord. "If you do not do to others what you would not want done to yourself, you will injure no one."

The poor man, who had often been abused, nodded his head. "Truly an incontrovertible moral truth," he said. "And what is the second?" "If you live each day as though it were your last, you will not waste one hour of your life." "True," said the poor man, his back breaking from an hour of carrying the heavy box.

They arrived at the palace, and the lord turned with laughter and said, "Now hear the third incontrovertible truth. If anyone tells you that in this world there is someone more foolish than you for carrying such a heavy burden for nothing but words you cannot eat, for heaven's sake do not believe him."

The poor man heard him thoughtfully, then opened his hand from the carrying pole, and the case crashed to the ground and down the stairs to the street. "Now hear a truth which invalidates all three of yours. 'A wise man who knows the truth but does not practice it is as foolish as one who trusts his porcelain in the hands of a man he has abused.' "[14]

The foolish man in this story is the man who does not practice what he knows. He thereby proves that he does not really know it. Both self-knowledge and "blessedness" come from living the good.

But be doers of the word, and not merely hearers who deceive themselves. For if any are hearers of the word and not doers, they are like those who look at themselves in a mirror; for they look at themselves and, on going away, immediately forget what they were like. But those who look into the perfect law, the law of liberty, and persevere, being not hearers who forget but doers who act—they will be blessed in their doing. (James 1:22-25)

The difference between "the desirable" and "the desired." The importance of "praxis," the practice of theology or theory in experience, is revealed by the profound difference that exists in all cultures between words and deeds. Crosscultural research by E. Deutscher has shown that people's stated values are often an unreliable guide to their actual behavior.[15] Sometimes words are consistent with actions, but sometimes what people *say* indicates what they believe is desirable whereas what they *do* reveals what they really desire.

Geert Hofstede cites a comparative study of patients in doctors' waiting rooms in Jakarta, Indonesia, and Sydney, Australia, that illustrates this point.[16] Sixty-two percent of Indonesian patients and 43 percent of the Australians said they would be unlikely to initiate a conversation with a stranger in the waiting room. However, previous observations of those same patients showed that 56 percent of the Indonesians and 76 percent of the Australians had actually been silent. Australians had a higher stated value of being sociable with strangers, but Indonesians were actually more sociable.

Praxis means living our theory or theology. Learning goodness from praxis means taking small, concrete steps to act out our stated beliefs. By action we gradually transfer what we believe is desirable into what we actually desire. For Christians this means trusting the Holy Spirit to convert our interior affections through our exterior practices.

Preparation as praxis. A common error in Western-influenced thinking is to separate theory from practice and preparation from life. Not only *what* is learned but also *how* it is learned forms a person and expresses the direction of her life. All of our life is preparation for something else. And all of our life is also the thing for which we prepare. Living the goal cannot begin after preparation. Nor can it wait for adequate understanding. The search for understanding, like the search for adequate experience, is endless. Now we must live the goal to the utmost extent that we know it. In such praxis the meaning of our faith is revealed to ourselves and those around us.

Nowhere is this more urgent than in a crosscultural situation. Most of the time

48

a person spends in another culture is spent learning how to adapt. No matter how long a Batak spends in Java, he will never be Javanese. No matter how long a Singaporean spends in the United States, she will never understand American customs the way they are understood by the "natives." Frank Cooley, a highly respected Presbyterian missionary who spent many years in Indonesia, revealed the secret of his success in a casual comment about the purpose of a trip to East Java. He said, "I'm only going to listen and to learn."

After arrival in another culture, most people naturally seek out friends from their own culture. If they are really serious about cultural adaptation they may study the local language and culture. Many people think cultural skills are theoretical "facts" that must be mastered before they can be applied effectively. Many sojourners depend on friends from their own culture in learning the ropes of their new context. From the beginning they learn to see the new culture from the perspective of other foreigners. This reinforces the idea of their own perspective as an objective, neutral view of an unusual culture. The praxis of their initial orientation reinforces an alienated and/or paternalistic perspective.

Bonding as praxis. Elizabeth and Thomas Brewster argue that the first few months of a person's sojourn in a new culture are the most crucial for his work there.[17] They believe that just as newborn infants bond to their parents or surrogate parents in the first months of life, so newcomers can bond to a new culture in the first months of their sojourn. Upon first arrival in a foreign culture, people are especially open to seeing the world in a new way. The excitement and novelty of discovery are not yet blunted by culture fatigue. Like newborn babes, they are ignorant and dependent. And their humble dependence begins a bond that can lead to service.

In practical terms, the Brewsters suggest that newcomers bring only as many possessions as are allowed on an airplane (twenty kilos' worth), live with a local family, travel only by local transportation, learn language by systematic contact with local people and avoid contact with people from their own culture for the first few months. By being forced to communicate about basic issues of survival with local people, not only do they learn language skills more quickly than through classroom instruction, but they also make friends. The Brewsters argue that such language learning is not just preparation for ministry, it *is* ministry.[18] It is praxis.

Ironically, it is the local people who initially serve the outsider. In many cultures service is voluntarily offered to one who is in need. The humility engendered is opposite to the colonial mentality of the self-sufficient superior who demands service from the weak "natives." It is also different from the common Asian practice of gathering only with people from one's own ethnic group. A praxis that models reconciliation and justice from the start is the best way for any foreigner to jump into a new culture. Such a praxis includes not only what you do for others but how well you are able to accept their way of doing things for you.

The irony of dependency as a path to deep relationships was vividly presented to us during my family's visit to Indonesia in 1989. When both of our daughters got very ill, we had no choice but to rely heavily on our Indonesian neighbors. When we cried for help, not only did they respond to our basic needs such as transportation to the hospital in the middle of the night, but they also looked for concrete ways to care for us emotionally, such as bringing us rare American food.

Most of all they reached out to us spiritually. My daughter will never forget the time our house helper, Ibu (Mother) Ngatimah, first spoke English. When Jenny was fainting in the bathroom, Ibu Ngatimah overcame her shyness in a strange language to call out to her in English. While we were at the hospital with Rina, Ibu Ngatimah sat holding Jenny's hand in deep and fervent prayer. Experiences like this have bonded our family to Indonesia far more than if we had had Westerners to efficiently care for our needs.

"Ministry" as a barrier. An Asian leader I spoke with believes that subtle attitudes of superiority are often communicated by Westerners who think they are there to serve the people. She suggested that the very idea of "ministry" can be a barrier to effective service in Asia. Anyone who enters another culture in order to serve the people faces this danger. A praxis of giving must be balanced with a praxis of receiving. Only superiors never receive help.

Recently I asked a Batak pastor what she found most obnoxious about Westerners. Her answer surprised me. She said, "They are always giving and never want to receive anything." Christians forget that God is at work in all places and that the object of God's ministry might as easily be them as the local people. Of course Christians should not enter a foreign culture in order to be served. But neither should we go as saviors.

It takes humility to be served. The apostle Peter learned this the hard way. When Jesus tried to wash his feet, Peter refused. Jesus replied, "Unless I wash you, you have no share with me" (see Jn 13:6-10). When you are served, you are placed in debt to the server. You are in a position of dependency. Dependency creates relationship. Service creates solidarity.

Peter thinks he's got the point and gushes, "Then Lord, wash all of me!" When a host offers a service, it is not the place of the guest to demand more. It is a short step from a prideful refusal to be served to an arrogant expectation of being given first-class treatment. Both attitudes are woefully common among educated Christians in foreign cultures, and sometimes can be found in the same person!

Anthony Gittins points out that people in foreign cultures are *strangers* and *guests.* In fact, many languages do not distinguish between the two words. As guests we must always remember that our hosts are superordinate. We are on their turf. The history of crosscultural conflict gives local people good reason to fear strangers. Gittins says,

> So if missionaries were more willing to allow themselves to be contextualized as *strangers,* rather than trying to position themselves as controllers, dictators, initiative-takers or proselytizers, then perhaps mutual relationships would be more conducive to a responsible and creative sharing of stories—and thus authentic evangelization—than has so often been the case.[19]

Christians are often afflicted with a minority mentality. Evangelicals want to defend the faith and convert the lost. Therefore they are defensive and feel victimized for their faith when they are not accepted. Since they understand the gospel in abstract terms as a message that must be accepted, they easily slip into a professional-client relationship with local people. They have a product that they must sell to the locals. Even with the best of intentions, they separate themselves from the people they came to serve. More seriously, their purpose has become abstracted from their life. Ministry is something *extrinsic* to their own being.

A prominent Western theologian recently gave a series of lectures at an Asian university. It was obvious from his manner that he had come to give and not to receive. During question periods he hardly heard the students' questions or the complex issues that lay behind them, but launched into long, irrelevant expositions of his latest theory. No doubt he left convinced he had done a service for his underdeveloped brothers and sisters in the Third World. But one of the most brilliant students commented after one of his lectures, "This is just a new form of colonialism." The comment did not apply to his theory, which concerned the liberating effect of the gospel, but to his manner. He came to teach, but not to learn.

Meaning revealed in life. A rather stale debate revolves around whether "presence" or "proclamation" is more crucial for evangelism. Or, to use different terms, which is more important, "orthopraxis" or "orthodoxy"? A common resolution affirms that both are necessary. Christian presence, in the sense of a lifestyle of integrity, validates the Christian message. Proclamation of the gospel explains why Christians are good. While this is undoubtedly true, it may also conceal the extent to which the *meaning* of what we proclaim is not only validated by how we live but actually *defined* by our lifestyle.

Do we even know ourselves, what we mean by what we say, before we see how it is lived out in our lives? Jesus said, "Each tree is known by its own fruit" (Lk 6:44). What we really believe is shown by the results it has in our own lives. Often our words are in specialized religious language that protects even us from real understanding. Repentance, forgiveness, grace, regeneration, reconciliation, salvation, hope, the love of God, the fellowship of the Holy Spirit, power, resurrection—all these are but marks on a page before being defined in a person's life.

As these words give meaning to our own experience, we can learn new language to express that experience to our friends. An Asian friend commented to me that if non-Christians don't understand our language, there is a good chance that we don't understand it either! The deepest truths of Christian faith are goals, rather than possessions, of understanding and experience. If we speak of them as if we fully possessed them, we hover on the edges of hypocrisy. We are saved, redeemed, sanctified only in the sense that we believe God has offered these gifts fully, even though we have only partially received them.

Crosscultural praxis is a three-way dialogue between God, our adopted culture and us. By practicing the gospel with cultural foreigners, we learn from them to see God's goodness enfleshed in a novel cultural style. The stranger becomes God's gift to us of a friend.

Praxis as love and commitment. Christian praxis is determined by our deepest commitments. The great commandment expresses what is meant to lie at the base of our praxis: " 'You shall love the Lord your God with all your heart, and with all your soul, and with all your mind, and with all your strength.' The second is this, 'You shall love your neighbor as yourself' " (Mk 12:30-31). This command transcends all cultures. But how it is lived is culturally specific.[20]

The ultimate test of praxis lies in the meaning of our commitment to the poor and despised of our community. It is relatively easy to show love to those who, like us, are relatively rich, relatively respectable, relatively powerful. These neighbors may well reward us in one way or another for our efforts. The people who really need us the most are the easiest to ignore. Jesus' teachings are full of examples of God's concrete commitment to the castoffs of society. As he says,

> For if you love those who love you, what reward do you have? Do not even the tax collectors do the same? And if you greet only your brothers and sisters, what more are you doing than others? Do not even the Gentiles do the same? Be perfect, therefore, as your heavenly Father is perfect. (Mt 5:46-48)

Augustine observed that if you want to know if a person is good, you don't ask what the person says, thinks or believes; you ask what the person loves. Love is the ultimate praxis that breaks down cultural barriers. Our ability to love our neighbors, especially those who are victims of injustice or tragedy, requires that we understand both their needs and the appropriate ways to meet them. For this task we need more than commitment. We need cultural knowledge, dialogue and wisdom.

THREE

KNOWLEDGE, FRIENDSHIP AND WISDOM

P raxis, as discussed in the last chapter, is not an achievement but a process. Just as a violinist never reaches perfection, so in life we are always learning how to be good and live well. Knowledge is the necessary cognitive information—from the Scriptures, from Christian tradition and from our context—to make good decisions and act well. Communication-dialogue is what connects us to the community and orders our life in relation to others. Wisdom combines praxis, knowledge and communication-dialogue and makes our presence and our actions apposite to our situation. Friendship is the key to knowledge, communication and wisdom in a foreign context.

Knowledge

It is quite possible to have deep commitments to God and your neighbor that result in foolish or even sinful actions because of a lack of knowledge. Knowledge of how to act in a particular cultural situation depends both on accurate cultural information of the meaning of certain acts and on knowledge of biblical and theological frameworks to make Christian sense of the situation.

Ethnic solidarity as a barrier to crosscultural relationships. The best way to obtain knowledge in a crosscultural situation is to make friends with local people. Unfortunately, the very attributes that bind groups together make friendship with strangers difficult. Many people groups in the Third World are well known for their strong ethnic and family ties. Group solidarity among peoples from communalistic cultures is the envy of many isolated, individualistic Westerners. Ethnic solidarity is *performed,* or acted out, in a multitude of practices ranging from preferential business treatment for members of the group to common religious rituals and affiliation.

Among Christians this often takes the form of ethnic churches. In urban centers where many people are separated from their ethnic homelands, it is natural for Christians to find members of their own group and form a church. For many people it is very difficult to worship in a strange language and cultural form. Ethnic churches are a potent tool of evangelism because non-Christians from the same group are drawn to the church for cultural reasons. There is a great attraction to a group that speaks your language and shares a common cultural background. Displaced people are often hungry for new religious answers. Ethnic churches are sometimes the only institution strong enough to preserve the culture of a particular ethnic group in a strange environment.

Nevertheless, ethnic churches are a symbol for a profound barrier to crosscultural learning. Insofar as Christians in a foreign context seek all their needs for intimacy and understanding within their own cultural group, they will be unable to make deep friendships across the cultural barrier. The knowledge that is prerequisite to crosscultural ethics is best achieved through crosscultural friendships.

A Korean church in China, a Batak church in Singapore, an African-American church in North Chicago, a Chinese church in the Philippines, an American church in Germany and a Taiwanese church in Hong Kong may each preserve their group's cultural survival and at the same time provide the means by which their members remain isolated from the dominant local culture. I have met educated Chinese Christians who have lived in the United States for twenty years and still do not speak English. Almost all their interactions take place within the Chinese Christian community.

Ethnic churches sometimes practice a subtle form of racism. Even as they positively reinforce the ethnic pride of their group, they encourage the silent assumption that those on the outside are inferior. Racism involves negative stereotyping of the stranger and makes crosscultural understanding very difficult.

Knowledge of unique people in their own cultural context is cut off by prejudice.

Ethnic churches are not wrong. Particularly for oppressed or alienated groups, an ethnic church may be necessary for survival and effective for ministry to its own group. Members of ethnic minorities who spend their whole week in a strange dominant culture may be greatly refreshed by participation in their own ethnic church. But Christians who are serious about crosscultural ethics need to be aware that crosscultural friendships are the most effective means of gaining knowledge of another culture. Friendships require time—time that may not be available if it is all spent with people of your own ethnic group.

Knowledge and friendship. When I was a high-school student in Taiwan, I had a Taiwanese girlfriend. She taught me many things, but I will never forget when she taught me how to distinguish Taiwanese Chinese from mainland Chinese nationals of Taiwan. The difference was subtle and not easily stated in words. But with her guidance and practice I could soon pick out members of each group. More important, I learned to see her country through Taiwanese eyes. My other closest friend was a mainland Chinese. From him I learned a different perspective on the political and economic realities of Taiwan.

As a teenager I used to fantasize about coloring my hair black and traveling around Taiwan disguised as a Chinese. Unfortunately, my blue eyes and over-six-foot height made the fantasy unlikely. But having close Chinese friends was the next best thing. From them I learned how they felt about their cultural reality in a way that would be impossible from books.

If friendship is an irreplaceable source of crosscultural knowledge, it is also one of the hardest to achieve. Friendship is both the means and the goal of crosscultural knowledge. Sometimes a simple piece of information is a frustrating barrier to friendship.

An American couple living in Kenya experienced great frustration in their attempts to make African friends.[1] In North America the way to make friends is to invite someone over to your house for dinner. So for the first year of their stay Tim and Poppie Stafford tried again and again to have people over. But the Kenyans never seemed to want to come to their home. Appointments for dinner were set up far in advance, but people did not show up, or when they came they were stiff and uneasy. Most troubling of all, they never reciprocated. While the Staffords received many invitations from Europeans and Americans, they were never invited into an African home. Because of their loneliness, it was difficult to avoid spending their social time with Westerners.

Finally they found an African who explained why their efforts were such a failure. In Kenya, as in many other Third World countries, it is very unusual to invite someone to your home for a particular meal in the future. Such an invitation may create a feeling of obligation and is usually reserved for very formal occasions. If you want to honor someone or become their friend, you simply drop in at their house. An invitation, or even advance notice, is unnecessary. It's appropriate to bring a small gift, and you will probably be fed, no matter when you come. In the States even good friends do not usually drop in without warning at mealtimes, but in Africa this is a common way to make a new friend.

Thus the Staffords began to drop by at Kenyan homes.

As we visited them, they began to visit us, also without warning and often at mealtimes. We had to adjust, and no doubt we made many offensive mistakes in doing so. But mistakes could be forgiven and corrected. Until we found the way to mix freely, we made few mistakes—and few friends.

An almost impenetrable barrier between cultures had been formed by a simple and small difference of procedure. *A single piece of information* broke the barrier down. Yet we had found it astonishingly difficult to get that piece of information. Apparently others do too. Just a short time ago I heard of some missionaries in Tanzania who were troubled that Tanzanians had not been friendly to them: "They never invite us to their homes."[2]

The Staffords had a biblical understanding of reconciliation and friendship. A message of divine reconciliation means very little to someone who is alienated from the messenger. Whether you are a teacher, a scientist, a missionary or a technical consultant, the most lasting results of your sojourn in another culture are likely to derive from the relationships you make. Tim Stafford's job in Kenya was to begin a magazine. But he understood that the technical expertise he brought was secondary to the relationships he formed with his Kenyan colleagues. The Staffords refused to elevate their technical tasks over the people they came to serve.

The Staffords were advised to "find Africans who will tell you the truth, however unpleasant, and not the truth you want to hear."[3] Although they had to learn much through trial and error, it was Kenyans who gave them the vital tools for deeper cultural understanding. Advice from experienced residents from your own cultural group can be helpful. But genuine friendship with members of the host culture is indispensable. Success or failure in crosscultural learning may depend on how early you find a local "guide," someone to teach you a new way to live.

This principle also applies to foreign cultures within one's own country. A white person who lives or works in a black or Chicano community is unlikely to achieve much without friendship. A Chinese who cares about his Indian neighbors needs to make friends. This may appear obvious. But friendship has different rules in different cultures. To make friends, you need to learn the rules. Such rules are not moral absolutes, but they are coherent to their cultural context.

Coherent and absolute knowledge. George A. Lindbeck distinguishes between coherent truth and absolute truth.[4] Coherent truth coheres with or makes sense in a total relevant context or system of thought and behavior. Absolute truth is "ontological"; it refers to the ultimate reality of the way things are. Coherent truth is consistent with its context; it makes sense in relation to a total style of life and thought, but it may or may not be ontologically or absolutely true. Ontological truth is coherent in all contexts and makes absolute claims about the nature of reality.[5]

When we move into a new culture, even what we believe is absolutely true must be relearned if we are to understand how it is coherent with our new context. For example, the assertion "God is love" or "Jesus is Lord" must be experienced in a new situation where the words *God* and *love* and *Lord* have different connotations. The meaning of our words is demonstrated by the culturally appropriate practices to which they give rise.

When Mother Teresa says, "God is love," we can understand a little of what it means by the way she serves the poor and dying in Calcutta. "God is love" certainly means something different when Charles Manson says it. Manson attracted a following of young women with whom he engaged in free sex and mass murder. I talked with Manson in prison and found him quite willing to affirm that God is love. But he also believed that he is God and evil is good. It was not his talk that showed what he really meant by love, but his actions.

Responding to incoherent and conflicting views. Where people's needs, questions and context of meaning are different from our own, our stated beliefs may sound incoherent to them. The answers we offer do not fit the questions they are asking. The behavior we advocate does not make sense in light of what they desire or believe desirable. This may lead to (1) reinterpretation or expansion of our beliefs to match their needs, (2) a new description of our beliefs in language that makes sense in their worldview, (3) a confrontation between radically dissimilar ways of understanding the world or (4) a suspension of understanding in the face of unresolvable experiences of reality.

1. Reinterpreting what we know. A middle-class Singaporean whose experience of personal guilt led him to see salvation as personal forgiveness might find that a black South African yearns primarily for salvation from the principalities and powers of racial oppression. Consistent with Scripture, the Singaporean might expand his understanding of salvation to include concepts that are foreign to his experience. Such a reinterpretation requires a denial neither of the ontological truth of God's love nor of the belief in the importance of forgiveness and reconciliation for all people. But it brings with it an expanded awareness of how God's love may be expressed in different situations.

The Willowbank Report stated, "The gospel is like a multi-faceted diamond, with different aspects that appeal to different people in different cultures. It has depths we have not fathomed. It defies every attempt to reduce it to a neat formulation."[6]

2. *Saying what you know in new ways.* Bruce Olsen provides a striking example of the description of reality in new thought forms that cohered with the views of a remote South American tribe.[7] When "Bruchko" wanted to offer disinfectant to the tribe as a way of combating disease, he went to the local shaman with a microscope. She was chanting spells to rid a house of the malicious spirits that cause disease. Because Bruchko had already established a relationship of trust and mutual respect with her, he was able to invite her to look at a drop of water in his microscope.

He said, "Auntie, if you look through this glass you can see all the little evil spirits who cause disease, wriggling about." When she was suitably impressed, he added some disinfectant and showed her how all the little spirits were killed. From then on the shaman sprinkled disinfectant while chanting her spells to cleanse a house from disease.

Olsen had learned to see the world through the eyes of the tribe. For years he looked for keys by which to introduce new ideas, beliefs and practices in ways that were coherent with their experience of reality.[8]

3. *Rejecting what you know is wrong.* The Willowbank Report relates how Christians in nineteenth-century Fiji successfully confronted cannibalism, widow-strangling, infanticide and patricide.[9] The report suggests that there is a category of cultural customs that Christians must "renounce immediately as being wholly incompatible with the Christian gospel (e.g., idolatry, the possession of slaves, witchcraft and sorcery, head hunting, blood feuds, ritual prostitution, and all personal discriminations based on race, color, class or caste)."[10]

If you care about people, a time will come when you must oppose those things by which they oppress themselves and others. If you care about truth, you will not remain silent forever if you believe they are making a terrible mistake.

Paul describes a classical clash of traditions that lay at the heart of his mission. A crucified savior was an incoherent concept to the traditional Jewish and Greek worldviews. Nevertheless, Paul believed this "folly" was the key to set people of both groups free: "For Jews demand signs and Greeks desire wisdom, but we proclaim Christ crucified, a stumbling block to Jews and foolishness to Gentiles, but to those who are the called, both Jews and Greeks, Christ the power of God and the wisdom of God" (1 Cor 1:22-24).

When foreign Christians are expected to participate in cultural practices that are antithetical to their basic values, confrontation, or at least open disapproval, may be necessary, even if it is not always effective. Someone entering a community that abuses drugs need not take cocaine in order to identify.

A Scandinavian scientist in a Middle Eastern country told me of a time when he wrote a grant proposal and submitted it with an Arab colleague. When they received the grant, the Arab colleague took the money and bought a Mercedes-Benz. "Hans" told his colleague how bad he felt about the situation. He explained that he knew he would have to stand before the judgment seat of God and answer to God for lying in this situation.

His Middle Eastern colleague was shocked that he felt bad and reassured Hans that he was innocent because he had written the proposal in good faith. The Arab professor explained that everyone was doing it. No one thought it was wrong. Another professor pocketed $1.6 million from a building program and only received a mild rebuke. In the face of corrupt practices that extended to the very top of the hierarchy, Hans felt that all he could do was express his pain at the situation in language understandable to a Muslim. He never again submitted a joint grant proposal.

Even more painful are situations where local Christians ask an expatriate to stand with them in exposing the oppressive or cruel practices of high officials. In one case members of a Christian development organization were asked to sign a document exposing a government atrocity in which hundreds of people were killed. In another case an agricultural adviser was asked to stand up for a woman in her just conflict with her chieftain husband. In both cases opposing the powerful could lead to the expatriates' being expelled from the country. Open confrontation could lead to severe restrictions that would hamstring or terminate the work of their organizations.[11] In both cases the intrinsic rightness of the cause had to be weighed along with the consequences of the action.

Sometimes local practices that are evil must be addressed immediately out of obedience to Christ and love for neighbor, no matter what the consequences. At other times entrenched cultural "law" (for example, bride price or polygamy) cannot be quickly changed without severe social dislocation. It may take years of careful planning based on acute social analysis to bring about the necessary social changes that will provide a foundation for a change of cultural practice.

Foreigners need to be very careful about confronting objectionable practices that are imperfectly understood. Often practices that are clearly evil from a Western Christian perspective do perform a vital social function within a particular social structure. Removing the offending practice may not be possible without a revolution in social structure. This may be needed. But it would far better come from local Christian leaders who have deep knowledge of the culture and will have to bear the long-term consequences. Foreign guests know too little. In many cultures direct confrontation hardly ever brings good results. The church has yet to find a simple solution to problems such as caste in India, polygamy in Africa, compromise with the state in China, ethnic rivalry in Indonesia, segregation in America and patriarchalism almost everywhere.

4. *Knowing what you do not know.* Crosscultural Christians are quite likely to face situations where they do not *know* how to resolve differences in values that stem from radically different worldviews. When confronted with an experience that defies your assumed categories of explanation, it is prudent to suspend judgment. There is no reason that Christians should think themselves capable of always explaining even their own moral experience, let alone the experience of other cultures.

Pak Mesach Krisetya of Satya Wacana Christian University in Java, Indonesia, relates the following case study:

A counselee, recently converted from Islam to Christianity, is troubled by the magical talisman that has given him power, success, and prosperity in the past. It is a gold coin, visible beneath the skin on the underside of the forearm. There is no scar, no sign of an incision. He reports that it was placed there by a Muslim priest who laid the coin on the arm, covered it with his hand, chanted the incantation, and when he took away his hand the coin was beneath the skin. The young man, having now rejected such magic, wishes to have the coin and its powers removed. He leaves the counseling interview, having decided to request prayer in the public worship service. The next

Sunday he goes forward asking that this symbol and its powers be removed. The pastor shows the arm and visible coin to the congregation, then lays hands on the talisman while all pray. At the end of the prayer, the coin is in the hand of the pastor; the arm is clear, scarless, and with no sign of the previous implantation.

In other cases, the pastoral counselor reports, prayer removes the special powers experienced by the person with the embedded coin, then a surgeon at the Christian hospital removes the coin but stitches mark the operation scar.

Such actual material phenomena are outside the categories of hypnotic, hysteric or psychosomatic description that we use to label symptoms from psychologically induced blindness to psychosocial death. The insertion of coins in the arm or diamonds in the temples, the ability to walk barefoot over live coals or to pour boiling oil over oneself from head to foot in temple ceremonies with no visible burn damage—these have been empirically verified by witnesses from within and without the culture. Such persons must be counseled from within the reality of their experience, though one possesses no scientific explanation for the phenomena observed.[12]

While examples such as this, which defy a rational, scientific worldview, may appear exotic, the puzzlement may be no less when foreigners are faced with moral dilemmas that spring from a little-known social structure. How should you counsel an African Christian who has just taken his brother's widow as his second wife? What do you say to a Christian who has joined the guerrillas to fight against an obviously corrupt government? What do you do about gifts from clients which may influence business arrangements? How do you treat needy employees whose work does not meet your expectations? How do you respond when someone tells you a lie?

In some cases where you lack cultural knowledge, you can refer the problem to a local person who understands the context. In some cases you can seek advice and support. In some cases you can simply admit your ignorance and attempt neutrality. In some cases you can give your opinion in a nondogmatic manner. But in some cases you must act.

If you cannot get advice or help, you must act on what you know. If so, it is helpful to recognize what you don't know. The meaning of your action will be construed in relation to an imperfectly understood context. While you may act on the basis of firm values, your action may communicate other values than those of which you are aware. Even values that you believe are universal may be expressed differently in culturally nuanced actions. What to you is a lie may be a widely recognized way of communicating need or respect for your interests.

Knowledge is essential for learning crosscultural goodness, both theological knowledge that will unlock the Scriptures and cultural knowledge that illumines the context of our actions. Some kinds of knowledge can and should be acquired before you enter another culture. But crosscultural goodness requires, a lifetime of learning in its proper context. The best way of learning ethics comes through communication and dialogue.

Communication, Dialogue and Friendship

The previous section, by itself, might give the impression that learning goodness in a crosscultural situation is a heroic individual pursuit. Crosscultural types are often adventurous individualists who relish the challenge of crossing new frontiers and learning through experience and study how to serve God in a foreign culture. But even experience and knowledge grow more from communion with others than from individual experience. Goodness is the gift of God through a community to its members. It is not the private achievement of a moral athlete.

A crosscultural Christian is in dialogue with at least three different communities. First there is the community of faith, which spans the authors of Scripture, the exemplars of the church through history and the living members of the church in all cultures today. Second there are the culture and subcultures to which the person is native. Finally there are the adopted culture and subcultures that the person has entered.

The community of faith. I was raised in a family that emphasized prayer and Bible study. Because my father worked for InterVarsity Christian Fellowship, I was taught at an early age to value a "quiet time" of prayer and Bible reading every morning.[13] As a student I learned to lead inductive small-group Bible studies. Inductive Bible studies were more oriented to the group's discovery of conceptual knowledge about God's Word and will. The goal of the study was to understand what the Bible says, what it means and how it is relevant.

I now see that a whole theological and cultural tradition was forming me through its rituals. I read the Bible with InterVarsity eyes. A theological tradition that grew out of English Pietism and the nineteenth-century missionary movement shaped what I saw and didn't see in the Bible. I will never forget my shock and puzzlement when, after years of reading the Bible, I discovered how much of it focused on the problems of justice, poverty and wealth. I had never seen it because my tradition assumed such matters were peripheral to the message of salvation.

The tradition that formed my ability to understand is theological and intellectual, social and cultural. It was shaped by the individualism and rationalism of the Enlightenment, the struggle against the anti-intellectualism of fundamentalism, the historical conflict with modernism and the social gospel, and the many polarities that provide the furniture of Western thought. Dichotomies such as "being and appearance," "self and role," "substance and accident," "noumenon and phenomenon," "reality and experience," "fact and value," "theory and application," "objective and subjective," "spiritual and material," "individual and social" are seldom articulated as part of a popular theological tradition. They are like glasses we wear or air we breathe. By them we live and see. But we never see *them* until we learn to question them.

The theological and cultural traditions that shape our study of the Bible are a treasure. We could never understand anything without the conceptual tools and presuppositions that give form to our minds. To be free of our tradition is neither possible nor desirable. As we become aware of the historical "conditionedness" of our own thought, we are humbled by the partialness of our understanding. When we understand the perspectival finiteness of our knowing, we can see the necessity of *dialogue* as an approach to truth and goodness.

A dialogical approach to knowledge and goodness is as old as Plato. As Frances Adeney has observed,

> The dialogical method emphasized the partiality of all our knowing. Plato set up the question; classic positions were adopted by participants in the dialogue. Then the positions were argued and each found to be lacking, although containing some aspects of the truth. By showing the partial nature of the truth in the positions taken, each dialogue unearthed a deeper question, i.e., a more fundamental issue that was at stake. . . .
>
> The striving itself pointed to the possibility of a deeper kind of knowledge that seemed to recede as one approached it. Movement toward fuller knowledge was possible; total knowledge was beyond human reach.[14]

Plato's method of seeking truth has been echoed since by many other thinkers, among whom G. W. F. Hegel is significant. Hegel suggested that historical progress takes place through a *dialectic*, a struggle between opposing ideas. When a thesis is presented in a given culture, it provokes an antithesis (a contradiction), which comes into conflict with the thesis. Through the dialectic between thesis and antithesis, eventually a new synthesis is formed out of the opposing ideas. The synthesis becomes a new thesis provoking its own antithesis, and the round continues, with each step coming closer to Truth.[15]

Hegel's view was evolutionary and cosmic. Both the doctrine of the Fall and the horrendous historical events of the twentieth century give us very little reason to share his optimism in the steady progress of civilization. Dialectical thinking can be wishy-washy and avoid the unpleasant fact that sometimes when there are opposing views, one is true and the other is false.

Nevertheless, the truth is often bigger than any one person's ability to grasp. By recognizing dialectical aspects of truth we are free to look for wisdom in opposing opinions without compromising what is valuable in our own. Elements of a foreign conception of goodness may be coherent in their own context, just as our own view of morality may be coherent in our cultural context. By dialogue between two internally coherent truths we may come closer to an understanding of ontological Truth. But this cannot be done alone. It is the product of community.

For Christians, the Bible is an authoritative partner in the dialogue. The world and thought forms of the Scriptures question our own world and assumptions. By "conversation" with the text we learn to see our own world differently. God's revelation in history is a story to which we fuse our own story. By doing so we learn to make sense of our lives as a coherent narrative. As Stanley Hauerwas states,

> The metaphors that determine our vision must form a coherent story if our lives are to have duration and unity. Such stories create the context of meaning for the concrete moral rules and principles to which we adhere. There is no principled way to separate the "religious" from the "moral" in such stories.[16]

When we face contradictions between our story and the biblical narrative, we are sometimes forced to reexamine our interpretation of the text in its context. By reexamining our interpretation of the text, we recognize our own assumptions and the presuppositions of our community of faith. We may discover that our account of our experience needs to be reinterpreted in light of the biblical story. These issues will be examined in the next chapter.

If we need a dialogue with the Bible to understand how we can understand goodness, we also need a dialogue with our tradition to see how it has influenced our theology. Our theology is heavily influenced by the heroes of our tradition who have demonstrated what it means to live as a Christian. Whether the hero is John Sung, Teresa of Ávila, John Calvin, Simatupong, J. N. Darby, Martin Luther King, Thomas Aquinas, Dorothy Day or Watchman Nee, our communities have interpreted the faith by the wisdom and examples of their best members.

Christians who enter another culture should enter into dialogue with their own theological tradition, not to pass it on slavishly but to understand how their own thought has been shaped. Most countries of the world do not need more divisions and denominations. They do need Christians who understand how their faith is culturally shaped and theologically partial. Only such Christians can begin to see the cultural elements in their own expression of the good news.

But dialogue with the Bible and tradition should not take place primarily in a library. This is one of the things for which the church exists. Over and over again, Christians who work in another culture emphasize the value of being in regular communication with a specific body of believers. A church that is contextualized in the local culture is an excellent resource for exploring the meaning of faith in that culture. For some people this is not possible, and a church from their own ethnic group or in their home culture remains their primary community.

A dialogue with two cultures. One of the benefits of entering another culture is the perspective it gives you on your own culture.[17] Of course it is all too possible to absolutize your own culture and judge everything from its perspective. Usually this is not done consciously. An absolutized culture is not even recognized. It is simply taken to be the perspective of truth and goodness. Patterns of time, space, government, business, family, group solidarity, politeness and work are perceived as the standpoint of truth and goodness. Not only does such an approach lead to alienation between cultural foreigners, it shuts off a person from coming to understand either culture. Cultural absolutism is simply a form of ignorance.

The first step to learning crosscultural goodness is to understand your own cultural specificity. For example, a young Chinese man from Hong Kong attended college in Canada and rented a room in the house of a local family. "Ying-chow" enjoyed good relations with the homeowners, who were very kind to him. He was a serious student with a strong sense of responsibility and a hierarchical view of the family. All went well until he gradually built up resentment over the behavior of the five-year-old daughter of his landlords. "Suzy" left her things around, was cheeky to him and pestered him to play with her.

One day she teasingly blocked the stairs of the house as he was hurrying to class. He fixed his eyes on her in a stern frown and ordered her to get out of his way and stop bothering him. She seemed genuinely frightened, broke into tears and ran to her mother for refuge. From then on not only did Suzy avoid him but the whole family became distant and cool. Ying-chow, suffering from loneliness already, did not understand such disapproval and retreated further into his isolation.

Later, as we talked, he began to recognize how his views of proper behavior of children in a family differed radically from those of his hosts. He thought children should be quiet and respectful to adults. Playing with someone else's child was certainly not his responsibility and might even be inappropriate for a single man. Flirting and talking back to adults was wrong for a small child. The girl clearly needed discipline. A stern rebuke from a resident adult was justified. He had always fulfilled his responsibilities and treated the older adults in the family with deference and respect. Ying-chow missed his own extended family acutely. He liked living in a home and felt unjustly blamed because of the actions of a naughty child.

From the family's perspective he had been unfriendly from the start. Suzy, innocently puzzled and a little afraid of the strange foreign man who had invaded her nuclear family, had made brave attempts to make friends with him. Her parents had taught her to be open and express her feelings to adults, even when she disagreed with them. Suzy was used to receiving hugs and laughter from adults when she acted "cute." In fact, she was the center of the family. She and her parents were puzzled by Ying-chow's aloofness and constant work. But she innocently went on trying to reach him till one day he turned on her in inexplicable rage. The threat in his eyes and his authoritarian tone were a new experience. Suzy was terrified. From then on the whole family felt uneasy about their brooding guest.

The differences between egalitarian and hierarchical family structures are obvious causes for this misunderstanding. But the real villain is ignorance, ignorance that such a thing as cultural approaches to familial relationships even exist. Ying-chow did not know what questions to ask or how to begin to unravel the mystery of his landlords' behavior. Since I had grown up in Hong Kong but knew North American culture, he thought I might know what he had done to offend.

Actually I did not need to say much. As soon as he began to talk, to communicate his experience, he began to see the broad patterns of how his cultural virtues of filial piety conflicted with the assumed practices of a Canadian family. Communication and dialogue with someone attuned to the importance of cultural differences was enough to open his eyes to the contours of his own worldview.

Communication was the key to his understanding. His assumption that children should be quiet and respectful to adults needed to be confronted with a cultural antithesis, that children should be expressive and affectionate. Only then could Ying-chow work on a new synthesis of behavior that retained what was essential to his Chinese Christian identity yet respected the cultural style of his hosts. Ying-chow wanted to know which approach was right and biblical. But that question was far too big for a simple answer. Each approach was coherent and intrasystemically true. Each had wisdom. Neither could be easily transferred to another cultural context.

Ways to cope with value differences. Richard Brislin suggests that there are five coping strategies for dealing with crosscultural conflicts.[18] I have adapted the following in relation to value conflicts: (1) *nonacceptance* (reject the new value and behave as you would in your own culture), (2) *substitution* (replace your native values with the new values appropriate to your new context), (3) *addition* (retain both sets of values: sometimes use behavior from your own culture and sometimes use behavior from the host culture when it is helpful), (4) *combination* (combine and integrate elements from both sets of values) and (5) *synthesis* or creation/integration (create a new, innovative value system that draws from the values of both cultures).

While it might be tempting to read these as a hierarchy, in the real world all five strategies are necessary to healthy interaction with conflicting values. If a businessman is offered a female companion or a teacher is given plagiarized material, the only possible response may be *nonacceptance* of the foreign value, no matter how commonly it is practiced. Cultural sensitivity is needed to guide the visitor's way of handling the situation. But some values cannot be harmonized with Christian moral commitments.

Some behavioral patterns, like visiting someone's house rather than inviting them to dinner, can easily be *substituted* for Western conventions. Nevertheless, the values of hospitality might remain essentially the same. A little more problematic is how far one might substitute patterns of frank communication with indirect or misleading conventions of local usage. Even though it is conventional in some cultures to bargain for a lower price because "my goat has died and my wife is sick," a Christian may enjoy such fabrications without resorting to them.

On the other hand, Sherwood Lingenfelter relates the following story in which substitution of indirect patterns of communication proved valuable:

> During my research on Yap in 1979, I was faced with the unpleasant task of firing a Yapese man. He was part of a group being trained to administer an island wide survy, and I discovered that he had made up the responses on survey forms he returned to me. He was obviously having difficulty understanding my objectives so I decided I could not employ him any longer.
>
> Knowing that Yapese generally cover up weakness, I determined to handle this matter as gently and as privately as possible, hoping to help the man save face and to maintain a positive relationship with him. I called him aside one afternoon, and as gently as I could, I told him he had lost the job. Paying him for work I felt was worthless, I thought that I had managed the situation in a generous and Christian manner.
>
> To my chagrin the young man, while very polite, took the matter very hard. He had indeed lost face, and from that time on, no matter what I tried, he refused to have anything more to do with me. . . .
>
> Sometime later I experienced difficulty with another Yapese employee who was fabricating responses on the survey. Wanting to avoid, if possible, the alienation I experienced with the first man, I asked a Yapese pastor friend for advice. Without hesitation he said, "Send somebody to talk to him." I was astounded. How could I do that? It was completely against my nature to take the cowardly way out. But my pastor friend persisted and persuaded me that it was the only way to handle the problem.
>
> I asked one of the older men working for me if he would take my message of reprimand to the errant worker, and without hesitation he agreed to do so. We drove to the worker's village, where my colleague went alone to the man's home and in a very tactful but effective way told him of my frustrations with his work and of my intent to fire him if the problems were repeated. We then returned to the office and for a period of two weeks waited to see how the man would respond. When he returned to the office with a new batch of questionnaires, he greeted me as a long-lost friend. We engaged in warm and lively conversation, and our relationship appeared more solid than ever before. His work was not merely acceptable, it was excellent; and he became one of my most reliable and helpful employees.

I was puzzled as to why the second worker had responded so positively whereas the first man had rejected me so completely. My pastor friend explained the matter quite simply. In Yap, to tell a man to his face that he has failed is to treat him like an insignificant child. My sending a messenger to the second man meant that I considered him as my equal or superior and that I could not to his face rebuke or expose his weakness. He accepted the respect that my sending the messenger had shown him, and he returned that respect by giving me the quality of work that he knew I desired from him.[19]

In this story Lingenfelter *substituted* a Yapese cultural style of confrontation for the Western pattern to which he was accustomed. The story can also be seen as an example of the *addition* of new values to a Western orientation. As an anthropologist, Lingenfelter had a task to do which assumed values that were foreign to his employees. When faced with their disregard for the purposes and values of his survey, he did not discard the task-oriented values of social science research. He retained the values of his objective but added new procedural values that respected his context. He could not have done this without advice from the local pastor. Thus the story also shows the value of communication with a trusted informant about good practice in an unfamiliar social context.

The addition of new cultural values to old patterns of behaving may be particularly effective in situations where global culture has modified the patterns of local behavior. An obvious example as to do with the meaning of punctuality. In many places, values of efficiency have been superimposed on cultures that traditionally value relationships more highly than the clock. Certain kinds of appointments are kept to the minute, while others are defined very loosely. The efficiency values of capitalism are utilized in some business and social events but are not allowed to dominate all of life. In such cultures skillful social interaction requires perception of where traditional and "modern" concepts of time are most appropriate.

Some years ago I was engrossed in conversation with an Indonesian Batak student and was surprised to learn that he had been waiting over a year to take an examination from his major professor. He could not graduate because he had been unable to see his professor for some months. My surprise turned to distress when I found out that he had a three-o'clock appointment with the professor that very day. When he told me this, it was already three-twenty and he seemed in no hurry. "Don't worry," he said, "it's rubber time." To arrive an hour late was perfectly acceptable, especially as he was having such a good conversation with me. On the other hand, when he took me to a church service the next morning, it started exactly on time. If you arrived an hour late the service would be over.

Sometimes diverse cultural values that are coherent in their own context can be *combined*. For example, an American who values human equality very highly will find it difficult to adjust to a hierarchical Javanese or Japanese social setting unless he is able to combine the values of equality with those of respect for those who are older. In America, egalitarian ideology leads to patterns of informal familiarity in communication regardless of the real feelings of those involved. In contrast, Javanese show great deference to social superiors regardless of their private opinion of them. Either style can be sincere or hypocritical, but it is quite possible to combine a fundamental conviction of the equality of all people with a humble respect for those whose age or role is above yours in the social hierarchy.

Friendship. Aristotle talks about three kinds of friendship: (1) friendship in which a weaker person receives help from a stronger person and the relationship is focused on this help, (2) friendship in which two persons relate because of reciprocal need, and each party maintains the relationship for what they can get out of it, and (3) the deepest kind of friendship, in which equals care for each other out of something like pure virtue—this is, so to speak, friendship for friendship's sake.[20] In real life all three types often overlap. Crosscultural friendships may begin with the first type, as the stranger is very dependent on the host, and develop into the second, as the stranger learns how to contribute to the community. The miracle of the third, ideal type of friendship is that it can bridge any barrier. True friendships are both costly and very precious. They sometimes cross not only cultural barriers but also class barriers.

The film *Driving Miss Daisy* provides a vivid example of a combining of disparate values which ultimately led to a new *synthesis*, a highly unusual friendship. The film is set in the Southern United States during the 1940s and 1950s. The son of a wealthy, eccentric elderly Jewish woman hires a black driver to be her chauffeur. While Miss Daisy affirms racial equality, the structure of her relationship with her driver is strictly hierarchical. Yet the driver's respectful dignity and indefatigable sense of humor overcome the oppression of his situation. Without either destroying the fragile hierarchy of his relationship to her or compromising his own human dignity, he becomes her best friend.

While ideally we might wish to see the social and cultural barriers between them abolished, in reality neither they nor their context could achieve such a leveling. Each remained socially and culturally distinct from the other. Neverthe-less, the honesty, commitment and love of their relationship, within their hier-archical roles, was a tremendous moral achievement. The positive values of Southern patterns of respectful communication were combined with a growing recognition of their essential equality. The result was a new relationship that transcended the possibilities of either of their cultures.

Perhaps Paul anticipated just such a transcending of social roles when he counseled slaves to remain in their position but regard themselves as free in Christ. Paul does not discount the oppression of their situation and advises them to become free if they can. But neither does he consider their social condition determinative of their true identity.

> Were you a slave when you were called? Don't let it trouble you—although if you can gain your freedom, do so. For he who was a slave when he was called by the Lord is the Lord's freedman; similarly, he who was a free man when he was called is Christ's slave. You were bought with a price; do not become slaves of men. (1 Cor 7:21-23 NIV)

It is not possible to draw up rules to guide the choice between strategies of nonacceptance, substitution, addition, combination and synthesis. Sometimes when we are confronted with alien values the right choice is apparent to reason or intuition. At other times, as in the case of the anthropologist in Yap, dialogue with someone fluent in the foreign culture is essential. The ideal informant is a mature Christian member of the host culture who is familiar with your culture. In cultures that value politeness and harmony, it is difficult to find someone willing to be frank about your failings.[21] True friendship with such a person, in any culture, is a gift beyond price.

Wisdom

As we live in another culture, our goal is to become bicultural—to become fluent in two languages and two cultures. The ability to be bicultural is a continuum that is never fully achieved. The novice in bicultural wisdom may serve God as well as the expert, though at a lower level of insight.

Inculturated wisdom. Crosscultural wisdom combines biblical knowledge, the power of the Holy Spirit and cultural experience to produce the fruit of goodness. The result is not disconnection from culture to some objective standpoint but identification with the moral aspirations of more than one culture. David W. Augsburger observes,

The intercultural person is not culture-free (a hypothetical and undesirable state). Rather, the person is culturally aware. Awareness of one's own culture can free one to disconnect identity from cultural externals and to live on the boundary, crossing over and coming back with increasing freedom. Disidentification of the self from old cultural identifications leads to rediscovery of the self in at least three contexts—one's own culture, a second culture, and in that unique third culture that always forms on the boundary between the two. This third-culture perspective enables the intercultural person to make communication easier, interpret cultural conflict, and function with acceptable competence without any inappropriate switching or confusing of behavior.[22]

The process of "disidentifying" the self from a monocultural perspective is painful and futile unless accompanied by a "rediscovery" of your identity in both your native and adopted cultures. A "third-culture perspective" is possible only through a synthesis of cultural values achieved through reidentification with both cultures. Another way to put this is that wisdom is not possible without love. Only as we love people in another culture can we begin to identify with them and see the truth they understand. As we make their truth our own, we become new people, formed from the synthesis of two cultures.

Wisdom as openness to truth. Wisdom cannot be equated with cognitive knowledge. Cognitive knowledge is safe. It can be bundled up in propositions and possessed by the knower. But wisdom comes in the confrontation between knowledge and an unknown reality. It requires an openness to the stranger and her unknown knowledge. It involves the risk that what we have assumed to be true will be exposed as our own prejudice. As Hans-Georg Gadamer observes,

> Understanding always implies a pre-understanding which is in turn prefigured by the determinate tradition in which the interpreter lives and which shapes his prejudices. Every encounter with others therefore means the "suspension" of one's own prejudices. . . . Always something more is demanded than to "understand the other," that is to seek and acknowledge the immanent coherence contained within the meaning-claim of the other. A further invitation is always implied. Like an infinite idea, what is also implied is a transcendental demand for coherence in which the ideal of truth is located. But this requires a readiness to recognize the other as potentially right and to let him or it prevail against me.[23]

To enter into another culture means to allow yourself to feel the pull of another way of seeing the world. This is not for the self-protective or timid. It is to be open to the possibility that another system of values and beliefs might be equally valid or better than my own. Cultural relativists accept this not as a challenge but as a premise. There can be no risk to the security of truth if all truth is relative. Christians do not assume the equal validity of all cultural perspectives. Those who believe in a good God who transcends all cultures also believe that some perspectives may be equally valid and others simply wrong.

Yet there is also the possibility, indeed the certainty, that some of our own perspectives are skewed. Christians believe there is a moral universe that exists outside human attempts to define it. Of all people, Christians should not be afraid of truth. While our culturally conditioned religious ideas may provide us with security, Christian faith is founded on the God of Truth, who is bigger than our religious ideas. Simone Weil said, "If ever I have to choose between God and Truth, I always choose Truth. And I have found that whenever I do, I run straight into the arms of Jesus."

Wisdom and the relativity of culture. There is little reason to suppose that our own cultural conceptions of goodness are more accurate than any other cultural viewpoints. Some people have assumed the superiority of the West based on its long history of interaction with Christian ideas. But the West has also been formed by Enlightenment humanism, scientism, capitalism, analytic psychology, deism and many other forces. Sometimes Western Christians mistakenly identify their cultural standpoint with their faith.

During a conversation with several Christian North American businessmen, I was amazed by their anti-Japanese sentiments. Not only was Japan seen as a threat to American business interests, but they believed that the temptation to sell a new product for production by a Japanese company was a great evil. Risking accusations of heresy in the face of what seemed so self-evident to them, I asked why this was so. Would it matter, I wondered, if the Japanese company was owned by Christians and the American company owned by egocentric materialists?

Their response surprised me. They affirmed that in general American business is conducted by Christian principles while Japanese business is not. The questions such an affirmation raised were beyond the scope of our conversation. But their assumptions were at least not self-evident. It is possible that Japanese productivity stems in part from closer adherence to the true relationships between work and community. Perhaps expressive and utilitarian individualism has a greater impact on American industry than Christian faith. The issues are

74

complex, and whatever conclusions are reached will be highly debatable.

Wisdom rooted in commitment. Simone Weil remarked, "Morality is not a matter of will, but of attention."[24] We pay attention to the things we care about, and that determines our perspective. Commitments and affections are not so much the result of a cognitive process as the fruit of experience. If I concentrate my time primarily on money-making, that is where my heart will be. If my focus is on academic prestige, that will be my treasure. If my eye is fixed on power and security, whether through a business or through a church, that will be my own special darkness (Mt 6:22-23). If the attention of my heart is on God's kingdom, everything I see will be lighted by that concern. Faith is more than assent to doctrine; it is rooted in the ultimate concern of a person in community.[25]

Latin American theologians such as José Míguez Bonino accuse Western theology of being deeply influenced by privileged social and economic conditions.[26] It is not difficult to see why this might be so. White middle-class Christians are naturally committed to their community. There is nothing wrong with that. Such commitment provides a standpoint from which to understand our faith and experience. At the same time the practices of commitment to our own social group, especially if our "in group" is comparatively rich and powerful, may shut us off from the wisdom that springs from a commitment to the poor. Middle-class perspectives are not invalid, but like all perspectives they are informed by self-interest and easily become narrow and superficial in face of an acutely suffering world.

Dietrich Bonhoeffer suggests that the "underside of history" is a more fruitful perspective for viewing reality than a position of comfort and privilege. The ideology of commitment to the poor is widespread in both Protestant and Catholic communities. But ideological commitment rings hollow if it is unconnected to vivid relationships with people who are suffering and oppressed. We cannot effectively think or act on behalf of people who are only an abstraction. Those who wish to see more of reality must be willing to really know those who are oppressed.

During the U.S. bombing of Libya in the Reagan era, I was given unusual insight into the situation by one of my students who had worked in North Africa for many years. "Jane," while a perceptive observer of North African politics, did not have any special political understanding of the causes of the bombing. What she did have was a deep love for North African Muslims. Her ability to identify with their way of perceiving the American bombing raid did not resolve geopolitical questions of the effectiveness of the action for global peace or American policy objectives. In any case there was not a unitary meaning that could simply explain, justify or condemn the bombings. There were many meanings.

But in the anguished face of Jane I could see the meaning of the raid from the perspective of an American who was deeply committed to the well-being of Libyans. The wisdom of her love was in shocking contrast to the jubilation of many Americans at this display of military power.

Tacit wisdom rooted in caring. There are depths of wisdom that can come only through love. Such wisdom is "tacit" or unstated for the simple reason that it is far more complex than "technical reason." It cannot be fully described in words. Without knowing quite how, a person who really cares about another may "see" many things invisible to a detached observer. Just as a lover can see beyond a surface smile to the tension behind the beloved's eyes, so a foreigner may see beyond the strangeness of inexplicable custom to the real person, if he really cares about him or her.

In a book on expert nursing, Patricia Benner argues that the wisdom of an expert nurse cannot be encapsulated in propositions or rules.[27] Benner relates stories of many "exemplar" nurses whose expertise in medical treatment far exceeds the established procedures of diagnosis and treatment. "Technically" they could never have known how to treat their patients so well. She suggests that their ability to see patients and know exactly what, out of a thousand options, is the best way to care for them is rooted in their care for the whole person.

The wisdom of caring draws on tacit knowledge that is derived from long experience. While tacit knowledge by definition cannot be codified, neither is it to be equated with unfounded personal intuition. Rather it is preserved in practices that are common to a community of caring and are passed on by example. Expert nurses are living examples of medical wisdom that can be imitated but not learned from a book.

Cultural wisdom has this same indefinable quality. A day spent carefully observing an expert in a culture may be of more value than reading a whole book of cultural rules. Rules are helpful for shielding the novice from blatant mistakes. But cultural rules, like the rules of grammar, have many exceptions and often derive from meanings that lie below the surface of consciousness. As grammar derives from speaking, so cultural rules derive from practice. Practices are learned through relationship with the community in which they are embedded. Michael Polanyi argues that this is ultimately true of all knowledge: "Tacit assent and intellectual passions, the sharing of idiom and of a cultural heritage, affiliation to a like-minded community: such are the impulses which shape our vision of the nature of things. No intelligence, however critical or original, can operate outside such a fiduciary framework."[28]

Wisdom as friendship with God. Traditional Western theology had very little room for the experience of friendship with God. How can a human being be friends with an infinite, all-sufficient, "Unmoved Mover"? At best, friendship with God might be conceived in Aristotle's first sense of an unequal relationship of need. The experience of radical dependency and grace (unmerited favor) is, in fact, the beginning of friendship with God. We can never be equal friends with the God of the universe!

On the other hand, Jesus told his disciples that he considered them his friends. Where servants simply receive and obey, Jesus' friends find that he loves them, tells them what God is doing and lays down his life for them (Jn 15:9-17). In return he wants something from them: that they obey his commandments, love one another and love him. In a sense this implies at least the second level of reciprocal friendship in Aristotle's scheme. To be sure, there is no comparing what we give with what God gives. But even if we give very little, it is something that God wants. I am not sure it is helpful to speculate about whether God *needs* a human response of love in some metaphysical sense. It is enough to know that God, like a mother with her baby, wants a return of love from God's child.

It's possible that such a person as Moses ("the friend of God") enjoyed elements of Aristotle's third level of virtuous friendship in his relationship with God. Moses spoke with God face to face like a friend and had arguments with God and won (Ex 33)!

Real friendship with God, at any of the three levels, gives a whole new perspective on life. While friendship with God entails a worldview (there is a just and loving God of the universe), the worldview is not the primary factor that brings wisdom. A Christian worldview is necessary to experience friendship with God. But it is not sufficient. "Even the demons believe—and shudder" (Jas 2:19).

Rather, wisdom stems from the gift of a new location in the world from which to experience life. A friend of God experiences God's forgiveness and is enabled to forgive. A friend of God experiences dependence on God and knows he or she is ultimately safe. Insofar as a friend of God experiences the love and justice of God, she or he is able to seek first the kingdom of God and God's justice on earth (Mt 6:33; see also 6:10). Wisdom comes not from assenting to doctrines but from knowing God in experience. Wisdom involves a different way of experiencing the world.

If "the fear of the LORD is the *beginning* of wisdom" (Prov 9:10), then the love of God is the *telos* or fulfillment of wisdom. In the wisdom of friendship with God, we are enabled to love God in our neighbor. "Those who say, 'I love God,' and hate their brothers or sisters, are liars; for those who do not love a brother or sister whom they have seen, cannot love God whom they have not seen" (1 Jn 4:20). The neighbor whom we can see, even if culturally strange, is the one we are called to love. It's much easier to love humankind, or "the oppressed," than to love the strange immigrant who just moved next door.

In order to experience the wisdom of God that is revealed in love, we must be changed. The commandments of Jesus, or for that matter the advice in this book, are "dead letters" unless we are enabled by the Spirit to love the stranger. Transformation into the likeness of Christ (Phil 2) is a mysterious process. It entails a kind of wisdom that is foolishness to those who have not experienced it (1 Cor 1:18-31). This wisdom may be in reach for a young child while a brilliant theologian cannot grasp it. The wisdom of friendship with God can be received only by those whose hands are empty.

The gift of being a friend of God is beyond my power to explain. Paul gives us a glimpse of it when he writes, "And all of us, with unveiled faces, seeing the glory of the Lord as though reflected in a mirror, are being transformed into the same image from one degree of glory to another; for this comes from the Lord, the Spirit" (2 Cor 3:18).

Friendship with God entails values that are both alien and familiar to every culture. They include qualities of character or virtue:[29] "love, joy, peace, patience, kindness, generosity, faithfulness, gentleness, and self-control" (Gal 5:22-23; compare 1 Cor 13:4-7); they include commandments such as the Decalogue (Ex 20:2-17), which is summed up in the great commandment to love God with all your being and your neighbor as yourself (Mt 22:37-40); they are revealed in the great narrative of salvation history with its clear portrayal of the justice of God and God's continual advocacy of the rights of the poor (Lk 1:51-53);[30] they include the reconciliation of all people with each other and God, and the breaking down of barriers based on race, class or gender (Gal 3:28); they include the formation of disciples in every nation on earth (Mt 28:19-20); and they include the call to imitate God's own self-sacrifice in the person of Jesus, who came to serve and die for his enemies (Mt 5—7; Phil 2:5-8).

FOUR

THE BIBLE
AND CULTURE
IN ETHICS

———————————

C hristians believe that the Bible is the primary, authoritative guide to faith and life. Cultural conventions do not have an authority that overrules Scripture. When Christians differ, whatever their culture, they rightly search the Scriptures to find wisdom.

William Dyrness has argued that "it is scripture, and not its 'message,' that is finally transcultural."[1] The message of the Bible, or the way it is interpreted, is always perceived and stated in human language that reflects the priorities of particular people in a particular culture. The entire canon of the Bible, on the other hand, is constitutive of what it means to be a Christian in every time and place. David Kelsey writes that to call a text "scripture" is to say

1) that its use in certain ways in the common life of the Christian community is essential to establishing and preserving the community's identity. . . . 2) It is authority for the common life of the Christian community. . . . 3) It is to ascribe some kind of 'wholeness' to it. . . . 4) The expression, "Scripture is authoritative for theology" has self-involving force.[2]

The term *scripture* implies commitment. In every time and place, believers define themselves in relation to Scripture. Whatever their differences in doctrine or practice, all accept a common written source as the vehicle of the revelation of God in Christ.

Yet the Bible is not self-interpreting. While all accept the text,[3] what they think it means differs widely.

The Cultural Context of the Bible

Not only the culture of the reader but also the many different cultures that lie within and behind the text compound the task of understanding. We can understand what we read only in relation to our cultural experience. But everything that is written in the Bible is located within the cultural experience of its author or editor.

There is an overlap between the cultures of the Bible and the cultures of its readers in every age. If there weren't, the task of reading such a foreign text would be impossible. But there are also pervasive differences. If we do not understand these differences, the ethical teaching of the Bible remains incomprehensible.

Christian commitment to the Bible reflects the conviction that God is revealed through this text. As Robert McAfee Brown has commented,

> Christians make the initially bizarre gamble that "the strange new world within the Bible" is a more accurate view of the world than our own and that we have to modify our views as a result. This means engaging in dialogue with the Bible—bringing our questions to it, hearing its questions to us, examining our answers in its light, and taking its answers very seriously, particularly when they conflict with our own, which will be most of the time.[4]

The problem comes when the Bible's questions and its answers seem totally foreign and incomprehensible to us. Whatever their doctrine of Scripture, most Christians simply ignore the parts that seem irrelevant. But more difficult to ignore are differences in interpretation between different believers or even in the same person at different times.

Devout Christians sometimes marvel that each time they come to a familiar passage they learn something new. The Holy Spirit opens their eyes to new insight. Whenever a person reads a text again, she comes to it from a slightly different context. This week she has different problems and concerns from those she faced a year ago. As the context of her interpretation changes, she sees new things in the text. Just as two photographs of the same scene can look dramatically different because of how they are framed, what focus is used, the light setting chosen and the type of film and camera used, so a text looks different to us as we visualize it from different vantage points. With dramatically different cultures, the range of vantage points widens.

This does not mean that the text changes. The number and types of legitimate interpretations are controlled by what is really in the text.[5] What is in the text itself is ruled by the finite number of meanings possible in its original context. Ethical instructions, laws, examples and narratives cannot be abstracted from the context without affecting their meaning. Whether the Bible says, "do not kill," "greet one another with a holy kiss" or "Jesus wept," the meaning of the text cannot be understood without the context.

Without this understanding much of the Bible would be even more puzzling than it is. For example, in Exodus 23:19 the Israelites are commanded, "You shall not boil a kid in its mother's milk." Knowing that "a kid" means a baby goat does not get us much closer to understanding why there should be such a prohibition. While animal-rights activists might be delighted with this verse, it is unlikely that prevention of cruelty to animals was the motive for the law. Archaeological discoveries concerning Canaanite fertility practices provide a much more plausible explanation. Boiling a kid in its mother's milk was evidently part of a common fertility rite. Thus the law should be understood as forbidding syncretism with Canaanite religions. Those who have no connection with fertility rites may find the literal meaning of the law irrelevant. On the other hand, insofar as we can find analogies in our own culture, we may still learn from this rule.

In many parts of the world, rites to appease spirits and assure fertility are common. In such a context this law is very relevant. It teaches us how God viewed fertility magic in the context of ancient Canaan. Even in contexts where such rites are rare, the meaning within this law may have relevance today. For example, a cosmopolite might extrapolate that in some situations, use of a dangerous fertility drug (trust in the magic of sciene to manipulate what rightly belongs to God) is an unwarranted means of increasing fertility. Perhaps Asians who hunt the rhinoceros (and are threatening its extinction) because of the purported powers of its horn in Chinese medicine should also take note.

Some biblical commands cannot be understood apart from their original context. Others are clear enough but should not be followed in most places today because the cultural conditions that gave them meaning are no longer pertinent. Whether the command is Peter's instruction to "greet one another with a kiss of love" (1 Pet 5:14), Paul's observation that "any woman who prays or prophesies with her head unveiled disgraces her head—it is one and the same thing as having her head shaved" (1 Cor 11:5), or the Deuteronomic law that rebellious children should be stoned (Deut 21:18-21), the commandments of Scripture must be understood for what they meant to people in a specific time and place before we can begin to understand what they might mean in *our* time and place.

In the Old Testament, God does or commands many things that appear abhorrent today. It is hard to imagine anything good that can be learned from a law that allows parents to have their children executed. We might speculate that since the law provided for a legal procedure that involved the whole community, it was unlikely to be used except in very extreme cases. Thus in addition to protecting the community from a youth who was entering a life of crime, the law protected children from arbitrary execution by parents who in that culture had unlimited power over their offspring. At the very least, the law required the agreement and participation of the entire community in the death sentence.

The meaning of the law can be understood only in relation to the actual conditions of its context. Possibly the law was intended to prevent even crueler practices. If so, like the divorce law ("because you were so hard-hearted," Mt 19:8), it did not legislate something good but only prevented something worse.

Even so, I am not happy with this law and do not pretend to fully understand it. I don't think that under any circumstances disobedient children should be killed. Apart from the hazard of allowing my modern consciousness to stand in judgment on Scripture, I am culturally too distant from the events reported to fully understand them. But it is clear that the meaning of goodness is sometimes understood differently by the authors of the original text from the way we understand it today.

For example, in Numbers 15 Moses is instructed by God to have a man stoned to death for gathering wood on the sabbath. Functionally the man was doing exactly the same thing as Jesus and his disciples did when they plucked grain to eat on the sabbath (Mt 12:1-8). But Moses, in accordance with the law, had the wood-gatherer stoned.

Korah, one of Israel's leaders, was outraged by Moses' seeming abuse of power. Korah said, in effect, "Moses, you have gone too far. Why should you have such power to act unilaterally? Are you the only one who knows the mind of God?" (Num 16:3).

Korah was not alone in his concern. He brought with him 250 well-known community leaders who had been appointed members of the council, a group meant to serve as judges of the people. Korah argued that all of God's people are holy. "All the congregation are holy, everyone of them, and the LORD is among them. So why then do you exalt yourselves above the assembly of the LORD?" (Num 16:3). As far as I know, this is the first biblical approximation of an argument for the priesthood of all believers.

When we read with modern eyes, Korah was admirable. He didn't grumble off in a corner but responsibly brought his concern to an appointed council. His concerns were ethical and related to human rights; his instincts were democratic; his methods were responsible; and his theological arguments were sophisticated by modern standards. Ah, therein lies the rub. Korah's actions cannot be judged by modern standards. Their meaning can be accessed only within the context of the birth of the nation of Israel in the early bronze age.

The meaning of Korah's action, in his cultural context, was rebellion against Moses and against God, threatening the very existence of the nation of Israel as a unified people of God. In this context, not only was Moses' leadership challenged, but God's leadership, God's law and the discipline required for the formation of a nation were at stake. Apparently the Ten Commandments were also at stake, as gathering wood was a violation of the sabbath.

According to the account in Numbers, God considered Korah's sin so grave that Moses had to plead before God for the survival of the whole nation. As it was, God created an earthquake that scared the Israelites half to death. "The ground under [Korah and his family and followers] was split apart. The earth opened its mouth and swallowed them up. . . . And fire came out from the LORD and consumed the two hundred fifty men offering the incense" (Num 16:31-32, 35).

The point here is not whether Moses was intrinsically right or wrong to cast a death sentence on someone for gathering wood on the sabbath, but that Korah was horribly wrong to challenge Moses' leadership at this pivotal moment in the formation of Israel. Korah's action cannot be judged in itself, apart from his cultural context. This is the story of a power struggle. The action of God leaves no question that Korah's action was wrong in that time and in that place.

It does not follow from this that stoning people who gather wood on the sabbath is a good idea today. The conditions that existed during the time of the exodus will never be repeated. Does this mean that the passage has nothing to teach us? Of course not.

We might learn that keeping the sabbath is very important in the eyes of

God—an important lesson for those enslaved by the twin gods of workaholism and materialism. We might learn that democracy is not an absolute good—an important lesson for those who think liberal political culture is the apex of civilization. We might learn that community solidarity and respect for leadership can be more important than individual human rights or even the deaths of 251 people—an important lesson for those who have elevated individualistic autonomy to the central place in ethics.

The story is rich with ethical content. But the content cannot be abstracted into timeless truths that are alienated from real times and places. The story as a whole is far more fertile for ethical learning than any principles abstracted from it. The principles may prove false if they are applied at the wrong time, in the wrong place, by the wrong person. Fortunately, the lessons I drew from the story of Korah are not absolute. From other stories we might learn opposite kinds of lessons.

From the story of the disciples plucking grain we might learn that human need can be more important than legalistic forms. From the story of Nathan the prophet's rebuke of David we might learn that leadership should not have unlimited power and that it is important to stand up against leaders when they violate the rights of individuals (2 Sam 11—12). From the story of Jesus and the woman taken in adultery we might learn that mercy in the judgment of sinners is wise for leaders who are also sinners (Jn 8:2-11). Even from other stories in the life of Moses we might learn lessons balancing the story of Korah.

For example, when the people worship the golden calf, Moses pleads for their lives: "Alas, this people has sinned a great sin; they have made for themselves gods of gold. But now, if you will only forgive their sin—but if not, blot me out of the book you have written" (Ex 32:31-32). Presumably worshiping a golden calf was more serious than gathering firewood on the sabbath, but in a different context, in a different life situation for God's people, a different ethical judgment is brought into play.

Does this mean that biblical ethics are relativistic, that there are no absolutes and we must make all our decisions according to subjective criteria? By no means! Ethics in the Bible are contextual. They are incarnated words. But they derive from the character and will of God, which do not change.

Eugene Nida, followed by Charles Kraft, suggests that the Bible teaches a "relative cultural relativism."[6] The point is not that all truth is relative, but that all truth is enfleshed in specific language that relates it to specific cultural concerns. We can have an adequate but never an absolute understanding of moral principles: adequate because we can clearly see goodness and evil at work in biblical and modern times, never absolute because goodness and evil are grounded in specific realities of which we know only a tiny part. Nida goes so far as to say,

> The only absolute in Christianity is the triune God. Anything which involves [a human being], who is finite and limited, must of necessity be limited, and hence relative. Biblical cultural relativism is an obligatory feature of our incarnational religion, for without it we would either absolutize human institutions or relativize God.[7]

The poles of absolutism and relativism in ethics will be explored further in chapter seven. For now we must turn to the question of how ethics are learned from the Bible.

Learning to See the World Through the Stories of the Bible

The primary way we learn goodness from the Bible is by making the story of the Bible the interpretive framework through which we view all of life. This approach does not deny that we learn propositions or doctrines from the Scriptures. But unlike traditional conservative theology, we do not view these doctrines as propositions that we learn and then apply to various contexts. Rather, they are a lens through which we see reality. They help us to see the truth. The lens is not the truth, but it helps us to describe what is true.

George A. Lindbeck writes,

> A comprehensive scheme or story used to structure all dimensions of existence is not primarily a set of propositions to be believed, but is rather the medium in which one moves, a set of skills that one employs in living one's life. Its vocabulary of symbols and its syntax may be used for many purposes, only one of which is the formulation of statements about reality.[8]

Like a culture or language, it is a communal phenomenon that shapes the subjectivities of individuals rather than being primarily a manifestation of those subjectivities.[9]

Christians are inescapably influenced to see and experience the world through the lens of their culture. The reality we experience is socially constructed. It is difficult for even a strong-minded individual to maintain a belief that is contradicted by everyone else. There is a well-known story of an anthropologist who went to study a tribe and ended up becoming an animist. The story of reality the tribe told became the interpretive framework through which the anthropologist perceived all of reality.

A friend of mine experienced a radical loss of faith while studying for his Ph.D. One day he looked out the window in Cambridge and was overwhelmed with the feeling that the buses below, and all the material things he saw, were all that mattered, all that existed. The story of the universe he imbibed day after day from the university and from popular culture was in stark contradiction to his faith The result was radical doubt.

Our lived morality is a result of the way we perceive reality. People usually act in relation to their interpretation of the way the world really is, far more than from a set of beliefs or principles. Iris Murdoch has observed that "we are not isolated free choosers, monarchs of all we survey, but benighted creatures sunk in a reality whose nature we are constantly and overwhelmingly tempted to deform by fantasy."[10] In this situation, morality is, as Simone Weil suggested, a matter of attention. We act in accordance with what we think matters, what we see as true. Our actions toward our family or colleagues, or employees or bosses, are more a natural outflowing of the story we are living than a rational choice of good or evil.

Our perception of reality derives from a tradition. In modern liberal culture, reality is perceived as an object accessible to universal, scientific, liberal rationality. In contrast, Alasdair MacIntyre argues that rationality itself is determined by particular traditions and by the social institutions and relationships that embody them. He writes, "What each person is confronted with is at once a set of rival intellectual positions, a set of rival traditions embodied more or less imperfectly in contemporary forms of social relationship and a set of rival communities of discourse, each with its own specific modes of speech."[11]

Modern liberals reject this position and continue to impose their own brand of rationality on everyone. The great temple to universal, scientific rationality is the modern university. Adherence to any particular tradition, especially if it is explicitly religious, is ruled out of the classroom. In contrast, "postmodern" thinkers have radically "deconstructed" or destroyed the pretensions of universal, scientific rationality, along with its liberal institutions. They acknowledge diversity along with the assumption that there is no truth and every tradition is equally untenable.

MacIntyre critiques both the pretensions of liberalism and the cynicism of some forms of postmodernism.[12] He argues that we can be coherent about reality only if we perceive it out of a coherent way of seeing the world. Much of the incoherence of the modern world derives from the fact that people live out of half-believed liberalism, an incoherent mixture of traditions or no tradition at all. The fact that we need a tradition, along with its community of practices, does not imply that only one tradition is true or that all are false (or equally true). All traditions are limited by the perspective of their histories, their institutions and their standpoint in time and place.

In order to escape the deformed fantasies of our age, Christians believe we must see the world from the perspective of God's work in history.[13] The stories of the Bible provide the language and categories through which we see the world truly. Lindbeck says,

> It is important to note the direction of interpretation. Typology does not make scriptural contents into metaphors for extra scriptural realities but the other way around. It does not suggest, as is often said in our day, that believers find their stories in the Bible, but rather that they make the story of the Bible their story. The cross is not to be viewed as a figurative representation of suffering nor the messianic kingdom as a symbol for hope in the future; rather, suffering should be cruciform, and hopes for the future messianic. . . . It is the text, so to speak, which absorbs the world, rather than the world the text.[14]

Christians learn to be good from the Bible by telling themselves and each other the story of their lives as a part of the story of the Bible. More important than the stories believers tell are the stories they live. Goodness comes by the work of the Holy Spirit when a person lives as part of the people of God. That happens when she has learned the story of Israel, of Jesus and of the church so well that her life becomes a continuation of the story. Then a Christian becomes "a letter of Christ . . . written not with ink but with the Spirit of the living God, not on tablets of stone but on tablets of human hearts" (2 Cor 3:3).

The great problem for ethics is, of course, *How* do we learn the story of the Bible? There seem to be many stories in the Bible. The stories that are there do not all seem consistent with each other. The cultural contexts of the stories are often strange to us. And the way the same stories are related by different parts of the Christian community are sometimes unrecognizable to each other. These are very large questions which are beyond the scope of this book. As a start, however, let's consider several of the many ways in which we are formed by the biblical narratives.

Ethics in the Context of a Narrative

Stanley Hauerwas once commented that we can learn more ethics from reading novels than from reading ethics books. The Bible is not an ethics book. It does not contain many systematic treatises on ethics. Where ethics are explicitly addressed, it is usually in the context of a story. The Old Testament law is recounted in the context of the saga of the exodus; the Sermon on the Mount is an integral part of the story of Jesus. To borrow an expression that David Kelsey uses to describe Karl Barth's view of Scripture, the Bible is like a "vast, loosely-structured, non-fictional novel."[15]

We learn ethics from a story by allowing its way of seeing the world to become our own symbolic structure of meanings. For example, when we read the story of the prodigal son we may identify with the father, the prodigal, the elder brother or even the riotous friends. As we identify with one or more characters, their behavior and relationships become symbols of our own behavior and relationships. The meaning and moral evaluation of our own behavior are clarified by the meaning assigned to the actions of the characters in the story. The prodigal son's riotous living may symbolize our own rebellion and teach us that forgiveness is really possible.

Within the biblical narrative we see a moral outlook on life that is expressed in many literary forms. In stories, poetry, history, prophecy, apocalypse, law, sermons, proverbs, letters, songs, biography, prayers and other kinds of literature, good and evil are revealed and symbolized within a particular cultural context.

When Christians read the rich profusion of biblical material, four common questions emerge: (1) How do we deal with all the intense and messy emotions expressed by biblical authors? (2) How relevant are biblical commandments for life today? (3) Are biblical principles the heart of Christian ethics? (4) Does the Bible tell us *why* we should live in one way rather than in another?[16] Many other questions could be added to these four, such as the place of moral examples (positive and negative), visions, aesthetic expression, tragedy and so on. All are best understood in the context of a story. Nevertheless, in order to limit my task I will examine these four questions.

1. Expressions of emotion. The Bible is full of emotions. From the fear of Adam and Eve to the exultation of David, from the erotic love of Solomon to the anguish of Jeremiah, from the depression of Job to the calm courage of Esther, from the tears of Jesus to the joy of his disciples, every book of the Bible bears the mark of breathing human beings whose moral lives are expressed with emotion.

At the emotional level there can be no precise formulation of what are appropriate responses to specific situations. Usually such responses are recorded without comment. Emotional responses cannot be easily labeled good or bad. They are more amenable to the terms *honest* or *dishonest, appropriate* or *inappropriate*. For a priori reasons, only Jesus' emotive responses may be labeled good. The psalmist who expressed happiness at the thought of Babylonian babies' having their brains smashed in is clearly not a guide for our emotional response to our enemies (Ps 137:9).

Nevertheless, the scope and range of emotions expressed by biblical writers gives valuable insight into the way God's people saw the world around them. In their emotions we see their honest response to what they saw as God's work in the world. Because they did not always see clearly, their emotions were not always appropriate. In many cases we are not able to judge whether the responses were appropriate. Their situation is too far from us. Their experience is too foreign. Even so, in most cases the emotions expressed enable us to identify with the biblical writer. While we may not uncritically imitate biblically expressed emotions, those emotions often provide a window into the heart of the situations the writers faced.

Sometimes within a story we see the destructive effects of negative emotions. Sometimes we see how God addresses human beings in the midst of their emotions. And sometimes human emotions are vehicles for the revelation of the heart of God. In Jeremiah, the prophet's own feeling of anguish at the coming destruction of Jerusalem is not distinguished from the Word of Yahweh. Gerhard von Rad comments that Jeremiah's unwanted vision contains a "darkness so terrible . . . that it constitutes a menace to very much more than the life of a single man; God's whole way with Israel hereby threatens to end in some kind of metaphysical abyss."[17]

Unlike Jeremiah, we are not meant to curse ourselves and our parents and wish we had never been born. But if we ever do, if we ever experience despair that is even remotely like Jeremiah's, then his story and the way that God dealt with him in it may become vitally important to our moral life. Although Jeremiah's specific responses to his situation are not presented as a model for us to follow, within the context of the story of his life with God his emotions reveal the depths of evil and despair that exist in the world. We cannot judge him. Perhaps his response was far more appropriate than that of anyone else in the city of Jerusalem at the time. Certainly he saw more than anyone else. His emotions teach us to see.

2. *Moral rules and law.* It is tragic how many Christians try to reduce the Bible's moral teaching to the level of rules, commandments and laws. When ethics and law are equated, the primary questions for biblical interpretation become, Am I bound by this law or may I safely ignore it? Is this commandment absolute, or is it relative to its original context? Is this instruction a commandment for all times and places, or is it a specific rule for a particular culture? Is this law relevant or irrelevant? Is this a moral or a ceremonial law?

The problem is not that these questions are invalid. But they do not go deep enough. Jesus said,

Do not think that I have come to abolish the law or the prophets; I have come not to abolish but to fulfill. For truly I tell you, until heaven and earth pass away, not one letter, not one stroke of a letter, will pass from the law until all is accomplished. Therefore whoever breaks one of the least of these commandments, and teaches others to do the same, will be called least in the kingdom of heaven; but whoever does them and teaches them will be called great in the kingdom of heaven. For I tell you, unless your righteousness exceeds that of the scribes and Pharisees, you will never enter the kingdom of heaven. (Mt 5:17-20)

There is no part of the law that is irrelevant. The common distinction between ceremonial and moral law has no substantiation in the Old or New Testament. So-called ceremonial laws are interspersed with clearly moral commandments. The ancient Israelites knew no distinction between the two. The religious and moral life of Israel were a single tapestry. Furthermore, as we have seen, some of the "moral" laws, including those calling for capital punishment, are the most difficult for modern people to understand.

The attempt by some "theonomists" to argue that all the laws of the Bible must be literally followed is in stark contradiction to a narrative reading of Scripture. When we abstract the laws from their context, their very source of meaning is lost. At the other extreme, some dispensationalists would discard some of the most profound teachings of Scripture by assigning them to a dispensation or period that does not concern Christians. For example, some say that the "Sermon on the Mount" is addressed only to Jews who will remain on the earth after the rapture.[18] The narrative structure of the law is honored, but at a cost of deleting some of its greatest insights. Theological liberals sometimes do the same but with different criteria.

Perhaps the most common and damaging "criticism with a penknife"[19] is the practice of rejecting the "difficult" Old Testament law in favor of New Testament grace. Not only does this contradict the practice and teaching of Jesus, but it deprives the believer of a great portion of the Old Testament. New Testament commandments are not necessarily more authoritative than Old Testament laws. Neither can be understood or blindly followed apart from their context. Their meaning is their source of authority and derives from God's will for God's people in a particular time and place.

Christopher Wright has classified the Old Testament law into five categories, each of which functioned within a specific sphere of ancient Jewish life. These categories include criminal law, civil law, family law, cultic law and charitable law.[20] Each of these areas of law was relative to the specific social structures of Israel. The law helped create and maintain these social structures. Today our social structures are different. Insofar as our societies are not agrarian, monarchical, slave-based, patriarchal, tribal, theocratic, polygamous, Middle Eastern and so on, we will have to develop our own laws to govern ourselves.

Laws are functional within their spheres of authority. They reflect an orientation toward love of God and neighbor within a specific social setting. Insofar as our setting is similar, these laws provide wisdom and instruction to us today.

Jesus said, " 'You shall love the Lord your God with all your heart, and with all your soul, and with all your mind.' This is the greatest and first commandment. And a second is like it: 'You shall love your neighbor as yourself.' On these two commandments hang all the law and the prophets" (Mt 22:37-40). Every kind of biblical literature must be understood both in relation to its context and in relation to the great love commandments. These commandments are the motive that lies behind every other commandment. We can learn from every law in the Bible when we understand how each law makes the love commandment specific in a particular context.

Biblical moral rules are usually simple and outline the boundaries of acceptable conduct rather than the specifics. For example, the prohibitions of the Decalogue (Ten Commandments) mark the edges of God's will and must be understood within the context of God's liberation of the people from Egypt and their revelatory purpose for Israel. The command not to steal, for example, does not elucidate the details of Christian economic relations. It does provide a basic boundary for acceptable economic behavior which has significance for every society. But the meaning of stealing may differ from culture to culture with varying definitions of property rights.

The prohibition of theft, like the other nine commandments, is not a timeless ethical principle that we must translate into different cultural idioms. Still less is it a criminal law code. The Decalogue includes no detailed legislation or penalties. Rather, it is a commandment that derives its meaning from the countless rules and regulations that are given in the criminal, civil, family, cultic and charitable law. Taken together, these laws provide a picture of the kind of community God wanted Israel to be in the early bronze age.

In order to understand the kind of community God wants us to be today, we must understand the picture drawn by the biblical narrative of the people of God. The laws enflesh that paradigmatic picture. We are not freed from the laws in the sense that we need not follow them. Rather, we are bound to follow the *meaning* of the law as it is contained in the account of God's will for Israel. As we can see from Jesus' commentary on the prohibition of adultery, that task may be far more rigorous than merely obeying the law. Jesus suggested that the meaning of adultery encompasses all male lust which objectifies women in the secret of the heart (Mt 5:27-28).

All of the classic "four uses of the law" may be understood as elucidating the symbolic structure of meaning revealed in the biblical story. (1) The theological or revelatory use of the law shows us the nature of the world and the meaning of our relationships and actions. (2) The moral use of the law convicts us of sin and drives us to Christ. (3) The political/social use of the law utilizes the paradigm of society revealed by the law to help create modern legal norms that will function in our society with similar purposes to the biblical law. (4) The didactic, teaching use of the law seeks concrete, applicable rules that are as relevant today as when they were first given by God, because the contextual meaning of the law still holds.

Luther and Calvin had a classic debate over the four uses of the law. Both accepted the first three, but Luther argued that because of grace we are freed from the fourth. My position combines the two Reformers' positions. Like Calvin, I do not think we are freed from the law. Like Luther, I do not believe we are bound by its particulars without consideration of context. Insofar as we can discover it, we are bound to the *meaning* to which the law points. The meaning of the law can be understood only in relation to the story of which it is a part.

3. Moral principles and themes. A common approach to ethics is to seek the basic moral principles that lie behind all the rules, laws and instructions of the Bible. The rule may then be disregarded in favor of the principle. The strength of this approach is that it seeks the meaning of the law. The principles of the great commandment to love God and your neighbor are the foundation of all Christian ethics. We are to interpret all the moral instruction of the Bible through the lens of these great principles.

Jesus is very harsh in his condemnation of those who meticulously follow every biblical rule but have forgotten the meaning and purpose of the law: "Woe to you, scribes and Pharisees, hypocrites! For you tithe mint, dill and cummin, and have neglected the weightier matters of the law: justice and mercy and faith. It is these you ought to have practiced without neglecting the others. You blind guides! You strain out a gnat but swallow a camel!" (Mt 23:23-24).

Justice, mercy and faith are foundational to a moral life. Through them we can understand the meaning of the law. But there is danger in seeing them as the basic meaning behind the law. Even the greatest principles are abstractions that live primarily in the world of thought and words. What does it mean to love God and do justice? The law tells you how in a specific situation. Even better, a story tells you how. If the great principles that may be deduced from the parable of the good Samaritan or the parable of the prodigal son are listed, some might think we have clearer teaching. But the principles listed are not *more* than the story. They are very much less. The idea that God loves sinners may leave a person cold. But the image of the father rushing to embrace his rebellious son grips the heart. It tells us how God loves us by giving us an image that relates to our experience and imagination.

Principles are indispensable to biblical ethics, but they should not be elevated to become the central source, still less the *only* source, of ethics. Principles are a tool for understanding the meaning of God's will, divorced from any specific situation or context. They lack the specificity of contact with cultural reality. Christians who make principles central often attempt to prioritize them to overcome situations of value conflict. For example, if the principle of protecting life is higher than the principle of telling the truth, then Rahab's lie can be justified.[21] Others absolutize certain principles in such a way that a sociocultural interpretation of the principle is treated like a moral rule that gives the same answer in every possible situation.[22]

With the exception of the great commandment, principles should not be rigidified into a strict hierarchy. It is not clear from the biblical record that a life is always of more value than the truth, or that, to quote Norman Geisler, "a complete person is more valuable than an incomplete person."[23] Nor should a

93

particular cultural interpretation of a principle be taken as a rule for all time. Honoring parents (a principle) does not necessarily mean patriarchy (a socio-cultural structure).

Just as principles help us see the meaning of biblical laws, so laws reveal the meaning of principles in a particular context. The real meaning of a principle can be understood only as it touches reality. But where it touches different realities, its incarnated meaning changes. The principle does not change at the level of abstract words. Justice and love remain the ideals. But whether they mean a person should be forgiven or stoned depends on the context.

Often moral rules point beyond themselves to principles. Take this moral rule: "If you take your neighbor's cloak in pawn, you shall return it to him by sunset, because it is his only covering. It is the cloak in which he wraps his body; in what else can he sleep? If he appeals to me, I will listen, for I am full of compassion" (Ex 22:26 NEB; this is categorized by Wright among the "charitable laws"). Taken as a moral rule, this may not give us much direct help for specific economic relations in the modern world. Coats are not usually taken in pawn today, and even if they were, they are not usually the only thing in which a person can sleep.[24] The law points beyond itself to the principle of compassion for the poor. The principle teaches us that God cares about the poor and how we treat them.

The meaning of the principle of care for the poor is derived from this and many other rules about how one should treat a poor person in a particular situation. Principles are tools to help us reincarnate moral practice from one context to another. By abstracting some of the meaning from a law in a simple form, they help us see how God's will in the biblical context might be relevant to us, even though our context is different. But the real meaning of the principle is revealed only in good practices in actual life.

The prophets continually appeal to ethical principles that go beyond the limited scope of moral rules. Often these appeals come in the form of warnings against evil practices. For example, "Woe . . . to those who issue oppressive decrees, to deprive the poor of their rights and withhold justice from the oppressed of my people. . . . What will you do on the day of reckoning, when disaster comes from afar?" (Is 10:1-4 NIV). Legal oppression is denounced with an appeal to the principle of justice for the poor. The meaning of the principle derives from specific practices of oppression.

Moral rules and commandments should not be stripped of their power by abstraction into principles or dispositions, as if the rule could then be discarded as merely local. The rules put flesh on principles. It is more helpful to think of principles as abstractions from rules rather than rules as applications of principles. A theological, narrative understanding of the commandments protects them from an ahistorical legalism and makes possible their application in altered form to new historical situations. Principles help transfer the meaning of good and evil from one context to another.

Principles lack the sharp definition of laws but provide an intermediate step through which contextual laws can be "reincarnated" in another cultural context. A good biblical example of this process is provided by Jesus in the Sermon on the Mount. "Eye for eye, tooth for tooth" (Ex 21:24) was an Old Testament law meant to protect a neighbor from excessive retaliation in the context of tribal warfare. Jesus does not simply discard the law but reformulates its deep, original meaning in terms of love for one's enemy. The original law protected the people against feuds and extremes of vengeance. Its meaning was rooted in respect for the rights of the enemy. Jesus does not eliminate that meaning but shows its logical implication.

4. *Why should we be good?* The fourth level of moral discourse has been called the "postethical" or "meta-ethical" level. Here the question is asked, Why be moral? What is the foundation and meaning of goodness?

There is an extensive philosophical debate over whether theology and morality are interdependent.[25] The Bible does not offer logical or philosophical arguments for the meaning or basis of morality. Nor does it offer such arguments for the existence of God. Without entering into the debate over whether all morality is logically dependent on theology,[26] we can say it is clear that faith in the God of the Bible requires or entails moral behavior. In both testaments those who identify themselves as God's people are called to be like God in character and moral practice. God's people are to be holy because God is holy (Lev 11:45). They are to be merciful because God is merciful (Num 14:18-19; compare Hos 6:6). Jesus said, "Be perfect, therefore, as your heavenly Father is perfect" (Mt 5:48; compare 5:43-47).

But the basis of biblical morality is not an abstract demand that we imitate God; it is an appeal to respond to the inherent nature of who God is and what God has done. God is first of all presented in the Bible as our creator. Because God is both loving and creator, we are to be good because God made us to be good. Goodness is good for us because we were made in the image of God and can become who we are meant to be only by being like God. God created us as cultural creatures; therefore our goodness must be expressed in and through our cultures.

The Bible also pictures God as our parent. The Bible simply assumes that certain responses to one's creator and parent are appropriate and good. The definitions of creator, father and mother are assumed to carry self-evident moral requirements. In the West, with its tremendous emphasis on individual autonomy and personal freedom, some may find this assumption more difficult to follow than those in other parts of the world. The majority of cultures in the world see obedience to parents as basic to membership within the community. Those who have been abandoned or abused by their father or mother may find the analogy of obedience to God as Father and Mother less than self-evident.[27] Nevertheless, whether or not the assumption of God's rights as parent are accepted, in the Bible they are assumed as universal for all God's created offspring.

The biblical story of God's love for his children is the paradigmatic story from which we are to understand our rights and responsibilities in human families. God is pictured as both a father and mother to us, but we are not to see God primarily as like our earthly mother or father, who may or may not be good.[28] Rather, we should be parents who love our children the way God loves us. The image is transcultural and rooted in biology, even though its realization on earth will vary according to different cultural patterns of family structure. Matriarchal, patriarchal, egalitarian, nuclear, extended and other family structures are all capable of reflecting God's love through the parents to the children.

Third, we are to be good because God is the lawgiver and judge of all the earth. God reserves the right as our creator and parent to judge the whole earth. As judge, God demands obedience. Richard Mouw has written a carefully nuanced book that argues that all Christian morality is founded on the idea of "moral surrender to the divine will."[29] As Mouw points out, surrender to God's authority need not be founded on fear of judgment; nevertheless, God's judgment is an inevitable aspect of God's authority. This image is prominent in Islam, which means submission.

The biblical picture of God as judge assumes that morality makes sense because there is goodness and justice at the heart of the universe. Justice and righteousness in the present make sense because, in the biblical story, God will someday establish them on earth. The coming kingdom of God is both motive and goal of Judeo-Christian ethics. The God of justice and the God of mercy are one and the same. God will judge the earth because God loves the earth.

Fourth, we are to be good because we are partners with God in a covenant. There is a paradox in the Bible on this point. On the one hand this covenant is a gift. It is unearned and eternal. On the other hand it is a mutual agreement that entails promises. The requirements of the covenant are religious fidelity (God is pictured as a husband and Israel as his bride) and social justice. In the New Testament, God's people have been accepted and forgiven through the new covenant sealed with the blood of Christ. Membership in this covenant is confirmed by obedience to Christ (Jas 2:17; see also Mt 25:31-46; Heb 6:4-8).

This points us to what I take as the central ethical image in the biblical story. We are to live well as the fitting response to God as our lover and redeemer.[30] Morality in the Bible is fundamentally seen as a response to God's grace in choosing, liberating, blessing, forgiving and judging us. The focal point of revelation is the mystery of the incarnation. God's Son, Jesus, took upon himself the agony of history and died to set God's people free. If we are really free, then we must live in the true freedom of obedience. (Gal 5:1).

Biblical goodness is linked to gratitude, reverence, loyalty, faith and hope. These virtues transcend all cultures. Above all, goodness is revealed in love. The law of love opposes and denies the validity of every cultural custom that restricts the flow of God's love in the community. God's love in Christ breaks down all ethnic, social, economic and sexual barriers that lead to the oppression of one group by another (Gal 3:28). The Bible tells us a story in historical, cultural terms of God's character and action in history. This story tells us why we should be good.

The Cultural Context of the Reader

It is not possible for us to understand the story of the Bible "objectively." As I have already indicated, all of knowledge is "subjective" in the sense that whatever we know, we know from a particular perspective. The goal of biblical understanding is not the formulation of some transcultural set of ethical principles but obedience to God in a particular time and place. People in different sociocultural situations may understand different things from the same story, in part because the will of God (but not the character of God) is different in different contexts.

The following story illustrates how a new cultural setting may raise disturbing new questions about a situation that had previously seemed clear and simple.

"Jane" taught English in a university in China. One day she saw "Kwei-feng" looking at someone else's paper on the final examination. Kwei-feng had often been in Jane's apartment, teaching her how to cook and engaging in deep conversations. They had become good friends. Jane had threatened failure to anyone caught cheating, but if she failed Kwei-feng, she knew Kwei-feng's job prospects might well be destroyed for life. If Kwei-feng failed this class she would be dismissed from the university with very slim possibilities for another chance at higher education or a decent job. Failure in the university could result in lifelong economic dependence on her parents. Her whole future might hang on this one exam. Besides, Kwei-feng was one of the most capable of Jane's students.

Jane could not recall any direct biblical passages on cheating, but she knew that dishonesty is wrong. The rules were clear, and academic standards were at stake. But was Kwei-feng really cheating, checking her answer with a friend or just allowing her eyes to wander? If she was cheating, did it really warrant dismissal from the university? Did cheating mean the same thing here as in America? If it did, was it valued differently? Jane knew that her Chinese colleagues were very lax on cheating. But did the fact that they were lax mean she should be too?

What was the real meaning of Kwei-feng's wandering eyes? What was Jane's responsibility in the situation as a young American visiting teacher? Jane had gone to China with a very black-and-white view of right and wrong: rules should never be broken. But in this situation she was all at sea. When she confronted Kwei-feng in the hall and saw the anguished horror in her eyes, Jane's heart felt leaden and her rules hollow. Kwei-feng was her most promising student. How could she know what was good in this situation?

The question whether Kwei-feng was right to allow her eyes to wander is only a small part of the ethical dilemma in this story. In her own context Jane would not have hesitated to fail a student caught cheating. She felt strongly about the biblical principle of honesty. Failure for cheating was simple justice. But did justice demand the same action in China?

Jane had to make a portentous decision quickly in a situation that she did not fully understand. If she had had more experience as a teacher in China, if she had understood the nature of the Chinese educational system better, if she had perceived a wider range of possible responses, if she had been able to consult a trusted Chinese Christian teacher, she would have been in a better position to know the will of God in this situation.

Jane approached the dilemma not only as a teacher in China but also as a

North American with a well-established set of norms on things like cheating, plagiarism, intellectual property rights, academic competition, educational opportunity and vocational freedom. None of these norms can be directly derived from the Bible, because in the biblical narrative there is no comparable sociocultural educational structure as now exists in the West. Nor, for that matter, is there a biblical educational structure comparable to that of China. Jane had to decide what to do based on a synthesis of educational values from her culture of origin, an understanding of the values of her new social situation and a critical assessment of both, based on the biblical story.

Since Jane's cultural situation in China was so far from the structures of education in the Bible, there were no concrete biblical laws or rules to tell her what to do.[31] General principles like honesty and justice seemed to be in tension with other principles like gentleness and mercy. Jane's emotions seemed to be in conflict with her rational, rule-oriented side. Perhaps of greatest importance was what kind of person Jane had become as a result of living her life in accordance with the Scriptures. If Jane was a person of integrity and compassion, a person of prayer and sensitivity, a person of self-control and wisdom, then she had a much greater chance of acting rightly in the situation. There is no law against the fruits of the Spirit (Gal 5:22-23). The guidance of the Holy Spirit might make up for her lack of cultural knowledge. On the other hand, even a godly person can make horrible mistakes. She would do well to learn the ropes of the Chinese educational system.[32]

The Bible is not an ancient puzzle to be solved but a narrative of God's action in history. As Brevard Childs has explained, "The central task is not the objective understanding of the Bible's ethical passages but the understanding of God's will."[33] It is impossible to know God's will apart from doing it in a particular human context. Knowledge is partial and dangerous when divorced from obedience and experience.[34] We cannot blithely say that we know what the Bible means before we have actually tried to do it.[35] In many instances we cannot know how to do God's will before we understand the sociocultural context in which we are placed.

The Sociocultural Context of the Bible: Model or Paradigm?

One of the knottiest problems for biblical social ethics is how to interpret the social structures assumed in the Bible. Are the structures of Israel an essential part of God's revelation? What is their ethical significance for us? The social, economic, political and cultural structures assumed in the Bible are very foreign to most of us in the modern world. Most of us no longer live in a world of absolute monarchies, slavery, tribal and clan warfare, patriarchy (in its ancient Middle Eastern form) and animal sacrifice.

The entire Old Testament assumes that God's people are a political entity who are ideally ruled by God. Today most Christians assume that a theocracy is both impossible and undesirable. Apart from a few Islamic states, most countries of the world now assume a religious pluralism that is foreign to the world of the Bible.

Instead of the agrarian world assumed in much of the Old Testament, the world today is undergoing rapid urbanization. Instead of a world of assumed male superiority, many parts of the world have vigorous movements for women's equality. Instead of absolute monarchy, democracy is a pervasive ideal. Instead of an all-encompassing religious, economic, political and social legal system, we have a patchwork of laws that govern different aspects of life in relation to social realities that are very different from those assumed in the Bible. Instead of face-to-face economic relations in which usury was forbidden, most of the world is structured around credit.

It is tempting to respond to these pervasive differences by simply rejecting at least the Old Testament as irrelevant to our time. The extent to which this is done by Christians of all theological convictions is one of the great tragedies of the church. Equally unacceptable are the attempts to require that all the Old Testament be literally followed or to limit the Old Testament to a source of "spiritual" typologies of Christ.

Christopher J. H. Wright offers a persuasive argument that the social shape of Israel is an essential part of its biblical theological significance.[36] The social laws of Israel cannot be easily separated from their theological motivation. Jewish law is continually justified with reference to the character of God. The revelation of God in the Bible is inseparable from an understanding of the kind of society Israel was meant to be. The story of God's work in the world cannot be divorced from the way God is revealed in the peculiar social structures of Israel.

In his massive study of the sociological world of the Old Testament prior to 1050 B.C., Norman Gottwald concludes that Israel was

an egalitarian, extended family, segmentary, tribal society with an agricultural-pastoral economic base . . . characterized by profound resistance and opposition to the forms of political domination and social stratification that had become normative in the chief cultural and political centers of the ancient Near East.[37]

With the ancient law God offered Israel an opportunity to be different from the surrounding nations. Within the context of a social structure based on slavery, Israel was to free all slaves and give them a nest egg every seven years (Deut 15). Within the context of a political system of monarchy, Israel was to know that monarchy would become a vehicle of oppression (1 Sam 8) and that even its greatest king was not above the law of God (2 Sam 12). Within the context of an agricultural economy, Israel was to ensure that everyone had a fair share of land and that both land and animals would be respected (Lev 25). Within the context of patriarchy and polygamy, Israel was to protect the rights of women (Deut 21:10-14; 22:13-29).

It would be nice if all these points were unambiguous—even better, if the institutions that we find abhorrent were simply outlawed. The seeds of the destruction of monarchy, slavery, racism, sexism and polygamy are all found in the Old and New Testaments. But these seeds were beyond the perception of most of the biblical writers. In the Law and Prophets and the letters of Paul, structures of oppression are questioned, denounced and ameliorated, but there are few calls for their abolition. In fact, these structures were usually embedded in the thought patterns of the biblical writers.

The commandments of the Old and New Testament do not assume an ideal social structure for all time. Rather, they assume the social structure of *their own* time and outline ways in which Israel, or the church, was to be different. Israel provides a paradigm of God's will in relation to actual social conditions. Israel is not a model of how the church, still less any secular state, should be structured. The Old Testament tells a story of God's work in the ancient Near East that is relevant not only to the church but also to modern politics.

Theologians like Elisabeth Schüssler Fiorenza have argued that we need a "hermeneutic of suspicion" that ferrets out the influence of sexism on the biblical writers.[38] Fiorenza's hermeneutic of suspicion comes dangerously close to making her own subjective view of feminism into the critical standard by which everything else is judged. Nevertheless, a carefully used hermeneutic of suspicion can reveal how the social structures of the cultures of the Bible shaped its message in ways that are not relevant to our culture. Fiorenza suggests that in order to do this we must

not understand the New Testament as an archetype but as a prototype. Both archetype and prototype denote original models. However, an archetype is an ideal form that establishes an unchanging timeless pattern, whereas a prototype is not a binding timeless pattern or principle. A prototype, therefore, is critically open to the possibility of its own transformation.[39]

The cultures of the Bible are no more authoritative than our own. Most of the Bible's moral exhortations were practically directed to people who were not living by idealized structures but according to the pagan practices around them. I suspect that things are not too different today. Biblical patterns of the extended family, home education, agriculture, usury, defense and medicine are rarely seen as authoritative today. One of the great tasks of biblical interpretation is to distinguish between the will of God and the particular cultural homes in which it was biblically incarnated.

Bridging the Gap Between Text and Today

The basic argument of this chapter has been that the biblical story, understood in context, teaches us to become good as we learn to see our lives as part of the same story. By guiding our interpretation, the story leads us to experience reality in a way that is consistent with God's work in the world. The story of God's work with Israel and revelation in Christ is our story too.

But it is not our only story. There is also the story of our lives that is inseparable from our cultural context. Our culture provides us with a symbolic meaning system from which we can never fully escape. We read the story of the Bible through cultural eyes. Our own cultural experience is not higher in authority than the Scriptures, but it is our starting place. It is also our goal. The Bible's teaching must be lived in our own cultural experience before we fully understand it.

This requires a process that is often called *contextualization*. We do not translate the Bible directly into a new cultural setting. Nor do we even "transculturate" it, as if the message of the gospel were an abstraction that could simply be expressed in different cultural forms.[40] It is the Bible, not an abstract interpretation of its message, that is authoritative. The message of the Bible can be understood only as it is perceived from a specific cultural standpoint. God's Word is always incarnated, and different parts of the church may incarnate it differently.[41] In other words, the content of the gospel cannot be separated from its cultural form.

The Reverend Nelly Hutahaean is a Batak pastor from North Sumatra, Indonesia. The following story relates how she tried to obey the God of the Bible in her own cultural context.[42]

One day Ari, a close friend of Nelly, came to her to ask for help. Ari's father had been killed and her mother imprisoned for many years because of involvement with the communists. Ari was rescued as a baby and raised by a foster family. She was now eighteen years old and only two months away from graduation from high school. Ari was a conscientious student, well respected by her teachers and friends. Recently she had been chosen to represent the school in a traditional Batak dance performance. As Nelly met Ari, she saw that her eyes were swollen and her body covered with black and blue marks from the most recent beating she had received from her foster father.

Every day Ari was required to come straight home from school and work in the house: washing clothes, cleaning, ironing, cooking, washing dishes, etc. She had been forbidden to take part in any extracurricular activities. Ari's foster father had very strict rules for her, and any deviation brought severe punishment. When the foster father found out she had accepted the honor of representing the school in the traditional dance, he locked all her school uniforms and books in the closet and forbade her to return to school.

Ari could not stand the pain and degradation of her position in that house any longer. She received regular beatings and now was being denied the chance to finish high school. She asked Nelly to help her escape and run away to Jakarta. There she hoped to see her mother in prison and start a new life. Nelly's dilemma was over whether or not she should help Ari escape.

My first response to this story was outrage against the foster father and the conviction that Nelly should help Ari escape from such abuse. From my (Western) perspective, an eighteen-year-old had every right to flee from such a situation. Ari's foster family treated her like a slave. They would not allow her to finish high school. Her foster father abused her. And she wanted to meet her long-lost mother.

But Nelly was not so sure. She wanted to make sure that her response would be faithful to Scripture and wise in relation to the cultural situation. She pointed out that if Ari ran away and broke her relationship with her foster family, it would have a grave impact on the rest of her life. It would also bring severe repercussions on the whole foster family and even the whole community. Fleeing from the family would break one of the most basic taboos of the Batak people. It would be considered the greatest possible sin. Ari would be excommunicated not only from the family but from the entire community. Not only would she not finish high school, but she would be an outcast for life. As part of a Batak family, she was guaranteed material security for the future by the clan. If she ran away, she would become as one who is dead.

By breaking the most basic *adat* (tradition) of the society, Ari would also bring irreparable shame on the family and father who had raised her. Within the patriarchal, close-knit family structure of the clan, the father would be seen as having failed in his duty, and the whole family would suffer. He would be shunned. His business might well be boycotted and go bankrupt. The whole community would be divided and suffer the loss of his participation. The *adat* was so strong that no woman had ever dared flee before.

Nelly wanted to understand what she should do, both within this context and in the context of the Bible. On the one hand, the biblical story highly values the family. The fifth commandment requires that father and mother be honored and suggests that such honor brings with it a long and fruitful life (Deut 5:16). For almost eighteen years this family had raised Ari and paid for her schooling.

On the other hand, Ari seems to come under the category of an oppressed orphan. The Bible is full of commands like "Seek justice, rescue the oppressed, defend the orphan, plead for the widow" (Is 1:17). The God of the Bible is the defender of the weak.

Within the context of Batak culture, how could Nelly honor both themes in the Bible? Nelly believed that honor was due to the foster family that had raised Ari. On the other hand she knew Ari needed help and could not be abandoned to face her suffering alone.

After a process of reflection, biblical study, counsel with trusted members of the community, study of possible alternatives and repercussions, and planning,[43] Nelly arranged for Ari to be hidden with another local family. An elder of the community was selected to approach the foster father, reassure him of Ari's safety, tell him Ari's perspective, and ask him to forgive her and give his permission for her to finish school. Meanwhile, Nelly prayed that God would forgive her for her boldness and help Ari to be able to meet her mother. She also prayed for eventual reconciliation between Ari and her foster father.

In retrospect, Nelly reflected that within a paternalistic, collective and family-oriented society such as hers, conflict such as this can seldom be solved by an individual. The leaders of the community are the only ones able to bring about a tolerable solution.

I learned much from this story. I saw that my Western, individualistic, human-rights approach to a solution was inadequate. I also saw an example of a wise woman who took her culture and her faith very seriously. Nelly did not accept the patriarchal assumption that a father has unlimited power over his daughter. But she did not reject the communal resources of her culture for problem-solving. Nelly did not approach the Bible as a narrow rule book requiring a daughter always to obey. Nor did she simply resort to the popular "poor-and-oppressed" passages without consideration of the importance of family and communal structures. In her values and actions Nelly combined respect for authority, loyalty to the oppressed and cultural sensitivity.

Because we live in a fallen world, we cannot be assured that stories such as this will all turn out right. In Ari's case the results were mixed. Ari is still not reconciled with her foster father, but she was able to finish high school and go on to university without being alienated from the community. Her mother is now free, and Ari is married and has children of her own. Nelly's story provides an example of someone who interpreted a moral crisis in her own culture through the lens of the biblical narrative. Nelly combined the story of the Bible with the story of her culture in such a way that her praxis was the product of wisdom.

Those of us who live in a foreign culture have a double task. We must continue to integrate the biblical story with the perspectives of our culture of origin. Beyond that, we must begin to understand our new home deeply enough so that its story may be seen and transformed through the Word of God. In the next chapter I will examine how crosscultural studies can help us understand the story of our adopted culture.

FIVE

CULTURAL VALUE ORIENTATIONS IN CONTRAST

T he following experience was related to me by a Western professor at an Asian university. After several years of teaching, "Robert" was very disturbed to find that students were being accepted into his department who were not qualified. He felt that the "culture of connections" was working in an unfair way for the benefit of the children of high officials. Robert discussed the problem with Asian faculty colleagues, who appeared equally indignant at this seeming abuse of power. However, no one wanted to do anything about it. Robert took the courageous step of writing a letter of protest to the dean of the university. He felt that his colleagues could not afford to protest for fear of retaliation by those in power. Since his salary was not paid by the university, he could afford to go out on a limb.

Robert was deeply offended by the result. He received a stern letter of rebuke from Dean Wong, to the effect that foreigners should not meddle with the internal affairs of the university. He was told that his job was to teach, not to criticize. Robert was so indignant that he leaked his letter and the reply to the local newspaper. The dean was extremely embarrassed and asked Robert why he did not come to talk with administration officials before going to the newspaper. Robert considered this a typical authoritarian way to avoid the issue. If he had gone to the administration, it would have tried to intimidate him into silence. Eventually he discovered that his actions were only a small part of a much larger power struggle in the university.

Robert's actions were apparently effective, but he is still not sure they were right. There was a decrease in unqualified admissions, and eventually Dean Wong resigned from administrative work.[1] At the same time a great deal of hurt, anger and embarrassment was caused to many parties in the university. Robert's own sense of alienation and ruptured relations was considerable and had not completely disappeared at the time of our conversation, which occurred a couple of years after the event. In the eyes of some colleagues and students, Robert was an aggressive and insensitive foreigner who did not know what he was doing. Others saw him as a hero.

Robert's experience involves differences of perception and communication. Robert was from a Western culture, but the same problems could have occurred if he were a visitor from another Asian country.[2] Misunderstandings in crosscultural communication are a major source of moral conflict for sojourners in another land.

This chapter will examine some of the problems of communication and their impact on ethics. Complex problems of communication inevitably lead to stress and alienation. Culture shock and the experience of being a stranger can have an enormous impact on a person's identity and behavior. So here I will look at some of the good and evil that can result in the process of adaptation to another culture.

Principles and Practices in Human Cultures

Michel de Montaigne said, "There are truths on this side of the Pyrenees which are falsehoods on the other."[3] To this Blaise Pascal replied ironically, "A strange justice that is bounded by a river! Truth on this side of the Pyrenees, error on the other side."[4] Nevertheless, the strange changeable truth that Montaigne elaborated so vividly is contextual truth, cultural truth, relative truth—that is, truth that is located in a unique social structure and worldview. As I have already argued, cultural relativism does not imply that universal values do not exist. Various writers have documented an impressve number of moral principles that appear to be transcultural.[5]

The limitations of crosscultural moral principles. Lawrence Kohlberg and his followers have tried to demonstrate that there is a universal pattern to the way all human beings learn ethics. Kohlberg claims that "the development of moral reasoning about the social environment follows a universal, invariant sequence, toward the same universal ethical principles in all cultural settings."[6] Kohlberg's work has aroused unprecedented interest. It seems to hold out the possibility that people in all cultures are maturing toward the same form of principled moral reasoning. Universal codes of moral conduct appear to be possible. Crosscultural empirical research has built up impressive evidence that many people in many cultures follow Kohlberg's sequence.

On the other hand, weaknesses in Kohlberg's theory have also become clear. Kohlberg's claims have been hotly challenged.[7] Kenneth and Mary Gergen suggest that

> it is dangerous business to posit a hierarchy of moral dispositions when that hierarchy allows the highly educated adult male a disproportionate likelihood of being on top. In effect, Kohlberg's theory places men of Western society in a position of moral superiority. By implication, others are placed in inferior positions.[8]

In a similar vein, Carol Gilligan suggests that women's moral reason is often based on concern for significant people in their lives rather than on abstract moral principles. This is classified as stage 3 reasoning in Kohlberg's theory but could easily be judged as a higher level than stage 6 (principles) if relationships were valued more highly than rights and principles.[9]

John Snarey's survey of crosscultural empirical research based on Kohlberg's work is relatively supportive of Kohlberg's theory.[10] Nevertheless, Snarey found that Kohlberg's stage 5 and 6 (reasoning from universal moral principles) were entirely absent from tribal or village societies. Even more striking is his discovery that group- and community-oriented groups had categories of moral reasoning that did not fit into any of Kohlberg's categories. Kibbutzniks in Israel, village leaders in Papua New Guinea and Chinese in Taiwan all used moral arguments based on community solidarity which do not fit into Kohlberg's more individualistic model. For example, when asked if a man should steal expensive medicine to save the life of his dying wife, villagers deflected the question by placing moral responsibility on the whole community: "If nobody helped him [save his dying wife], and so he [stole to save her], I would say we had caused that problem."[11]

Kohlberg's list of moral universals (or anyone else's list) are inadequate. Even though we might find universals we would all agree on, they would remain extremely abstract and of limited value in helping us know much about what is good. If, for example, we agreed on the principle "do justice," we would still be a long way from knowing what we were talking about. What justice *means* can be determined only in the context of a coherent set of assumptions, beliefs, institutions and relationships. Different communities and different cultures have different conceptions of justice, because they have different histories, different social structures and different conflicts.[12]

It is difficult to imagine, for example, a discussion of justice that would satisfy both Israeli settlers and Palestinian refugees. Each group's historical experience, cultural style, religious commitments, social institutions and assumptions about the world may give internal coherence to its own conception of justice in the Middle East. At the same time, that group's conception makes very little sense to the other group, which does not share its tradition.

It is not belief in principles that makes a person good or evil but cultural practices that make sense within their own context. How then do we evaluate a case like that of Robert and the university? One approach is to analyze the different religious worldviews that undergird different cultural practices. But Robert and the academic leaders with whom he differed were all Christians. Sadly, some of the most heated crosscultural value conflicts occur between Christians. It's easier when there is a non-Christian religion to blame!

Cultural values are more basic than principles. Culturally held values are not usually based on moral principles, although they may be justified by them. According to Geert Hofstede, "Because our values are programmed early in our lives, they are non-rational. . . . Values determine our subjective definition of rationality."[13] D. J. Bem says, "Values are ends, not means, and their desirability is either unconsciously taken for granted . . . or seen as a direct derivation from one's experience or from some external authority."[14] In other words, usually either we feel our values are simply logical, rational and obvious from experience or we attribute them to God or some other authority. Since we take in our cultural values with our mother's milk, they are more basic than rationally held principles. Robert's outrage when his protest was spurned stemmed in part from his expectation that all rational Christians would agree with him.

Cultural values are rooted in basic human needs. There are certain clear similarities in the structure of values and their expression in all cultures. Hofstede suggests there is a "universal level of mental programming." He says, "This is the biological 'operating system' of the human body, but it includes a range of expressive behaviors such as laughing and weeping and associative and aggressive behaviors which are also found in higher animals."[15]

Clyde Kluckhohn suggests that even culturally very distinct behaviors may have roots in the same biological needs.

> There is a generalized framework that underlies the more apparent and striking facts of cultural relativity. All cultures constitute so many somewhat distinct answers to essentially the same questions posed by human biology and by the generalities of the human situation. . . . Every society's patterns for living must provide approved and sanctioned ways for dealing with such universal circumstances as the existence of two sexes; the helplessness of infants; the need for satisfaction of the elementary biological requirements such as food, warmth, and sex; the presence of individuals of different ages and differing physical and other capacities.[16]

Kluckhohn's concept of a "generalized framework" is too mechanistic a concept to be congruent with more recent anthropological theory. Basic biological and social needs are not facts that can be posited apart from their cultural interpretation within a social narrative. Nevertheless, the fact that cultures are linked by commonly experienced physical constraints is intuitively obvious.

Of course, positing that human beings address these constraints as groups is already an interpretation that assumes that societies are fundamental to humanness. It contrasts with Thomas Hobbes's well-known "state of nature" in which every individual was perceived as being at war with everyone else in a battle for survival. The idea of the fundamental aloneness of the individual who enters into a social contract for purely pragmatic survival reasons is contradicted by the conception of human *community* as constituting the fundamental meaning of human *being*. Clifford Geertz argues that human nature should not be thought of as lying "behind," "under" or "beyond" culture, but within it.[17] Human beings are socially constructed.

On the one hand this accords well with the Bible's view of human beings as always in relationship. The existentialist longing to find individual authenticity independent of society and culture is doomed to failure. Who we are is always who we are in relation to others.[18] There is no authentic self that can be discovered or defined in isolation from the community.[19] This perspective is confirmed by many Asian cultures, which prefer the image of a family over that of a social contract as their basic conception of society.

On the other hand the biblical story of human creation in the image of God seems to indicate that certain human characteristics are not simply the result of biological *or* social necessity but were given as gifts that transcend all cultures, times and places. The capacities to love and create, to transcend physical necessity through intelligence and imagination, to invent symbols and tools, to worship and play, to be just and fair, to show mercy and joy—these and many other characteristics are common to persons in all cultures, times and places.

Shalom H. Schwartz and Wolfgang Bilsky argue that there are a universal content and structure to human values that stem from three universal human requirements that underlie all human cultures:[20] (1) the needs of individuals as biological organisms, (2) the requisites of coordinated social interaction and (3) the survival and welfare needs of the group. From these three basic needs Schwartz and colleagues have discovered, at last count, eleven "motivational domains" which they believe to be culturally universal. All values in all cultures are thought to stem from these eleven basic motivational areas.[21]

Studies such as this prove far less than they hope because of the unavoidable subjectivity and arbitrariness in the way the empirical data are gathered and interpreted. If all reality is divided into eleven (culturally biased) categories (or three or seven or twenty-five), it is not surprising that just those categories will be found through survey research. Nevertheless, claims for universality aside, it is certainly possible that basic social and biological needs underlie cultural value structures. "Motivational domains" are an intellectual construct based on cultural values and do not, as Schwartz and Bilsky seem to think, exist in the real world. But biological and social (and symbolic) needs are more plausible sources of cultural values than abstract principles. In the practices of surviving, relating and believing, cultural values are formed, re-formed and passed on.

Evolutionary theories of culture, which dominated early anthropological studies, have been widely rejected, both because of their implied racism and because of a mounting lack of evidence. They were replaced by an absolute cultural relativism that has also been increasingly abandoned for philosophical, practical and ethical reasons. The problem then arises, If we are to make moral judgments about the practices of various cultures, but we cannot simply rely on abstract moral principles or a scientifically determined structure of universal values, how are we to judge?

Practices give meaning to principles (not vice versa). Cultural practices demonstrate the meaning of cultural values. Moral principles are abstract generalizations that express the meaning of practices apart from the context from which they grew. Principles dilute the meaning of practices through abstraction but enable cultural values from one situation to be applied in another. In response to the unique problems of a given time and place, human beings create patterns of behavior (practices) that protect, preserve and pass on their values. Cultural values are experienced as good when they successfully help guard the basic biological, spiritual and social needs of the group. Thus values are functionally good—that is, they achieve the goals of the group in relation to their environment. A principle is a tool that enables cultural values to be seen in a wider context.

For example, if a Latino family wishes to protect the virginity of their beautiful daughter in a context in which males conventionally seek to prove their virility through sexual conquest, the family may enforce a practice that young women should never leave the house unchaperoned. The daughter's virginity is a social, biological, spiritual and economic value that is protected by cultural practices. The principle that families should protect the well-being of their daughters may give rise to different cultural practices in a context where unaccompanied women are not automatically considered legitimate prey for macho males. Thus confinement to the house may be replaced by a ten o'clock curfew.

Of course the change may go in the opposite direction. My twenty-year-old daughter was used to an active night life in California. When she attended university in Yogyakarta, Indonesia, she soon learned not to go out alone after dark. Unlike her experience in some American cities, she was not in physical danger. But the sight of a young blond woman alone at night in Java gave a different cultural message than it did in Berkeley, California, and the attention she received was not the kind she wanted. She stayed home at night not because of a rule or a principle but because she was not the kind of person who wanted to receive a lot of sexual attention from strangers.

Moral principles become practical and visible when enfleshed in specific practices. Principles lack specificity and may be understood only vaguely. For example, the principle of the equal worth and dignity of all human beings is an abstract idea that we are far from understanding clearly. Human beings in all cultures do not live up to it. It would be hard to find a mother who does not value her own child more than the beggar down the street. Even God does not appear to live up to the equal-value principle. Why did God choose Israel and not the Philistines? Does God favor those who are socialized to Christian faith over those who are not? Paul's answer seems to be yes, and we have no right to question the will of the Creator. For example, in Romans 9:19-21 he says,

> You will say to me then, "Why then does he still find fault? For who can resist his will?" But who indeed are you, a human being, to argue with God? Will what is molded say to the one who molds it, "Why have you made me like this?" Has the potter no right over the clay, to make out of the same lump one object for special use and another for ordinary use?

On the other hand there are abundant passages of Scripture that state categorically God's love for all peoples, his lack of partiality, his care for the poor and his removal of all ethnic, social, economic and sexual barriers.[22] Human equality is a powerful ideology affirmed by most people in the world today, especially those who follow Christianity or Islam. Yet its specific content as seen in *practices* is widely divergent.

There are vast differences over the definition of what is human and what is equal. Justice theories abound, human individual rights are pitted against distributive justice, and practices everywhere lag far behind the theorists. Some argue that basic human rights are not a matter of theory but of empirically verifiable basic biological needs to sustain life. But as Max Stackhouse has pointed out, such a linking of needs and rights is very rare in the history of human thought. He says,

> But that these needs ought to be met; that they should be met as a matter of social duty; and that they should be met for all, whatever the condition of age, strength, health, or status, entail a range of ideas that has been not at all obvious to philosophy, politics, law, natural law theory, or for that matter, the biological sciences themselves.[23]

In the face of such confusion it might be tempting to abandon the notion of human equality altogether. But this would be foolish. Christianity has a long and fairly consistent tradition concerning the nature and value of both individual human beings and human communities. The fact that a concept is not clear, precise or absolute does not mean it is not true. Our idea of human equality, flawed and weak though it may be, points beyond itself to a truth that transcends all cultures. What human equality really means can never be abstractly defined. But it can be demonstrated in specific times and places.

Some cultural practices are so far from the ideal of human equality that there is virtually unanimous agreement that they must cease. Such was the case with slavery, with footbinding in China and with Nazi extermination of "undesirable races." Unfortunately, such agreement does not extend to those who practiced such things. Slave holders in America were far from convinced that equal human value before God entailed an end to slavery. Nor does eventual agreement last forever. "Ethnic cleansing" operations in Bosnia and tribal warfare in Somalia remind us that "the final solution" is still being tried as a resolution to ethnic conflict.

Debates about what does not accord with the principle of equality are necessary and important. But far more important are positive demonstrations of practices that give meaning to the principle. The men who argue most strenuously for women's equality are not necessarily the most loving husbands. The churches that most clearly articulate the need for social justice are not necessarily the most effective in addressing the causes of poverty and oppression. Practices show the real meaning of words. As Jesus said, "You will know them by their fruits" (Mt 7:20).

Narratives or stories that demonstrate the principle of human worth and equality are not reducible to the principle. In answer to a question about the principle of love for your neighbor, Jesus told the parable of the good Samaritan. The story is richer than the principle because it has the details of real life. The principle of Jewish-Samaritan equality is only a shorthand, abstract way of talking about what happened on the road to Jericho.

In the case study of Robert, human equality was a serious issue in his conflict with Dean Wong. Robert's concern for equality of opportunity in admissions was valid and important. The principle of fairness or equality of opportunity would probably be agreed to by most fair-minded observers. Why then is Robert still uncertain about his actions? Whether his concern for procedural justice warranted his actions is a complex question because it is not abstract but real. To understand the meaning of Robert's acts, we need more information about the differences between cultures.

Maps or Models of Cultural Value Orientations

Many different attempts have been made to provide a conceptual model of differences that occur between cultures. Social scientists have repeatedly sought a universal paradigm that would render differences in cultural values understandable, or at least amenable to clear labels. Some, like Schwartz and Bilsky, try to derive a universal description of cultural values on the basis of basic biological and psychological needs.[24] Others, like Kohlberg, or for that matter Aristotle, propose a set of universal principles.

Third, some approaches simply list contrasting values. For example, a widely used simulation model for crosscultural training lists American values and Contrast-American values. Americans are optimistic, friendly and pragmatic, like a fast pace of life and stress equality. Another culture may be fatalistic, guarded, traditional, tranquil and class-conscious. Value lists have the advantage of greater specificity and descriptiveness but face the obvious danger of stereotyping. Lists of values may lack coherency. They provide little understanding of why a given culture holds certain values. On the other hand they may be too coherent, providing a cardboard characterization that ignores the complexity of human values.

An approach that has gained wide respect among social scientists is based on the concept of "value orientations." As does the basic needs approach, Florence Kluckhohn and Fred Strodtbeck have argued that there are certain universal problems and conditions faced by all societies. But instead of positing a universal set of motivations or values stemming from these needs, Kluckhohn and Strodtbeck suggest that there are a limited number of solutions to these problems, which may be called value orientations.[25] Kluckhohn and Strodtbeck compared five small communities and mapped out their value differences in terms of five problem areas, each of which contains three possible value orientations. For example, one problem area is the relationship of human beings to nature. The possible value orientations discussed by Kluckhohn and Strodtbeck in this area are (1) subjugation (nature as a lord to be served), (2) harmony (nature as a mother to be loved and respected) and (3) mastery (nature as a resource to be utilized).

Many different social scientists have taken the value-orientations approach, some expanding the problem areas (up to seventy-five different value orientations), others contracting the categories (down to three).[26] Some writers make unwarranted universal claims for their system; others are more cautious. Significant empirical work through international, multicultural surveys has been done to map out where various cultures stand in relation to each other's values. Perhaps the most impressive such work is from Geert Hofstede, who narrowed his focus to work-related values.[27] While Hofstede's intent is to be universal, he is well aware that the researcher's values and assumptions cannot be excluded from the research. Objectivity in discussing cultural values is a noble goal, but the researcher's own values are like the eyes with which he sees. Without eyes there is less distortion. Unfortunately, without eyes we cannot see anything!

A value-orientation approach from a Christian perspective is Marvin Mayers's basic values model of patterns of behavior.[28] Mayers's model was refined and usefully applied in a little book by Sherwood G. Lingenfelter and Marvin K. Mayers.[29] Lingenfelter and Mayers list twelve patterns that may be grouped into six pairs of polarities as follows:

1. a. Time orientation	punctual, linear, scheduled, concern for efficient use of time, versus
b. Event orientation	very loose scheduling, events allowed to proceed until complete regardless of time;
2. a. Dichotomistic thinking	polarizing life into right and wrong and analyzing experience in discrete parts, versus
b. Holistic thinking	looking at the whole and synthesizing without too great a concern for analytic harmonization of details;
3. a. Crisis orientation	a planning orientation which seeks to anticipate and plan for emergencies on the basis of precedent or expert advice, versus
b. Noncrisis orientation	take life as it comes and choose from various alternative courses of action only if the crisis occurs;
4. a. Task orientation	focus on goals and achievement, completing a task takes precedence over relationships, versus
b. Person orientation	good relations, friendships, conversations take precedence over goals and tasks;
5. a. Achievement focus	respect for achievement and ability regardless of rank or status, versus
b. Status focus	respect for status, position, role (as assigned by the social group);
6. a. Expose vulnerability	values frankness, transparency and sees exposure of fault as a virtue, versus
b. Conceal vulnerability	mistakes, sins or weaknesses should not be revealed or exposed.

This model is a useful tool for gaining insight into the crosscultural value conflict faced by Robert in his confrontation with the university administration. An irony of the model is that it is very dichotomistic and contrast-oriented. It is a Western model of value orientations. Nevertheless, its simplicity makes it helpful for the purposes of this chapter.

Value Orientations and the Case of Robert and Dean Wong

The following reflections do not resolve the conflict between Robert and Dean Wong. Readers who have a strong "dichotomous" orientation to ethics may find this frustrating! In order to understand the values of a foreign culture, a person must suspend judgment and "place him or herself imaginatively within the scene of belief inhabited by those whose allegiance is to the rival tradition, so as to perceive and conceive the natural and social worlds as they perceive and conceive them."[30] This is not always very comfortable. It requires that a person give up rigid categories in which the truth is always black or white. John Dewey wrote,

> One can think reflectively only when one is willing to endure suspense and to undergo the trouble of searching. To many persons, both suspense of judgment and intellectual search are disagreeable; they want to get them ended as soon as possible. They cultivate an over positive and dogmatic habit of mind, or feel perhaps that a condition of doubt will be regarded as evidence of mental inferiority.[31]

Time versus event orientation. Robert's confrontation of the administration over unfair admissions was taken shortly after he found out about the abuse. For him, time was urgent. Action had to be taken before any further injustice occurred. Robert's linear values encouraged him to act now for the sake of future goals. Those in the administration saw the problem in a much larger temporal context. Being more event-oriented, they felt no urgency to create unnecessary conflict now for the sake of hypothetical future goals.

Edward Hall's studies of cultures with "polychronic time" suggest that polychronic or event-oriented people focus on the present. They accept many different things that are all happening at one time, and relate them to each other.[32] Contradictions may be accepted (or ignored) in favor of harmony. As a linear-time-oriented person, Robert focused on one thing in relation to the future. Even those who shared Robert's concern for academic integrity did not publicly confront the problem, because they believed there was a process that must unfold in a different way. Taking immediate action to address a practice that is deeply

117

rooted in the social structure is dangerous. That does not mean it is wrong, only that if two parties are working within different time orientations there is ample room for misunderstanding.

Dichotomous versus holistic thinking. Robert perceived the problem as a discrete event or series of events that could be addressed separately from all the surrounding relationships and roles that made up the administration of the university. Not only did Robert not understand all the complexities of the larger picture, he did not think he needed to understand them. The big picture was probably too large to address, but individual corruption could be addressed.

It is possible that Dean Wong shared Robert's concern for academic integrity and fairness in admissions but faced powerful pressures to which, at that time, he felt the university had to submit. On the other hand, he or someone else in the administration may have received a large gift that he did not wish to see exposed.

Robert's action may or may not have helped the administration get free of outside pressures on its admissions policy. A holistic orientation considers individual problems primarily in terms of their impact on the whole, while the dichotomist breaks down the whole into individual parts that can be dealt with separately. Dean Wong saw the harmony of the whole as more vital than any particular abuses in its parts.

Crisis versus noncrisis orientation. A crisis orientation plans for the future so as to control or, if possible, prevent crisis. In contrast, a noncrisis orientation minimizes or ignores the possibility of future crises and addresses a crisis only when it is absolutely necessary. Robert's intervention was not intended to deal with a current crisis; he did not ask that any students be expelled or employees fired. Rather, he wanted to prevent the future injustice of qualified students' being displaced by unqualified ones from powerful families. As a crisis-oriented Westerner, Robert wanted to plan ahead to prevent future injustice.

For Dean Wong, Robert was creating a crisis where none had been before. By demanding a change in admission policy, Robert challenged the power structure. By making his communication public, Robert shamed the whole university and especially Dean Wong. In that context, the administration no doubt felt that Robert's creation of conflict in the present was worse than the future injustices he sought to prevent. Robert wanted to confront the problem now so that future injustices (crises) would be halted. Dean Wong wanted to protect the dignity of the current power structure.

Task versus person orientation. For Robert, the persons involved in this interaction were incidental to the task of bringing about positive change. He initially felt that the fact that he was a foreigner and not fully part of the university "family" should not have mattered if he was bringing up a valid concern. What was important was the task of creating greater justice and integrity in the university.

In contrast, a person orientation stresses relationship and informal, private, oral negotiation to resolve conflict. When Dean Wong suggested that Robert should have come to see him rather than write an official letter, Robert saw this response as a power play that avoided the issue. In fact, the administrators probably thought that preserving relationships between all parties (including, no doubt, the families of high officials) was more important than the task of rooting out all forms of nepotism. A person orientation does not imply that all persons are treated equally. Robert's status as a guest, at least in the eyes of the administrator, restricted his right to criticize.

Achievement versus status focus. Fundamental to Robert's concern about the admission of unqualified applicants was the assumption that when it comes to entrance into a leading university, what should count is a person's achievement. Status based on family rank or birth, wealth or political power should have no place. This is an area of tension in many countries where the achievement of an individual has traditionally been far less significant than the role assigned him by his birth and status. A person whose status calls for certain academic qualifications should receive them whatever his achievement level. In some Middle Eastern countries, members of the royal family always get 100 percent on their examinations! When one Western teacher refused to give unwarranted high marks to royal children, the task of grading was politely assigned to someone else.

Admission to most good universities in Asia is highly competitive, but that does not mean the status of the applicant does not have influence. Actually, some of the same dynamics work in the admission process to Western universities. The "old boy system" is alive and flourishing, especially in Ivy League universities. The offspring of alumni and wealthy donors are admitted to such schools in higher proportions than is warranted by their test scores. In an achievement-oriented culture this provokes a scandal if it is proved, but in a status-oriented culture it may appear far less significant.

Exposure of vulnerability versus concealment. Western values often assume that it is admirable to be frank, open and vulnerable. Robert believed that by bringing a questionable practice into the open he was serving the cause of truth. By exposing himself to criticism he was contributing to a noble cause. Those whose position shielded them from honest evaluation should be exposed to the light of day. However, in a culture that prizes harmony above many other values, his frankness was seen as a threat not only to wrongdoers but also to the established order. In Asia the protection of the reputation of those in authority is especially important. Concealment of the vulnerability of leaders of a university or another institution may take precedence over openness to objective review.

In this regard the popular distinction between "shame cultures" and "guilt cultures" may be useful. First proposed by Ruth Benedict based on studies of Japan, shame and guilt are best thought of as a continuum. David Augsburger suggests that all cultures contain both, but shame cultures place more emphasis on loss of face before significant others, while guilt cultures stress loss of integrity before one's own conscience.[33] A shame orientation emphasize the opinion of the group as a restraint on wrong behavior, while a guilt orientation focuses on individual subjective consciousness. Neither system is wrong; both have strengths and weaknesses. Asian cultures are much higher on the shame scale, and Western cultures higher on the guilt side. For this reason Augsburger cautions Westerners against judging Asian cultures (and vice versa).

Lucian Pye observes that in Asia

> leaders are concerned about questions of dignity, the need to uphold national pride, and other highly symbolic matters. Those in power want above all to be seen as protecting the prestige of the collectivity, which they are inclined to place above the goal of efficiency or of advancing specific interests in concrete ways.[34]

In Robert's case, regardless of whether the guilt involved in unfair admissions was a real concern of the university, the shame to the whole community caused by public exposure was felt much more keenly. Robert, on the other hand, used shame as a tool to get at what he felt was really important—the guilt of unjust practices.

The Moral Connotations of Communication

The moral dilemma Robert faced was primarily concerned not with fair admission standards but rather with what he, as a guest professor, ought to do about a perceived injustice. Assuming that his Asian colleagues were not agreeing with

Robert only out of politeness, they shared his opinion about the need for fair admission standards. While they had no authority over admission policies, the problem concerned both Robert and his colleagues because they had to teach poorly prepared students. Therefore the central moral dilemma involved cross-cultural communication. How should Robert communicate his values, which he thought were in the best interests of the university?

The simplest and certainly the most prudent answer would be for Robert to leave that up to his Asian colleagues who shared his concern. He might advise them and give moral support without jeopardizing his role as a guest. On the other hand, prudence might be a mask for cowardice. If his colleagues could not or would not address the situation, perhaps Robert should have done so. If so, it was critical that he understand the ways that cultural values are embedded in all kinds of communication.

Charles Osgood led a major study of the affective qualities of human communication.[35] He found that the connotation of words in over thirty cultures include the dimensions of (1) evaluation, (2) potency and (3) activity.

Evaluation. Regarding evaluation, Osgood says, "What is important to us now, as it was way back in the age of the Neanderthal Man, about the sign of a thing is: First, does it refer to something *good* or *bad* for me?"[36]

This is pretty basic. Everything that anyone hears, in any culture, is evaluated in terms of whether it's good or bad for me or for my group. Human beings have sensors in every language for threats and promises. Our perception may be of moral goods (such as love), moral evils (such as deceit), nonmoral goods (such as candy) or nonmoral evils (such as a revoked visa), but ultimately all communication in every culture contains a moral element. Human beings apply a culturally influenced critical standard to evaluate the meaning of even the simplest communication. Crosscultural communication requires that people learn to understand the critical standard of the other. What is it that threatens bad or promises good to the other?

Dean Wong received Robert's letter as a threat. We do not know all the reasons why. Since the letter was written by a Westerner in an Asian language that normally uses very indirect forms of expression, Robert's letter may have been quite direct and blunt, neglecting the normal polite forms of address. In any case, Dean Wong retaliated with an angry letter suggesting that foreigners should mind their own business.

Behind such a statement lies Asian sensitivity to hundreds of years of foreign imperialism, colonialism and neocolonialism. The evaluation of Robert's letter as a threat was intensified by his nationality. He was not just a professor but a Westerner. The threat thus had symbolic power that went beyond the criticism of Dean Wong's actions. The dean's response implied that Robert's letter threatened the university's freedom from foreign control. That threat touched a deeper distrust of Western paternalism, neocolonialism and racism.

The dynamic of threat and promise is intensified in a relationship between two people with unequal economic power. A Westerner abroad often receives a much higher salary than his Third World counterparts, and Robert may have had close ties with funding sources important to the university. Criticism from such a foreigner may contain an implicit threat, even if it is not intended. If such a threat is perceived, it may intensify the resentment.

In a case involving the admission of applicants from rich or powerful families, there may be a real threat of cutting off a valuable source of income or political influence. Criticism by a "rich" foreigner may be resented as insensitive at best. After all, the foreigner does not have to deal with the complex bureaucracy and the chronic lack of funds that plague many developing countries.

In return, Robert evaluated the letter of rebuke also as a threat. A common and intense desire of expatriates working in a foreign country is to be accepted for who they are and not stereotyped as foreigners. As someone sincerely seeking the welfare of the university, Robert resented being identified with "the oppressor." After working for years in the country and achieving fluency in the language, Robert longed for acceptance, if not as a "native," at least as a friend who could be trusted. This experience taught Robert that he would always be a foreigner. Perhaps it was the hurt that ensued that caused him to release the letters to the newspaper.

Potency. Osgood's second category has to do with the power of the person who authors the communication. We understand what is said partly in reference to who says it and what kind of power she or he has over us. The meaning of words changes according to our perception of the strength of the threat, or promise, implied by their author. The same words spoken by our boss and by the gardener have different meaning.

Robert's potency as a foreign guest professor was ambiguous. In one sense he was more powerful than a local faculty member, because he was less subject to the normal power structures. If he had been a lowly lecturer, he could have safely been ignored, been given an implied threat or actually received sanctions of one

122

kind or another. As a guest, he perhaps needed to be taken seriously. A guest has access to international resources and relationships that may be of importance to the university. On the other hand, as a guest he was always subordinate to his hosts. Dean Wong clearly did not think a guest professor had the right to criticize the university power structure. While a guest may not be demoted, he is there by an invitation that may not be renewed.

The potency of a message lies not only in the author but also in the form of communication. In many modern institutions, memos and letters are commonplace. But in some countries with a strong oral tradition, written communications are a mark of status, formality and seriouness. Usually they pass only from superiors to inferiors, or between equals. Thus Dean Wong's irritation with Robert's letter may have stemmed from a perception that Robert was claiming inappropriate status or power in writing at all. Dean Wong's harsh reply was meant to remind a disrespectful foreigner that this university was no longer under colonial domination! If such was his intention, the plan clearly backfired when Robert took the unexpected action of releasing the letters to the newspaper. By doing so he demonstrated his potency. Robert may have won the battle that lost the war.

Activity. Finally, Osgood's study suggests that people in all cultures consider the meaning of communication in relation to what kind of activity or behavior is demanded of them by the words spoken. There are two primary possibilities: activity or passivity. Simply put, this means we understand communication in terms of whether we must respond or can safely ignore the message. Richard Brislin suggests that cultural foreigners are often perceived as safer to ignore.[37] It may be hard to evaluate their intentions or their potency, but usually they are safe to ignore.

In the case of Robert, Dean Wong could not completely ignore Robert's communication, both because of Robert's status as a foreign guest and because the complaint came in a formal letter. On the other hand, the dean did not think he had to do anything about it. The letter was answered, but the demand was ignored. It is possible that if Robert had gone to the dean in person in the first place instead of writing a letter, he would have received a better result.

In any case, taking the dispute to the newspaper was an extreme response that cut off further communication. Even in the West, questioning a superior's integrity through a letter to the newspaper may be seen as a breach of professional ethics. While the immediate shame fell on Dean Wong, Robert's long-term standing in the community may have been even more injured, at least with those in power.

A conversation, or a series of conversations, could have opened a process of negotiation that would have been less threatening to Dean Wong yet perhaps harder for him to ignore. Robert might have been able to include other Asian faculty in the discussion with the prospect of gradually widening the forum of discussion if a satisfactory agreement were not reached.

Of course it is easy to speculate with hindsight. Nevertheless, the form of communication between people from different cultures is a significant factor in its ultimate moral impact. The next chapter will consider the effects of nonverbal communication and the role of the stranger in crosscultural ethics.

SIX

STRANGE
COMMUNICATIONS

E dward Sapir and his student Benjamin Lee Whorf are well known among linguists for their hypothesis that language is "a self-contained, creative, symbolic organization, which not only refers to experience largely acquired without its help but actually defines experience for us by reason of its formal completeness and because of our unconscious projection of its implicit expectations into the field of experience."[1]

Language and the Way We See the World

The assertion of the "Sapir-Whorf hypothesis" is that language is not just a neutral medium through which we express our ideas but a powerful structure that shapes all that we think, say and do. Most of what we see and understand is filtered through language. The implication for crosscultural ethics is that different languages produce different perceptions of the world. Language and culture cannot be separated. Therefore we cannot hope to really see the world through the eyes of another culture without learning the language.

George Kraft suggests that if a person spends two months, two years or ten years in a country, the entire time should be spent in learning the language. No other task better communicates the gospel.[2] The same advice could be given to a tourist spending two weeks in a country. Language learning is the best way to open the door to communication, understanding and human connection. By becoming learners and making the difficult effort to speak with foreign words, we demonstrate our care for people and allow them to show us how they name their world. Sometimes it is less important how well you speak than that you are trying. Halting phrases bring smiles and approval.

On the other hand, skill in a language acts like a passport to real relationship. Skill or fluency entails a deep understanding of the culture. Fluency is lacking as long as we translate *our* language into another. Fluency requires that we experience reality through the categories of the new language. Then we not only will communicate clearly but may also instinctively say the right thing, at the right time, in the right way. If we think in another language we may say very different things from what we would ever say in our own language. The following story illustrates the point.

> Sometime in 1906 I was walking in the heat of the day through the bazaars. As I passed an Arab Cafe, in no hostility to my straw hat but desiring to shine before his friends, a fellow called out in Arabic, "God curse your father, O Englishman." I was young then and quicker tempered, and could not refrain from answering in his own language that I would also curse his father if he were in a position to inform me which of his mother's two and ninety admirers his father had been. I heard footsteps behind me, and slightly picked up the pace, angry with myself for committing the sin Lord Cromer would not pardon—a row with Egyptians. In a few seconds I felt a hand on each arm. "My brother," said the original humorist, "return and drink with us coffee and smoke [in Arabic one speaks of 'drinking' smoke]. I did not think that your worship knew Arabic, still less the correct Arabic abuse, and we would fain benefit further by your important thoughts."[3]

Nonverbal Communication of Goodness

Communication includes much more than language. Ray L. Birdwhistell, who sparked the relatively recent interest in nonverbal communication, estimated that in a conversation between two people from the *same* culture, less than 30 percent of what is communicated is verbal.[4] It is reasonable to suppose that people from different cultures rely even more heavily on nonverbal communication. This is good news insofar as much can be communicated between people who do not share a language.

I will never forget a weekend we spent with a French family in 1970. My wife and I picked up Jean Marie, who was hitchhiking outside of Paris. We were just beginning to study French, and he spoke no English. When we let him off, he invited us to his home in a small village for the weekend. There, through music, laughter, food, wine, children, flowers, chores and shared grief over the injustice of the world, we became like brothers and sisters. Of the few words we were able to exchange, only one do I remember as significant: the French word *simpatique* expressed what we had found together.

Part of the rapport we shared stemmed from our common membership in the worldwide youth culture of the 1960s. But our whole family has enjoyed real, if less dramatic, nonverbal rapport with strangers in a dozen foreign countries. I once stumbled upon a hidden tribal village in the mountains of Mindoro, Philippines, far from the nearest road. There I met a teenage couple who lived in a simple bamboo hut and had no formal education or contact with the outside world. They invited me into their home to share a simple meal of wild root vegetables cooked in coconut milk. Not only did they make me welcome, we spent an hour in delightful communication without words. The human connection between us was enhanced by our mutual strangeness. When I left, surrounded in the warmth of their shy smiles, I knew I had received a great gift. The next day I tried to return, but I could never again find the secret path that led to their valley.

Such experiences may lead to the false conclusion that all human beings are basically alike and nonverbal communication is universal. Unfortunately, communication without words is a complex language that varies widely from culture to culture. An hour or a weekend may be all that it can bear without serious misunderstanding. Something as simple as a smile, or laughter, may signify widely different meanings in different cultures. With a certain hyperbole, a well-known travel writer suggests that a smile almost never means happiness in China.[5] More often it signifies something like "Westerners are so stupid!"

In Indonesia I am repeatedly amazed at the pervasiveness of smiles and laughter, especially in the countryside, where 90 percent of the people live.[6] Smiles and laughter often indicate genuine pleasure, friendliness or at least politeness. They are also used to defuse tension and minimize someone's embarrassment. Thus when a large American woman, who was feeling very self-conscious in a world of small people, tripped and spilled her drink at a party, everyone began to laugh. The meaning of the laughter was not, as the woman thought, ridicule of her clumsiness, but a socially conventional way to defuse tension and help her feel at ease.[7] Concern for her feelings (a virtue) prompted the laughter, not insensitive ridicule. Unfortunately, she did not know the nonverbal language.

In many cultures the values of pleasing a stranger and responding positively to their wishes is far more important than telling them the truth. Javanese almost never say no to a direct question. It just feels too impolite. In some cultures an affirmative answer is likely if your question is given with a smile or an upbeat manner—what the hearer interprets as the expectation of a positive answer—regardless of the question. Conversely, a sober or angry manner is likely to bring a negative answer. It seems to be what you expect. The listener's job is to be polite and say what is expected, not give factual information.

An amusing example of this happened in Oakland, California. Grace Dyrness, the director of an inner-city Christian ministry, had just returned from teaching a class on crosscultural communication at New College Berkeley and was on her way to Harbor House, which offers English classes for Southeast Asian refugees. In a friendly manner she stopped to talk with some older Laotian men who were sitting outside. She asked them if they had been to English class, if Irene was their teacher, if she was a good teacher and if they had enjoyed it. To each question they returned her smile and answered yes, yes, yes, yes. Grace entered the building with a warm feeling at the positive attitudes of the old men. Inside she learned that there had been no classes yet that day and the old men were not even enrolled!

Culturally specific forms of nonverbal communication include unconscious as well as conscious actions. When I first met an Indonesian graduate student in the United States, I was puzzled that although our conversations were very friendly, he always seemed somewhat tense. Somewhere I had read that in Indonesia it is more respectful not to look into a person's eyes when you talk to him. I decided to try it. It was very hard. My American conditioning made me feel that I was not being open and honest if I did not look him straight in the eye. Nevertheless, I was amazed at the results. As I talked to his chin or his chest with only occasional glances at his eyes, he began to relax and became more jovial than I had ever seen him.

This behavior is not a "rule" that you can follow with Indonesians or even Javanese. Often Indonesians do look each other in the eye with no indication of disrespect. My experience on this one occasion may only indicate that averting of the eyes is a traditional, refined Javanese way of honoring a superior in a society that highly values humility. Unconsciously, the meaning of downcast eyes registers as respect in Indonesia but as evasiveness in America.

Studies using high-speed film show that speech and bodily movement are totally synchronized. The body, even down to the blinking of the eyelids, follows the speech. Nothing is random or totally without meaning.[8] Not only the speaker's movements but also those of the listener are coordinated with the speech. Different languages and different cultures show different body movements. As John C. Condon and Fathi S. Yousef put it, "We dance to the rhythm of our own voice when we are talking and, as listeners, we dance to the tune of the speaker's voice."[9]

Unfortunately, the specific meanings of nonverbal communication are not all universal. Some have been shown to be very different from culture to culture. No one knows how much is transcultural. But certainly this makes "fluency" in another language much more difficult to attain. "Not only must we learn to hear and express the new sounds in new rhythms of another language, we must also learn to blink and twitch in a new rhythm!"[10]

Nonverbal communication includes facial expressions, posture and stance, hand gestures, use of space, touching, eye movement, smell, taste, timing, volume of voice and many other things. Edward Hall has illustrated ten different areas in which all cultures communicate: interaction, association, subsistence, bisexuality, territoriality, temporality, learning, play, defense and exploitation.[11] In Hall's model, each of his categories interact with every other category to form one hundred areas in which culturally unique communication occurs. An analysis of just these ten vectors of communication could yield virtually an infinite number of specific cultural practices, all of which are value-laden.

The following example displays a misunderstanding that includes crosscultural confusions in the areas of interaction, bisexuality and territoriality.[12] An American businessman was talking with a young Latino woman at a party in Central America. As they conversed, she took a step closer to him. Feeling uncomfortable, he took a step backwards to maintain what he felt was a comfortable distance. Over the course of their conversation they repeated the unconscious maneuver until they had moved the entire length of the room and he was cornered.

He arrived at the conclusion that she was aggressively "coming on to him," and suppressing his moral qualms about her behavior and his response, he invited her to his apartment. She was totally shocked and insulted. She felt that he had been extremely cold and aloof all evening. Each had a different cultural convention for the meaning of space between people in a conversation. Latinos feel comfortable standing closer to each other in a casual conversation than do North Americans. Each made value judgments about the other based on unconscious nonverbal communication that was misconstrued.

The literature of crosscultural studies is full of stories of major and minor disasters that befall those unskilled in crosscultural communication. Some are tragic, some are funny, many are freighted with moral content. But few are as outright delightful as the following:

A little golden girl of seven . . . brought in a coconut which she had opened under the tree outside, sat down, and offered it to me cupped in both hands, at arm's length, with her head a little bowed. "You shall be blessed," she murmured as I took it. I did say, "Thank you" in reply, but even after that I should have returned her blessing word for word, and after that I should have returned the nut also, for her to take the first sip of courtesy; and at last— when I received it back, I should have said "Blessings and Peace" before beginning to drink the milk. All I did—woe is me!—was to take it, swig it off, hand it back one-handed, empty, with another careless, "Thank you."

"Alas," she said at last in a shocked whisper, "Alas! Is that the manners of a young chief of [the white people]?" She told me one by one the sins I have confessed . . . but that was not the full tale. My final discourtesy had been the crudest of all. In handing back the empty nut, I had omitted to belch aloud. "How could I know when you did not belch . . . that my food was sweet to you? See, this is how you should have done it!" She held the nut towards me with both hands, her earnest eyes fixed on mine, and gave vent to a belch so resonant that it seemed to shake her elfin form from stem to stern. "That," she finished, "is our idea of good manners," and wept for the pity of it.[13]

Anyone entering a foreign land needs good teachers who will teach him or her the languages, spoken and unspoken, that reflect the goodness, truth and beauty of local custom. Above all, we need people who will tell us the truth about our mistakes. Would that we all had teachers as truthful and eloquent as that little girl.

Adaptation to the Role of a Stranger

Christians entering another culture frequently make two mistakes. First, although they know they have a lot to learn, they expect to make rapid progress within a few months. In fact, they are less skilled than a little child in how to communicate and fit in. Almost always they are disappointed in their progress. Learning another language and culture takes years of hard work.

If peak efficiency and productivity are your goals, it is probably better not to enter another culture. This is especially true for people from wealthy countries who go to the Third World. The material limitations of developing countries may be significant. But the structural barriers of a strange language and culture can be overwhelming. Crosscultural literature frequently warns people that if they can't succeed at something in their own culture, they will not improve in a foreign context.

Non-Western people who visit the United States often adapt more quickly than their Western counterparts who go abroad. For one thing, people who travel to the States are far more likely to speak English than Americans are to speak a given foreign language. Moreover, Asians, Africans, Europeans and South Americans often know far more about the United States than Americans know about their respective cultures. "Globalization" and U.S. domination of the world's media make American cultural values familiar (though perhaps in distorted form) to people from many parts of the world.

Second, Western Christians think they have a lot to offer. Many would not go to another country if they did not have motivations of ministry. Christians go to serve, to evangelize, to help build the church and the developing country. Probably they have more education, more money and more opportunity than many of their national colleagues. That makes them not only rich but also dangerous. As every parent should know, powerful people who try to help often do more harm than good. Apart from the risks of dependency or of help that is inappropriate, there are the subtle dangers of help that masks self-interest. A foreigner who comes to help may find less appreciation than he or she expected.

Beyond the physical, language and cultural difficulties they face is the immutable fact that they are foreigners, strangers in a foreign land. Even those who are totally fluent in the language and culture do not cease to be strangers. Even an American who becomes a citizen, who settles permanently in the country, remains a "white man," inexorably tied by skin color, birth and history to the imperial, colonial powers of the West. Similarly, a Nigerian or Indian who lives for many years in England will never be accepted as a true English person. In Indonesia, Chinese whose families have lived there for hundreds of years are still not considered "native" (*pribumi*).

The difficulties and dangers of strangers. A foreigner, in time, may be loved and respected. But he or she does not thereby cease to be a stranger. Anthony J. Gittins, an anthropologist at the Catholic Theological Union in Chicago, points out that in many languages the word for "stranger" is the same as the word for "guest." These words have a very different feel in English, but in many cultures the rules of hospitality require that strangers be treated as guests. Rules of hospitality are not taken lightly. The responsibilities of a host are significant. Being a stranger is not easy, but neither is being a host. Both must play their role if a crosscultural relationship is to be formed. Gittins asks,

> Do we show adequate and genuine deference to our hosts? Do we willingly acknowledge their authority in the situation, and their rights and duties as hosts? Do we allow ourselves to be adequately positioned as strangers, according to the legitimate needs of the hosts? Or do we try to seize initiatives, show them clearly what our expectations are, make demands on them, and thus effectively refuse the role of stranger, thereby impeding them from being adequate hosts?[14]

Strangers have no inherent right to credibility or trust. These must be earned. Legitimation is a gift from the host. Unlike a citizen, who has a right to be there no matter how obnoxious or foolish he is, a stranger/guest is dependent on his host for the right to remain. Thus the guest is always subordinate to the host. This is a moral relationship that is usually enforced politically through the necessity for visas and restrictions on foreigners. Unfortunately, it has not always been so enforced. In the past those with power came and did whatever they wished. One of the worst things a guest can do is to take away the rights of a host to be the host.

Today the older, more obvious oppressions of colonialism have given way to a more subtle neocolonialism. The paternalistic relationship between the United States and the Philippines is a sad example of how a host nation can politically lose the rights of a host over its own home. The Bell Trade Act, forced on the Philippines at the close of World War II, granted Americans the same rights as Filipinos to do business in the Philippines. Whereas in Indonesia foreign companies must form joint ventures with their hosts, in the Philippines local businesses must compete on equal terms with multinational corporations. During a ten-year period, for every dollar invested from the United States in the Philippines, five dollars returned to the States. Twenty-four of the fifty largest companies in the Philippines were owned by Americans.[15]

The history of colonialism and neocolonialism is a story of how guests came bringing gifts and then took over the home of their hosts for the sake of profit. Missionaries sometimes do the same. As one wag put it, "They came to do good and they ended up doing very well."[16]

This familiar story should not obscure the fact that missionaries and other foreign guests have often made great contributions to their host countries, sometimes at great personal sacrifice. In spite of the history of colonialism, and as testimony to the reality of forgiveness, Western strangers are still welcome in many parts of the world. But their welcome is not unconditional.

In the 1970s some Two-Thirds World Christian leaders caused shock waves in the West by calling for a moratorium on Western missionaries. Today the idea of a moratorium is seldom mentioned. Most churches in the Two-Thirds World appreciate missionaries, provided they can find the right kind.

During the Indian struggle for independence there was once a massive demonstration calling for all foreigners, and especially Britishers, to be thrown out of India. During a passionate speech by a fiery radical, a humble English priest came forward and asked if he too should leave. The priest had lived for many years in simplicity with the people, identifying with their struggles. A great roar of denial went up from the crowd, and the speaker replied, "Oh no, Father; you see, you are one of us."

Stages of assimilation. Gittins elaborates three stages of assimilation that were classically described by Arnold van Gennep.[17] When you first arrive as a stranger, there is a preliminary stage of mutual exploration. When the novelty wears off, you enter the transitional or liminal (threshold) stage, in which you are not given special treatment but are still exploring the meaning of your relationship with the culture. Finally, if you do not become liminoid (stuck in the liminal stage), there is the possibility of eventual incorporation. In real life these are not discrete descriptions of specific stages. Rather, they should be thought of as ideal types or as a continuum of the experience of inculturation. A stranger may move back and forth between the three stages.

The *preliminary stage* is marked by formality and tentativeness. If the stranger is also an invited guest, she may be treated with exaggerated politeness and respect. This does not mean the host is without caution. Strangers may be a valuable resource, but they are also dangerous.

Societies that are not cautious with strangers may not survive long: "there are no longer any indigenous Uruguayans or Tasmanians; and for every forty Brazilian Indians before the arrival of the Europeans, thirty-nine have been exterminated (from 1.2 million to 30,000)!"[18] If we look at what is even now happening to tribal peoples in many parts of the world, from the point of view of survival, those who skip the preliminary stage and get out their blowguns may be the wisest. Most strangers bring the threat of competition, paternalism, cultural change, economic and social domination, exploitation and dependency. Strangers usually bring gifts, but their motives and long-term impact are unknown. They may be powerful and dangerous.

Nevertheless, the preliminary stage is not usually characterized by suspicion. More often you are treated as an honored guest. In the popular literature on culture shock, this stage is often referred to as the honeymoon phase. All the attention and ritual are exciting. They are also tiring, both to you and to your hosts. If you do not leave first, they must come to an end as you enter the transitional or liminal phase.

In the *transitional stage* the stranger is no longer treated like an honored guest. If you have made it this far without fleeing the culture shock, you are now accepted as a normal part of the local scene. You are still a foreigner, but no longer noteworthy.

> No longer will there be the formal ceremonial relationships of hospitality and kindness; in fact the stranger may sense a certain cooling-off on the part of the hosts. What was relatively structured behavior in the early stages now becomes frustratingly unpredictable, changeable, even random. . . . The incomer is perhaps treated with casualness or even left to manage alone.[19]

This can be a relief, a cause of anxiety or both. Your presence is accepted, and it is assumed that you have adjusted to the culture. In a sense you are honored by not receiving special treatment. It means you are accepted. On the other hand, your adjustment is far from complete. While the highs and lows of the initial stages of culture shock are past, recurring experiences of culture fatigue are common and may sap your sense of identity and self-worth. By now, after six months or a year or three years, you expected to be fluent in language and culture. Instead you, and your hosts, are aware of how much you still don't know. Your body still does not "dance and twitch" in the appropriate manner to the rhythms of the new culture. And you suspect it never will.

The commitment of the hosts in this phase is still conditional and tentative. The guest is being tested to see how he or she will turn out in the long run.

Enough time has passed for the sheen to have worn off of both parties, and as in a marriage, either may wonder if they have made a mistake. Joy and closeness may be experienced one day, followed by alienation and disappointment on the next. The host wants to know how committed the guest really is and how long they are likely to stay. The guest wants to know if he or she is really still welcome and how long that is likely to continue. Neither side wants to be simply exploited for the interests of the other.

The important thing in the transitional stage is to keep moving, keep growing, don't let relationships stagnate and, as in marriage, stay committed. That is not so easy. The longer a stranger stays, the easier it is to become stereotyped into fixed functions or begin to compete with the hosts for power and status. Insofar as that happens, the possibility of becoming partners, fellow-learners and friends will be lost. The transitional stage can last for years. It can last a lifetime.

Three things can happen to strangers in the transitional stage: (1) they can remain in that stage till their task is completed and they leave (voluntarily or involuntarily), (2) they can become "liminoid," frozen in a more or less permanent state of cultural distance akin to alienation, or (3) they can become incorporated, or adopted into their new cultural home (stage three).

Some strangers come to do a job for a short or long period. They both give to and receive from the culture but have no intention of becoming incorporated into it. These may be called "utilitarian transitionals." They are like long-term tourists who are appreciated for what they bring and in turn appreciate the experience they receive, but there are no strings attached. They are like a couple that goes out for a casual date with no intention of any further commitment. When they leave they are thankful to be returning home, and they are not likely to be missed.

In every country I have visited, there is a community of expatriates, some of whom have been there forever, who seem to despise the country in which they live. The most common characteristic of these "liminoids" is that they continually complain about "the locals." In return they are heartily resented. A liminoid person is like someone stuck in a disastrous affair or a bad marriage. They hate it but for some reason don't leave. Tony Gittins remarks, "Liminoids do not get better, they get worse."[20]

Sometimes liminoids have had a healthy and productive relationship with the country, but for some reason it has gone sour. If you are a liminoid it is better to bail out and go home. Sometimes people become liminoid against their will.

Even though they have the best of intentions, gradually the stress of culture fatigue builds up and they become chronically unhappy with the country. Of course everyone is liminoid sometimes, even the "locals"! But a true liminoid is trapped in destructive attitudes.

An ideal goal of the transition stage is *incorporation*. A stranger is incorporated when she or he is fully accepted and integrated into the culture. Both sides have made a long-term commitment to the other which will not be terminated even if the stranger leaves. When you are incorporated, you have internalized the culture to the extent that it has become part of you. Incorporation does not occur at the initiative of the stranger. It is an act of the host to make the stranger a real part of the family. The closest analogy may be adoption. But it is also like marriage in that both parties make a commitment to each other.

As in adoption, a person who has been welcomed into a new family does not ever become structurally equal with his new "parents." The new culture may become family, but it will also remain your host, at least for a very long time. As an incorporated foreigner, you remain a guest, structurally subordinate to your hosts. Gittins suggests that if strangers are unwilling to accept this and show it in their attitudes, they are unlikely to be incorporated into the culture.

Acceptance by the host is no *carte blanche* for the stranger to forget the precedence due to the other. . . . If the stranger wishes to remain "free" and not be beholden to the host, then incorporation is not desirable; but where incorporation does take place, then *noblesse oblige* [requires] the guest to defer to the host and be loyal rather than critical. . . . If we sense that we are incorporated into a group, do we thereby acknowledge our responsibility to support and be loyal to our hosts? Or do we retain our "right" to criticize and judge others, thus effectively making it undesirable for us to seek incorporation? And what of our hosts: do we appreciate their relative slowness in accepting us fully? Do we understand how seriously they take the duties of hospitality? Can we accept that they remain superordinate, since we are on their turf and not our own? And do we nevertheless aspire to learning how to be appropriate strangers, or do we wish to repudiate the conventions and seize the initiative and control?[21]

It is possible that a stranger who has been "married" by a culture may be "divorced" if she acts disloyal or overly critical of the "family." On the other hand, it seems to me that Gittins confuses stages when he speaks of loyalty as a prerequisite for incorporation and incorporation as requiring absence of criticism. Before incorporation you may need to prove your loyalty through forgoing the "right" to criticize. But loyalty and criticism are not mutually exclusive. If they were, my marriage would not have lasted for twenty-five years!

If outsiders have lived in a culture long enough, proved their loyalty and been truly incorporated, their constructive criticism of those who remain their hosts may be part of their gift to the family. If so, incorporation is not a *barrier* to criticism but rather a *prerequisite* to constructive criticism. Those who remain in the transition stage, still less those who are liminoid, have very little right to criticize. Their loyalty to and identification with their hosts is not yet established. Their understanding of the context is too superficial. Only those whose commitment and acceptance are clearly understood have earned the responsibility (not the right) of constructive criticism.

In the case of Robert and Dean Wong considered in the last chapter, Robert may have misjudged the stage of his assimilation. After a number of years in the country, Robert may have believed he was incorporated into the culture and had earned the responsibility of criticism, at least within his university. Possibly he was incorporated by some members of the community but not by others. If so, he may have earned the responsibility to criticize the portion of the community that had "adopted" him but not the right to criticize more widely. In any case, criticism in any culture must be done with sensitivity to the local rules of social interaction.

This is tricky when it involves social justice issues. Those in power are seldom likely to appreciate criticism from a guest, no matter how well accepted he may be by other members of the community. In Robert's case, he felt he was giving voice to the feelings of colleagues who were powerless in the situation. If Robert had actually been asked to speak out against those in power by marginalized members of the community, his moral position would be stronger. He could then have been seen as risking his own security in the community because of his loyalty to the weak and oppressed.

This is a common dilemma for those who work in countries with repressive governments. In countries like El Salvador, Western missionaries have lost their lives because of their solidarity with the poor. In one Central American country, local Christian leaders pleaded with American development workers to stand with them in exposing a government atrocity. The Americans knew that if they did so, they and perhaps their organization would no longer be welcome in the country. On the other hand, if they did not go out on a limb, their courageous local friends could lose their lives.

In the final analysis, no firm rules can be made about whether a guest may criticize a host. If the situation is serious enough and lives hang in the balance, even a preliminary-stage stranger may be required to speak out on behalf of the weak. The rules of relationship between guest and host usually preclude open criticism. Even indirect criticism is a sensitive issue. If guests, for reasons of conscience, are forced to speak out, they should know that their privileged position as guests in the country may quickly come to an end.

The Gift of Strangeness

The strangeness of strangers is their greatest asset. Far from being an unmitigated disaster to be overcome as quickly as possible, the oddness of a foreigner is a treasure to herself and to her hosts. She is different from everyone else, and though she may be a threat, she is also a promise. Although she may be uncomfortable, she is likely to receive gifts of which she never dreamed. With almost monotonous familiarity, people who come to serve others in a foreign culture, whether across the ocean or just downtown, suggest that they have received far more than they have given in their attempts at "ministry."

The stranger is often valued for bringing resources that are unavailable in the local community. New wisdom, ideas, art, technology, music, education, spirituality, science, customs, money, food, health care, experience and relationships are all treasures that may come from across the ocean or across town. The church is a universal body in which all are enriched by the mutual sharing of diverse cultural gifts.

What is given to and received from a "successful stranger" is often unpredictable. Just as the dangers that emanate from the stranger are unpredictable, so is the treasure. A lawyer may enter a community to do legal aid work and end up caring for unwed mothers or taking meals to people with AIDS. The same lawyer may expect to help overcome institutionalized racism in the courts and receive in return cultural enrichment and gratitude. But her most valuable reward may be to see the courage and joy of people who daily face poverty and what her culture calls failure. Her whole view of the world and definition of success may change.

Often enough, groups will accept relatively rich strangers because of expectations for financial and technical assistance. Regardless of whether all the expectations for material or educational help are met, it is unlikely that the success of the assistance will be measured in physical terms. Material and even intellectual resources can deteriorate very quickly. But lives changed through relationship can last forever.

A gifted English scientist who taught for many years in an Arab university was very successful on a number of different levels. He helped his hosts establish a graduate program, obtained grants, wrote curriculum, developed materials, taught the faculty and so on. Thus when it came time for him to leave, he was surprised that in the official speech of gratitude only one thing was mentioned: that he was a deep man of God. This was all the more remarkable since he was a Christian teaching in a Muslim setting. His colleagues had recognized that he brought a treasure far more valuable than his scientific skills.

Groups that cannot defend their boundaries against strangers are often exploited and may lose their identity. But groups that seal their boundaries against all outsiders harbor the seeds of their own destruction. This is true biologically, socially, economically, culturally, politically and spiritually. Not only is new blood genetically good for human reproduction, it is also culturally good for a healthy society. That is why vigorous cultures are not static or fixed. They are in the midst of cultural change. The stranger, because of his or her strangeness, is potentially the bringer of life.

The stranger plays a significant role in both the Old and New Testaments. God's people are often pictured as strangers and sojourners on a journey through a strange land. Perhaps that is partly why both testaments stress hospitality to strangers. The Jews knew what it felt like to be alien. But there is also the recognition that the stranger may have a secret that is of great value. On more than one occasion in the Old Testament the stranger turns out to be an angel in disguise.[22] More powerfully yet, Matthew suggests that Christ is present in the stranger. When we welcome the stranger, we welcome Christ (Mt 25:35). Conversely, when we reject the stranger we reject Christ. When we are ourselves strangers, we represent Christ and are commanded by him to bring good news.

The central assumption of communication theory has been that understanding between people is based on similarities between them. Only insofar as people share the same assumptions and ideas can they communicate. This assumption has recently been cogently challenged by Zali D. Gurevitch, a sociologist at the Hebrew University of Jerusalem.[23] Gurevitch does not question the need for human beings to create a common world of meaning in order to communicate, but he suggests that this is only one side of what makes a meaningful dialogue.

The other side is our need to "make the other strange," to realize another person's foreignness so that we can encounter her reality.

The problem with people who are like us is that we know too much about them. As a result we enclose them in "a grid of familiar typifications" that effectively blocks their unique presence from view. We categorize and stereotype familiar persons such that we cannot see anything new, only what we already know. In order to have real dialogue, we need the ability *not* to understand them. We must see them as strange before we can really see them at all. Most of the time we hide from reality by seeing everything in abstract categories. Even the people closest to us may be seen as categories such as wife, student, neighbor or father. The problem is, as T. S. Eliot put it, "humankind cannot bear very much reality."[24]

When you become a stranger and enter another culture, the result is a radical "defamiliarization" of all you know. You are forced to open your eyes and really look. The simplest things do not make sense. The unexpected happens every day. What is normal to others is shocking or marvelous in your eyes. If you can handle the stress, your strangerhood becomes a powerful stimulus to understanding yourself, your own culture and the new world presented to your senses. The "honeymoon phase" of culture shock is a wonderful opportunity to really *see* the uniqueness, while your senses are still hungry for the newness of everything.

In a similar way, your strangeness shocks your hosts into recognizing a broader reality than before. Of course the host may just stereotype you into whatever image he has picked up about American Christians, Berkeley radicals or Cambridge intellectuals (pick your stereotype). But if dialogue really takes place he will soon be surprised to find that you are stranger than you seem. And the shock in his eyes may be God's gift, through you, to him.

The purpose of the stranger is not to become like the host (or vice versa). That is impossible, undesirable and probably immoral—probably immoral because it involves self-deception and/or hypocrisy. Strangers who pretend they are not strange at all are usually distrusted. Rather than being a chameleon who tries to be exactly the same as the surrounding people ("going native"), a good guest seeks a relationship that honors the profound differences that exist between cultures. In the words of Clifford Geertz,

> We are not, or at least I am not, seeking either to become natives . . . or to
> mimic them. . . . We are seeking, in the widened sense of the term in which
> it encompasses very much more than talk, to converse with them, a matter

a great deal more difficult, and not only with strangers, than is commonly recognized.[25]

Real conversation is a treasure that seems all too rare these days. When such opening of the heart occurs between people from radically different cultures, it is a miracle of grace. This may be one of the highest aims for which we were created. Each person, and each culture, has a unique secret. Each is capable of knowing something of God which no one else knows. In the meeting of strangers we have the opportunity to share that treasure with each other. George MacDonald says,

There is a chamber also (O God, humble and accept my speech)—a chamber in God's own heart, into which none can enter but the one, the individual, the peculiar person—out of which chamber that person has to bring revelation and strength for his brothers and sisters. This is that for which a person was made—to reveal the secret things of the Father.[26]

SEVEN

ETHICAL
THEORY AND
BRIBERY

I n interviews with Christians from all parts of the world working in "Third World" countries, the most commonly cited moral problem is corruption or bribery.[1] This chapter explores how Western ethical theory of moral choice might contribute to a sharpened perception of the nature of moral reality in relation to this thorny issue. I will examine a case study in order to consider how classical ethical categories and more recent conceptions contribute to an understanding of what is at stake in a particular crosscultural problem. This will provide both an in-depth ethical analysis of bribery and the outlines of an ethical method for evaluating other crosscultural dilemmas.

As an individual case, the situation presented in the following story is relatively trivial. But behind it lies a much larger problem of how to "act well" in a bureaucratic, patronage-based social structure in which relationships, and even survival, are structured through the giving and receiving of gifts.

The Case Study: Elusive Justice

Bill looked at the police officer with uncertainty and frustration. The officer had asked him for 200,000 rupiahs for the return of his driver's license. It was Bill's twelfth weekly visit to the headquarters since the license had been confiscated, and his resentment rose as he faced the possibility of yet another wasted week clouded with uncertainty and unpleasantness, unable to use his car. Must he sacrifice his principles in order to resolve the matter?

The problem began when Bill had returned from a missionary assignment out of town. He was coming into Bandung, West Java, along the main highway from Cirebon, the same road on which he had left the city two days before. The chaotic congestion was about normal in this heavily populated part of town. Animals, trishaws, and people were weaving their way in and out among the motorized traffic that crawled along the road toward the urban open market. For some time Bill had been caught behind a slow-moving, over-crowded bus, and there was little chance of getting past it, even when it stopped to allow passengers to alight.

Suddenly Bill was jolted to attention when something hit the side of the car. Before he knew what had happened, he caught sight of a policeman approaching the car and shaking his fist. By the time the officer had picked up his baton from the street, Bill was out of the car and prepared for the worst. Fellow missionaries had warned him never to tangle with the police. In fact, it was missionary policy not to call the police, even in the case of a house burglary. Experience had shown that it was cheaper to sustain the losses of robbery than to bear the frustration of red tape and loss of further property taken to headquarters to test for fingerprints.

Bill did not have to wait long to find out what he had done wrong. For several hundred yards approaching the market area, the highway became a one-way street. Buses and other public vehicles were permitted to use it in both directions, but private vehicles had to detour around back streets and rejoin the highway several blocks beyond the market. Bill pleaded that he had seen no sign and had simply followed the bus. The officer walked Bill back twenty yards and pointed out to him a small, mud-spattered sign obscured by a large parked truck. This did not seem to concern the officer at all. There was a law and a sign—and Bill was guilty.

Officer Somojo escorted Bill to the local police post in the market. Five other officers materialized from the stalls in the market, so Somojo began to explain how very embarrassing it was for him to have to prosecute a foreigner, and how he regretted that Bill had put him in this difficult position. After some time, Somojo suggested that the whole thing might be smoothed over quietly and without further awkwardness if Bill would pay a token fine of 2,000 rupiahs ($1.20) on the spot. Bill had been expecting just such a request. Without even asking if it was a formal, legitimate fine for which a receipt would be given, Bill quickly protested that although he might be technically guilty, Indonesian law had a system of justice and courts where such matters were to be settled. He would go through proper channels and requested to be allowed to do so. The officer scowled and told Bill that he would have to hold his driver's license until the case was settled. Bill could come to the police headquarters the following week to get it back. Since no receipt was issued for the license, Bill secretly feared that he would never see it again.

The following week, Bill went to the appointed office, only to be informed that the license had been sent to another department on the other side of the city. After a slow trip by trishaw, Bill finally found his way to the other office. The policeman in charge had a record of Bill's offense and said Bill could talk to the captain who would probably be prepared to settle the issue for 4,000 rupiahs. Bill suspected dishonesty and requested an official receipt for the money. The man just smiled. Bill told the policeman that he had come to Indonesia to build efficiency, justice, and a high standard of morality in the country. He would prefer to go through official channels. At that, he was told to return in a week's time. So week followed weary week, with hours wasted in travel and more hours spent waiting in offices. Each time the amount requested for settlement rose higher.

Bill worried about what he should do. He didn't want to be a troublemaker, but as a missionary he had to take a stand for honesty. His Christian witness depended on it. His whole upbringing as the son of an evangelical pastor had been one of strict integrity, and he had managed, so far, to maintain this standard in previous encounters with immigration officers and postal clerks. Yet, while he felt he had done the right thing, he still felt uneasy, for he knew full well that government officials were so poorly paid that they had to make at least double their official salaries on the side if they were to feed and clothe their families. The whole system was unjust, and he was caught in it. Bill talked to some other missionaries. They just laughed and said, "Let us know how you get on!"

Now it was the twelfth week, and he still did not have his license. More-over, the amount being asked to settle the case had risen to 200,000 rupiahs

(U.S. $120). Should he pay the official and end the case? Or should he appeal to a higher-level officer in hopes of a just settlement? Bill looked at the officer and said . . .[2]

Responses to the Case Study

As I have presented this case study to Christians from various countries, most felt that "Bill" should have paid the bribe or fine in the first place. Others, including Indonesians, Filipinos and a few North Americans, thought "Bill" should stand firm.

Of the minority who said Bill should refuse to pay, the Americans appealed to a moral principle: "Bribery is always wrong." The Filipinos explained that the only way for Christians to escape the straitjacket of corruption is for them, as a community, to become known as people who never compromise in such matters, no matter how trivial the situation. Some Indonesians suggested that because of his role as a Westerner and a missionary Bill should not pay. But of course Indonesian Christians would just pay; they would have no choice.

The majority from all nationalities felt that in this situation the money should have been paid in the first place. Various reasons were given in justification: (1) The situation involves a conflict of values—the values to be gained by paying are greater than the values lost by compromise. (2) Since the police are paid so poorly, the money should be thought of as a tip for services rendered rather than a bribe. (3) Bribery is an accepted mechanism for legal transactions in this context. Westerners have no right to impose their own legal norms on a context in which small-scale bribery has almost the status of customary law. (4) Corruption should be fought, but you must choose your enemy. If you refuse to compromise at such a trivial level, you will waste all your time struggling with the victims of the system and have no time to address the real villains—the structures of the system and those who enforce them at a high level. (5) Unless Bill has friends in high places he has no choice. He must pay and should be considered a victim of petty extortion, not a criminal.

Sources of Moral Decision-Making in Ethical Theory

How does Western ethical theory correspond to the reasons stated in these various opinions? The concern of this chapter is to clarify why some people think one way and others another way. What follows is a brief description of theoretical ways of moral thought. I will use two traditional, philosophical approaches to moral decision-making and see how far they take us in understanding why people differ on their opinions. More recent ethical theory attempts to move beyond the "decision" by focusing on the moral qualities of the person(s) within their particular tradition and social structure.

Deontological ethics: absolute right and wrong. The first traditional approach is often called "deontological" ethics, from the Greek *ontos,* which means "that which exists by itself." A deontological approach to ethics argues that goodness and evil are intrinsic to an act or an actor. Certain actions and attitudes are right or wrong *in and of themselves,* no matter what their effect on the world. Some Christians argue that we must do or not do certain things, regardless of culture, and leave the results in God's hands.

For example, a Christian pacifist may argue that it is always wrong to kill another human being. Even if by killing a person you save ten lives, it is still wrong. Some would say the same for lying. George MacDonald said, "I would not favor a fiction to keep a whole world out of hell. The hell that a lie would keep any man out of is doubtless the very best place for him to go to. It is truth . . . that saves the world."[3]

In this quote, lying is seen as deontologically wrong. A deontological approach draws the line at a certain point and suggests that if your behavior crosses this line it is wrong, no matter what your motives are or how salutary the outcome.

A simplified deontological approach to Christian ethics is sometimes labeled "moralism." There are clear moral rules derived from Scripture, reason or society. These are moral absolutes that should never be violated under any circumstances: don't lie, don't bribe, don't kill, don't drink alcohol, turn the other cheek, and so on. A value of this approach is that it is clear, uncompromising and objective, and it precludes rationalization. Some students who argued that "bribery is always wrong" exhibit this approach.

The biggest problem with moralism is that a person's choice of moral rules is likely to be deeply related to culture. No one follows all the rules of the Bible, so determining what is absolute requires selection. Bribery may feel wrong to me because it is considered illegal and "sleazy" in my culture. To someone from another context, small-scale bribery may seem perfectly all right. One Third World pastor told me that he felt great relief and peace after paying a small bribe to a police officer who stopped him for a minor infraction. He felt that God had rescued him from a potentially very dangerous situation!

Moralism ignores the fact that sometimes moral rules conflict with each other or with broader moral principles. Moralism can lead to legalistic self-righteousness and concentration on trivial rules at the expense of larger, less definable issues. For legalists, all morality is flattened out. All rules are equally important. Those in the fourth group, who argued for ignoring the small-scale problem and fighting against corruption at a higher level, were trying to avoid this problem. Similarly, those who felt a Westerner could afford to resist but they could not were applying different rules to different people according to their power in the situation: it is better not to pay, but for some it is just too costly.

Moralism is a shallow example of a deontological approach that insufficiently recognizes the complexity of reality. The narrow rigidity of legalism is an inherent danger of deontology.

Teleological ethics: goodness determined by the outcome. The second philosophical stream is called "teleological" ethics, from the Greek *telos,* which means end, result or goal. Teleological ethics argue that goodness lies not in an act or actor but in the act's real effect on the real world. People and actions are judged good or evil not by some inner quality but by the results of their action in human history. As Jesus said, "You will know them by their fruits" (Mt 7:20).

For example, some Christians would object to an absolutist interpretation of the commands not to kill or to lie. To kill or lie in order to save the lives of innocent people may be seen as good. Of course the results or "fruit" of an action cannot be measured only for the short term; the long term must also be considered. If the judgment of God is factored into a teleological approach, its distance from deontology is lessened. God's sovereign final judgment is the ultimate guarantee that good action produces good results and sin leads to death.

Situation ethics is a popular attempt to escape the dangers of moralism. Joseph Fletcher argued that since Christians are not "under the law," there are no moral rules, only the law of love. Every situation should be judged uniquely on the basis of love: what is the most loving thing to do in this situation? On the one hand, goodness is determined by motivation—does the action spring from love? On the other hand, it is based on realistic calculation of what action will most effectively show love to those involved. Situation ethics recognizes the primacy of love and the uniqueness of each individual circumstance. In regard to the case study above, those who considered the low pay of the police and the conventional acceptance of the system of "gift giving" exhibit a situational rather than a moralistic approach.

Situation ethics has many problems. There is the obvious danger of subjective rationalization. Almost anything can be justified by an appeal to love. As Stanley Hauerwas observed,

> The ethics of love is often but a cover for what is fundamentally an assertion of ethical relativism. It is an attempt to respond to the breakdown of moral consensus by substituting the language of love for the language of good and right as the primary determinate for the moral. . . . Love becomes a justification for our own arbitrary desires and likes.[4]

The short- and long-term effects of an action rarely can be accurately predicted. The true situation ethicist chooses the good by calculating what course of action will have the most loving results. Morality by calculation assumes that it is possible to know the moral results of an action. But the moral results of action are often unknowable, even after the event. What can scarcely be known in retrospect can hardly be known beforehand. Situations do not stand alone but are part of a larger historical, sociocultural and economic context that is impossible to master.

An Indonesian professor responded to the story of Bill by writing out his own hypothetical story of the policeman, showing how hard his life was and the desperate material needs of his family. His conclusion was that Bill should have paid out of love and respect for the policeman. But his imagined circumstances are just the sorts of things that a person cannot know on the spot, when a decision has to be made.

Situation ethics promotes an individualistic approach that exchanges the absolutism of rules for an absolutism of the personal conscience. By doing so, it ignores the usefulness of moral rules as a shorthand for judgments of society or the Christian community on right and wrong. Situation ethics devalues all principles except love and oversimplifies the relational meaning of morality. Love may be our highest norm, but it is not the only one. In a case of bribery, other principles such as justice, honesty, gentleness and obedience to the state cannot be ignored.

Finally, situation ethics is too time-consuming. To judge every situation afresh, without the benefit of rules, is impossible for human beings, for we must all categorize reality in order to avoid being overwhelmed by data. To be sure, emotivist situationalism is easy and quick. But if a situationalist is serious about calculating the most loving action, each decision could be long and torturous.

The dangers of a situational approach were recognized by respondents to the case study who argued for a principled rejection of all bribery. They saw a principled approach as the only way for a community to resist the enslavement of corruption. Some even argued that it was working, that officials no longer tried to receive payments from the Christian community because they knew it was futile.

On the other hand, the Indonesians who said that Bill should refuse to pay but that Indonesians would have to pay were not situationalists. Their conclusion was based not on the love commandment but on a power assessment of the situation: a Westerner might be able to get away without paying, but they could not. Furthermore, they thought it was appropriate for Bill to go through all the hassle of refusing to pay because of his role as a Western missionary who would be expected to bring unexpected values into the situation. At the very least they did not want to judge Bill in his decision to take a costly stand.

Situation ethics is a shallow example of a teleological approach that overestimates the power of an individual to calculate and bring about loving results without the restraints of law and community.

Distinctions, Synthesis and the Problem of Bribery

Deontological and teleological ethics are often treated as mutually exclusive. The polarization of means and ends, the antithesis between principles and results, is a characteristic weakness of Western dualistic thought. It leads to a war between the absolutists and the relativists. The absolutists are thought to be too narrow and rigid. The relativists are thought to be too wishy-washy.

Actually, the distinctions between deontology and teleology helpfully show two necessary and contrasting elements in moral choice. These are not contradictory but complementary. The way they fit together cannot be determined by abstract philosophical principle. The concrete situations in which moral choices are embodied reveal the ways in which principles and results interact.

Absolute moral principles. As a Christian I believe there are absolute moral principles and rules that reflect the character of God. These moral principles underlie all human behavior and are based in the fact that we live in a moral universe. Human beings were created in the image of God and have an intrinsic value. In the words of the Westminster Confession, we were created "to glorify God and to enjoy him forever." While these deontological absolutes are expressed and emphasized differently in different places and times, they are clearly affirmed by Christians in all cultures.

The central moral absolute that follows from these Christian affirmations is

" 'The Lord our God, the Lord is one; you shall love the Lord your God with all your heart, and with all your soul, and with all your mind, and with all your strength.' . . . 'You shall love your neighbor as yourself.' There is no commandment greater than these" (Mk 12:29-31).

Out of love for God and neighbor come the deontological proscriptions against idolatry and covetousness. From love of neighbor and the inherent dignity of the human person (rooted in creation and confirmed by redemption) come the absolutes of beneficence (the quality of charity or kindness) and the commands to seek justice and love mercy. Most would accept the further implication that one should never torture or degrade a human being made in the image of God.[5]

Some Christians see bribery as one of these absolutes. Bribery is seen as a form of dishonesty, of cheating, which favors the rich. They reject any compromise and are willing at any cost to resist the pressure to smooth their way with money. An American businessman in the Middle East has told me some marvelous stories of his absolute refusal to compromise on the issue of bribery. Though he faced enormous obstacles to his business, he always kept his priorities straight. He knew he was there not primarily to make money but to serve God.

Bribery as a general concept may be fit into this absolute category if a moral condemnation is included in the definition of bribery. If a bribe is defined as a gift intended to corrupt an official and cause him to act unjustly, then it must always be wrong to bribe. Some have tried to rigidly define bribery as *only* gifts given to obtain illegal favors. Given that definition, gifts to obtain just or legal service can be called tips.

But this is an unfortunate solution to a complex dilemma, because it allows proscriptions against bribery to be considered absolute while it disregards the most common kind of bribery in the modern world.[6] By this definition there is nothing amiss when individuals or corporations pay large sums of money for special treatment, provided the treatment is not illegal.

Certainly gifts, especially large gifts given to obtain basic services, easily become a means of oppression. As a result of such gifts, those who cannot or will not pay may be denied even minimal justice. Similarly, gifts given by large foreign companies to win contracts routinely squeeze out the local industries that cannot afford such gifts. As John Noonan has observed, size is an important clue to whether a payment is a tip or a bribe.[7]

But what about small gifts? Is there anything wrong with small gifts given to induce a poverty-stricken civil servant to bypass mountains of (quite legal) red tape? Whether such gifts are considered a bribe or a legitimate tip may amount to a matter of definition. The word *bribery* has strong moral connotations. Characterizing a transaction as a gift, tip or bribe makes a great deal of difference. Our tradition, our culture and the assumptions embedded in our experience usually determine how we describe a given activity.[8]

Some Christians reject an absolute prohibition on bribes because they believe that what a Westerner calls a bribe may be a necessary mechanism for sharing wealth in poor countries. A prominent scientist of unquestionable Christian integrity suggested to me that paying a bribe in the Soviet Union is permissible if it is really an accepted part of a person's salary. Where salaries are low, everyone knows that officials must require gifts in order to survive. The money is not meant to corrupt but to expedite a sluggish process. People need money to live, and you have to make small gifts in order to get things done.

A moral distinction may be made on the basis of whether a person has the freedom to give or not to give. If a small gift is freely given to obtain better service and there is no fear or threat involved, it is possible to consider it a tip. Presumably the service would be given in any case, but would probably take a little longer. The tip speeds up the process and benefits both parties. Little or no harm is done to the poor who either do not need the service or can obtain it with a little more time.

On the other hand, if fear or force is involved, or if the expected delays are extreme, the freedom that characterizes a gift or a tip is removed.[9] A gift or a tip is never compulsory.

While a gift is never compulsory, it may be strongly expected. When my neighbors bring me a bunch of bananas from their tree, they expect that sooner or later I will share with them the papayas that grow in our yard. Yet I would never suspect them of bribery! As Anthony Gittins has pointed out, gift giving is a rule-governed activity in which obligations are a constant.[10] The obligations, however, are not usually to be seen as the requirement to pay the person back on a tit-for-tat basis. Rather, the obligation is to continue the relationship that is symbolized by the gift: "gift exchange is seen to be patterned behavior embodying clear moral values; it creates and maintains personal relationships, not simply between private individuals, but between groups and between 'moral persons' or statuses."[11]

This is a far cry from bribery, in which either the briber buys special service from the bribee through an illegal gift or the bribee forces an illegal payment by refusing to give fair treatment. A gift helps create or maintain a moral relationship, while a bribe undermines it.

Small gifts paid to poor officials are ambiguous because they occupy a gray area between a gift, a tip and a bribe. Usually they are not compulsory, but neither are they free. They may help establish a relationship of trust and mutual help, but they are also underlined with the threat of poor service and time delays. Certainly they are a part of the establishment of status relationships, but they are also sometimes a pure economic exchange that takes place outside the law.

This ambiguity was echoed by many Christians I interviewed. For example, a Christian who worked in the Dominican Republic suggested that the clear definitions we assume in the West do not apply to some other countries. He suggested,

> In the U.S. there is a clear line between a bribe and a non-bribe. But in many places it is a continuum. In the States a person may get a 30% commission while their counterpart in the third world receives only 5% but expects a bribe. Sometimes you don't know you are paying a bribe. You may receive a bill for 125% import duty where 25% of it is a bribe. The equivalent of not paying the customs officer a tip is not paying a waitress a tip. He deserves a tip as payment for his services because his salary is so low.[12]

The complexity of the meaning and value of gift giving is reflected in the book of Proverbs, where there are three negative and three positive references to bribery (Prov 15:27; 17:8; 17:23; 18:16; 21:14; 22:16). John Noonan Jr., in his massive historical study of bribery, faults the Old Testament for having a double standard. He suggests that while the extortion of bribes is roundly condemned, the giving of bribes (or gifts to officials) is not condemned in the Old Testament.[13] Such equivocation in the Old Testament seems to reflect a recognition of the power differential between a poor person who gives a gift in order to stave off injustice and the rich who uses his power to exploit the poor. The powerful and the powerless are not judged by the same abstract absolute, but by the relationships and intentions of their situation. Thus

> If you close your ear to the cry of the poor,
>> you will cry out and not be heard.
> A gift in secret averts anger;
>> and a concealed bribe in the bosom, strong wrath.
> When justice is done, it is a joy to the righteous,
>> but dismay to evildoers. (Prov 21:13-15)

The way a moral act is described is part of the texture of a narrative. If the narrative experienced is of a righteous poor person who escapes injustice by giving a culturally appropriate gift to his or her potential oppressor, the reality described is very different from the narrative of a policeman who threatens torture unless he is given a large gift. The definition of what is going on springs not from a philosophical category such as "deontology" or "teleology" but from a much larger tradition and narration of experience.

The positive references to bribery in the Bible appear to reflect a utilitarian approach to ethics for those who have no other means of receiving justice. However, Proverbs unequivocally condemns those who accept bribes in order to do wrong: "The wicked accept a concealed bribe to pervert the ways of justice" (Prov 17:23). It also warns that giving gifts does not always work: "Giving to the rich will lead only to loss" (Prov 22:16). A single perspective on bribery cannot be forced on the Bible, because different verses were written at different times for different contexts and different people.

Certainly the great majority of Old Testament references to bribery are negative. The God of the Bible is one who does not accept šōḥaḏ (bribes), who judges impartially. We are called to be like God in love of righteousness. Nevertheless, there is enough ambiguity in the biblical record to allow for hesitancy in making the prohibition of bribes an absolute.

Right and wrong "on the face of it." A helpful intermediate category between the relativism of teleology and the absolutism of deontology has been developed by Roman Catholic moral theology. The concept of prima facie moral rules and principles is founded in the recognition that we live in a fallen, sinful world where what ought to be is sometimes impossible. *Prima facie* means "on the face of it" or "on first assessment." Prima facie rules ought to be absolutes in all cultures and all times. On the face of it, all things being equal, one must always obey these rules.

If you break a prima facie command or principle, you cannot escape doing evil. Nevertheless, there are tragic circumstances where, because of sin, values come into conflict and one commandment must be sacrificed if we are to uphold a higher value. Such an action, even though justified, should never be done without regret. In a real sense it still remains wrong. For there are tragic consequences from such a violation that undermine the fabric of society. Evil still clings to the act, even if it is morally justifiable.

William Frankena suggests that if certain actions are prima facie wrong, they are "intrinsically" wrong. In other words,

> They are always actually wrong when they are not justified on other moral grounds. They are not in themselves morally indifferent. They may conceivably be justified in certain situations, but they always need to be justified; and, even when they are justified, there is still one moral point against them.[14]

Commonly cited prima facie rules include the prohibitions against killing, lying, work on the sabbath and divorce. If you kill to stop a maniac gone amok, lie to save an innocent person hiding in your house, overwork to meet an urgent deadline, or divorce to end a situation of physical and mental abuse, in each case your action may be necessary and morally justifiable. But your action is not *good*; it is a necessary evil. Tragic consequences will follow. A fellow human will be dead, truth and human trust will be undermined, the quality of your inner harmony and worship will be threatened, what God has joined together will be torn apart.

The "necessary" evil that is done in all these cases will affect the actor, the immediate people involved and the broader society. Their effect is not only personal but also social. That is why these moral rules, on the face of it, should never be broken.

Some Christians deny this category and treat examples such as the above as absolutes never to be broken. But the prima facie category has the virtue of taking moral rules seriously without trivializing the power of evil to frustrate the best intentions of law. Prima facie principles may only be broken to avert some greater evil. Unlike in situation ethics, prima facie rules and principles are not nullified by moral calculation. They remain strong guides for behavior which must be reckoned with even when we tragically break them.

How can we determine when a prima facie moral law must be set aside in favor of a higher value? Some ethicists reject the implication that a Christian may face unavoidable evil. Instead of a prima facie category of morality, they suggest a fixed hierarchy of values in which to choose a higher value over a lower is not a lesser evil but a higher good. For example, to lie to save innocent life is in no sense wrong, but the highest possible good in the situation.[15] Others admit the tragedy implied by the prima facie category but also suggest a fixed hierarchy of values to guard against creeping relativism.

Unfortunately, no fixed hierarchy of values can be demonstrated from Scripture, reason or experience. Where is it written that death is worse than deceit? Is divorce worse than lying? Is neglecting the needs of your family worse than neglecting a friend in despair? Is stealing a car more honorable than allowing a criminal to escape? There is no abstract answer to such questions apart from detailed knowledge of the situations in which they are embedded. The fact that there is no fixed hierarchy of values does not imply that such values are relative, subjective or changeable. All of the actions in this paragraph are intrinsically wrong. But their relative seriousness depends on many factors not revealed in the moral principle itself. Cowardice may sometimes be worse than killing.[16]

One thing can be known for certain. The double love command does not admit exception. Augustine suggested that every other command of God must be filtered through the eyes of the command to love God and your neighbor. "On these two commandments hang all the law and the prophets" (Mt 22:40). The love commandment does not set aside the other commands but interprets their true meaning in a concrete situation. Unlike in situation ethics, love is not all that matters, but love is a part of all that matters. All moral situations receive their true weight in relation to the love of God and neighbor.

The category of prima facie rules is helpful for thinking about bribery. If bribery is defined as the giving of gifts in exchange for privileges or services that either are illegal or are meant to be administered impartially, then bribery is a prima facie evil. Each case of bribery undermines the cause of justice in society by making it difficult for the poor to be treated fairly. Bribery is officially illegal in almost every country in the world. On the other hand, it is possible to conceive of situations where greater harm may be done by refusing to pay a bribe. In the case of Bill, were fifteen hundred rupiahs ($1.50) and the principle of not paying an unofficial gift to an impoverished police officer worth the weeks or months of frustration and the possible permanent loss of private transportation? Should Bill be fighting other battles?

Whatever your answer, the effects are not simple. The escalating amount of money required symbolizes a growing alienation between Bill and the authorities. Is this a case of justice holding out against tyranny or a case of a foolish neo-colonialist foreigner insisting that his hosts conform to his rules? In either case Bill is unable to ensure that justice is done. If he pays, he violates his own conscience and may well reinforce the structural injustice of a society that treats those with money better than those without. If he doesn't pay, he may end up without a car because he quibbled over paying less than two dollars to a poor official.

Our individual actions cannot always overcome evil that is a structural part of a situation. Many Christians have told me stories of instances where they paid a small bribe to avoid what they understood as a far greater evil. Were they without sin in doing so? Perhaps not. The prima facie category does not absolve the lawbreaker from guilt. It only allows us to recognize our weakness in the face of a sinful world. Sometimes we are not wise enough or strong enough to act well in situations of ambiguity. Sometimes we cannot see any good course of action. Sometimes the law we break seems insignificant in the face of the enormity of our situation. If so, we dare not claim innocence. Nor may we rescind or denounce our action. It throws us on the mercy of God.[17]

Relative moral situations. Many moral situations are not determined either by absolute principles or by prima facie commandments. One need not be a relativist to see that many decisions are relative to a particular situation. Those who argued that the "bribe" was really a tip with the status of customary law are suggesting that what is a bribe in a Western legal context is best considered a tip in an Indonesian context. In that case Bill simply misunderstood the meaning of his situation in a foreign context. His refusal to pay was not so much wrong as unwise.

While in the case of Bill this argument may be oversimplified, there are many moral choices we make that are unique to a particular person, time or place. Such relative situations are not trivial. They may have large moral consequences. But they are not subject to abstract definition. They require deep understanding of a context and the subject's role in it. They require calculation of what actions will bring the most good and prevent the most evil in a particular context. They require the capacity of character and the commitment to care about what matters most. And they require the wisdom of God's Spirit so that we may choose the good.

Culture plays a major role in making morally relative decisions. How do we treat time? How do we decide how to live and at what socioeconomic level? How directly and forcefully do we communicate? How individualistic or communalistic are we in decision-making? How competitive are we? How do we spend our money? When do we give to those in need? How much time do we spend with our family? How do we honor our parents? How do we plan for emergencies? How authoritarian are we with our subordinates? Do we reach out to those in prison? How do we work for justice in society? How do we share the good news of our faith with people in need?

These, and many other questions like them, may be the most important moral questions of our lives. But there are no simple answers to them that are directly based on absolute or prima facie commandments.

An American evangelist once told a wealthy audience that a person could not be a Christian and drive a BMW luxury sedan. While such a statement could be considered neither an absolute nor a prima facie moral command, it provocatively dramatized what is at stake in our relative moral decisions. It is our relative moral decisions that demonstrate what we mean when we claim to love God and our neighbor.

In some cases the definition of a bribe and the meaning of a particular gift may be relative to the cultural intentions and expectations of those involved. In the Middle East the value of a service or a thing is often defined through emotional bargaining. The normal fee for installing a telephone may not be fixed but variable. Appeals to relationship, need, the ability to pay and other subjective factors are a vital part of defining the value of all goods and services. After all, why should we think something (like a telephone) has an objective value outside the relationships of those involved in the transaction?

A study by E. Glen, D. Witmeyer and K. Stevenson of negotiation styles within the United Nations showed that Arabs argued with an intuitive-affective style, expressing their positions through appeals to strong emotion. Compromises were often "indicated by strong expressions of personal friendship and esteem towards the intermediary."[18]

If relationships are the key to negotiations, it is not hard to see how the value of a service might be understood as contextual. For many people, relationships outweigh efficiency. If the feelings are right, for example, a seller may be willing to take a loss. While in economic terms it is a loss, in affective terms there is a gain—an established relationship of indebtedness. At the least the customer may come back, and she may encourage her friends to do so as well. On the other hand, if the feeling of relationship is wrong the seller may pass up a profit. An economic profit may not outweigh the cultural alienation of dealing with someone perceived as rude and arrogant.

What Westerners see as bribery or deceit may be understood in some countries as ways of maintaining or achieving the right relationships. The market conditions of modern capitalism are not necessarily a more moral way of setting price than a bargaining relationship between two people.

Sometimes if a right relationship is established with someone, the necessity for a monetary exchange is eliminated. The right word or the meeting of eyes (or the humble averting of eyes!) may signal the kind of respect or "in-groupness" that establishes relationship.

In our case study, Bill might have been able to avoid the situation of conflict altogether. By showing the policeman genuine love, by expressing greater respect, by demonstrating true humility, by a wise use of trust, by an appropriate invitation or nonmonetary gift, by speaking with meek authority, Bill (or Jesus) might have reached the policeman in his place of greatest need. He might have been able to avoid the request for a bribe *and* initiate a friendship.

Many situations that appear to be either-or moral dilemmas may have hidden within them a third way. A godly Indonesian pastor shared his surprise with me that one time when he was stopped by the police for a traffic infraction, he was released with no payment or charge after he had apologized with genuine humility for his error. The right word spoken by the right person in the right way at the right time may bridge the chasm to another human being.

Most people do not have such deep power for good in their character. Most do not have the wisdom to overcome the deep divisions in society which lead to conflict. Sometimes human evil or structural injustice cannot be overcome by goodness. Sometimes the best of people end up on one cross or another. The best course of action for one person may be disastrous for another.

The relative moral decisions we make are ultimately grounded in the absolute core values that guide our lives. They grow out of our habitual praxis, our knowledge (or ignorance) of our context, our relationship to a community and the gift of God's wisdom and guidance.

Bribery and Social Structure

Why is bribery so much a part of some societies and not of others? Are some countries more dishonest than others? Does poverty make people corrupt? The prevalence of bribery in poor countries may contribute to the paternalism or even racism of some Westerners who see it as evidence of "Third World" backwardness or moral inferiority.

One Englishman suggested that in India it stemmed from a Hindu culture in which there are no moral absolutes. Religion undoubtedly influences ethics, but if Hinduism is the culprit, why is there so much graft in many Roman Catholic and Muslim societies? Certainly moral relativism is no part of Catholicism or Islam. Moreover, it seems unlikely that the "Protestant" West is more honest or less greedy than other parts of the world.

A better explanation is that the social structures of some countries makes gift giving a far more extensive practice than in others. In Indonesia one seldom pays a visit without bringing a gift. In North Africa relationships are secured through mutual indebtedness. In Egypt nothing is done without a tip. In Latin America trust is ensured by a gift. In China connections are established through presents. Gift giving is not bribery; but when gifts become an obligatory mechanism for major social functions, the possibilities for corruption are obvious.

In many parts of the world, gift giving is radically shaped by a historical marriage between the structures of patronage and bureaucracy. Gift giving is an integral part of a patriarchal society. It is expected that the superior should care for the people under him by giving them gifts. Gifts are a means of buying loyalty and service. In the Marcos palace in Manila there were whole rooms full of merchandise for giving as gifts. Gifts mitigate an unjust and harsh social system. People are honored to have a patron, a protector. A person may be exploited, but he or she is also protected by the "father."[19]

The word *patron* is originally from Rome. But the idea of responsibilities that accompany patriarchy must go back to the dawn of history. When a bureaucracy is added to a patronage system, both systems are modified but continue to operate. Modern bribery is related to this historical marriage. In Latin America a semifeudalistic hacienda system was grafted onto a bureaucracy derived from the French. In Indonesia the feudalistic Javanese state was consciously married to the Dutch colonial bureaucracy. In the process, both were changed.

Bureaucracy is a different system from the hacienda system or the Javanese rule of the divine king, but a gift is still the accepted mechanism to buy loyalty or silence or service. Gifts are expected not only from the social superior but also from anyone who needs the "loyalty" or service of the bureaucrat.

In the traditional society, services were rendered and protection was given according to a strict hierarchical order. Gifts were simply a means of strengthening established relationships and rewarding good work. In a modern bureaucracy, relationships have to be established without the benefit of a clear social order. If the country is very poor, with high unemployment and a large, underpaid bureaucracy, civil servants are effectively paid with power and prestige rather than money. They must use their power to receive gifts if they are to support a family. The "patron" must demonstrate by gifts her worthiness of being served. This, of course, lends itself to corruption. But it is more than bribery in the Western sense. It also serves the social functions of sharing wealth and clarifying relationships. An Ethiopian church leader remarked,

> In Africa we do not have such a defined world as you do in the States. We
> give weight to different issues. It's not that bribery is OK, but it's not so central.
> In America money changes hands by different rules. People still get a share
> of the wealth that passes through their hands, but it is done by more highly
> defined rules. On the other hand, it can be very irritating in Africa.

When Bill refused to pay the policeman a small sum, he also refused to recognize
the status and power of the man. In America a police officer is ideally a servant
of the people and an agent of the law. But in Indonesia he is an important,
powerful man (albeit a very poor one) whose dignity must be upheld.

The linking of patronage and bureaucracy might be considered morally neutral
if it were not for the poor. Not only the relatively rich are served by the bureaucracy but the poor as well. An Indonesian professor remarked to me that the
Dutch ideal was that the bureaucrat was meant to serve the people.[20] But here
the bureaucrat does not serve the people, he serves the state. Or more accurately,
he serves his superiors in the bureaucracy. This can become very oppressive to
the poor who have nothing. It takes great sacrifice, or is simply impossible, for
someone who earns fifty dollars a month to scrape together a bribe. Of course
the poor are seldom expected to pay as much as the rich. To someone used to
the rule of law, this too feels unjust. Actually it mitigates the injustice of the
system.

The ability to break the bribery system depends on the power you have, what
is at risk and what values are at stake. Those who can afford to go without the
services of the bureaucrat, who can afford to wait, who have the power and
education to appeal to higher levels, whose goodwill and service are needed by
the country or who have connections to a powerful elite in the country can break
the system. Such people also "earn" the service they receive, though they do it
in an indirect manner.

Conclusion

Moral choice in every society is founded in the cultural character of a person
and the way he or she sees the world. We are cultural creatures who make sense
of our lives by means of a narrative that distinguishes between the good and the
evil, the important and the insignificant. What we pay attention to shapes our
ability to choose. This chapter suggests that neither relativism nor absolutism is
an adequate approach to moral choice. The structures of society are fallen and

pervaded by evil as well as infused with good. To cooperate with the good while exposing the evil is a task that requires character, sensitivity and knowledge.

First of all, we need to know our core, absolute values. These may never be compromised, though they may be expressed in different ways. Certain types of bribery are absolutely wrong. Paying money to subvert justice or hide our own evil is clearly wrong. The size of a gift is significant. Very large gifts that are given or demanded in exchange for services that are intended to be free signal serious injustice. Needless to say, gifts to secure illegal services are also wrong.

Second, we need to avoid situations of value conflict. When confronted with tragic circumstances we cannot control, we need to know how to choose higher values over lesser values. While some kinds of bribery are absolutely wrong, some may be wrong but unavoidable. They are wrong on the face of it, but less significant than the values that would be lost if we refused to pay. Some people have more power to break the bribery system than others. Therefore it is important not to judge those who make different decisions about what is a "lesser evil." Nevertheless, the greatest danger of the prima facie category is that it may become an easy way out, a means of justifying actions we know are wrong. Most of what we call bribery is evil and cannot be done without consequences that hurt other people more than the briber. If we bribe or kill or lie for what we consider a higher cause, repentance is advisable, for judgment lies ahead.

Third, we must constantly weigh our priorities and decisions on the basis of what fits our particular role in a particular context. Some things that look like bribes to Western eyes may be appropriate tips or gifts that serve a positive role in a given social structure. When there is ambiguity, the Westerner would do well to get advice from someone native to the culture. Bill might have gotten better advice from an Indonesian than he did from other missionaries. But to do so he would have to have the humility to be a learner and not a teacher in the situation.

Conversely, some kinds of payment that look perfectly legitimate to Westerners look like bribery to others. An Asian woman complained that some of the worst corruption comes when large Christian mission organizations lure gifted national leaders away from urgently needed, indigenously controlled work. The offer of a relatively enormous salary tempts gifted people to abandon locally controlled organizations to serve a Christian multinational. Local leaders may become discouraged as their gifted young leaders are made subservient to foreign organizations. Thus the power of money can perpetuate another form of colonialism.[21]

Sometimes patterns of foreign aid serve the same function as bribery. Aid brings dependence, fostered by a patronage system in which the foreigner has all the financial power. Paternalism may take the place of partnership.

Obviously these issues are not cut and dried. What may be right for one situation may be wrong for another. Gifts may be empowering or enslaving. The fact that *some* values are relative does not mean that *all* values are relative. The fact that there are some situations of structural evil where one cannot escape without fault does not suggest that whenever we feel tension we should give in.

Bribery is a serious evil in the modern world. The person who successfully navigates the shoals of corruption is likely to be someone who is living the right kind of story. At the point where we have to make a decision, we are unlikely to reflect on whether deontology, teleology or prima facie thinking is more appropriate. The kind of person we are and the way we are oriented to God, to our neighbor and to our own self-interest will most likely decide for us.

The God of Job and the God of Jesus does not accept bribes.[22] Bribes are the opposite of true gifts. Bribes seek to dominate and control. Bribes subvert justice for the poor. Gifts are given freely and establish a reciprocal relationship. Gifts are a sign of love. Gifts are at the heart of the gospel. Those who love God bring gifts, not bribes, to their neighbor.

EIGHT

THE ETHICAL CHALLENGE OF OTHER RELIGIONS

C hristians who live in a culture with several religions face deeper problems than differences in doctrine. In many countries of the world, including the United States, you do not have to cross national borders to find yourself surrounded by other religions. Christians have long been a minority in Western universities. But only in the last few decades have other religions become active competitors throughout society.

Christianity in the West faces what Peter Berger has called a "legitimation crisis." Religious plurality[1] is a threat to Christian faith when other religions are perceived as attractive and/or Christian faith is "delegitimated" as a foundation for life. In the United States, "secularism" used to be seen as the major opponent of Christian faith and indeed of all religion. But the feared (or hoped for) process of secularization has proved illusory. People in America are not becoming less religious. On the contrary, they are more religious, albeit not in relation to the mainstream institutional churches.[2]

In most of the world (excluding Western Europe) the deep religiousness of most people has never been in doubt. In Africa, Asia, the Middle East and Latin

America religion is seldom considered optional. Even in China and the formerly communist world religions of all different stripes are resurgent.

Comparative religion studies in universities, seminaries and Bible schools all focus on doctrine and practice. Anthropology, phenomenology, sociology, theology and apologetics are useful tools for such study. But *ethics* is the place where most Christians vividly experience the challenge of other religions.

Ethical Challenges to Christian Truth

The ethical challenge to Christian faith comes from three directions. First is the challenge of aesthetic and spiritual experience. The discovery of great beauty and deep spiritual experience in other traditions challenges the sometimes ugly and shallow practices of Christianity. Second, the virtues and goodness of some believers in other faiths puts to shame the crass egotism and materialism of many Christians. Third, there are great social, economic and political evils practiced in the name of Christianity. In some places, non-Christian cultures produce societies that display a moral excellence unusual in "Christian" countries. Western civilization has failed to provide a universal example for the rest of humanity.

The purpose of this chapter is to clarify and address these challenges to Christian faith. Several major theological attitudes to other religions will be examined. I will suggest a dialectical approach that holds in tension the good and evil in all religions. This perspective calls for dialogue, humility and honest conviction.

The Challenge of Aesthetic and Spiritual Experience

Buddhism. When I lived in Berkeley, through a consultation on ethics and nuclear weapons I developed an unlikely friendship with a prominent nuclear physicist. Michael May, formerly director of the Lawrence Livermore Laboratory, is a Zen Buddhist. One day he invited me to a *zazen,* or meditation sitting, at the local Zen center. Starting at 5:00 a.m., we meditated in utter silence and stillness for over an hour. Unlike the Buddhists there, I meditated on the goodness of God. But I was profoundly touched by the simplicity, beauty and tranquillity of the experience.

In later conversations May expressed his gratitude for years of disciplined Zen practice. He said that if he had found a Christian program of meditation with the disciple and rigor of Zen, he would have followed it. In any case, the differences in religious teachings were unimportant to him since "it is the experience and practice that matters." Sometimes when listening to a dull sermon or singing an inane hymn, I think back with regret to the fulsome silence of the Zen hall.

Shortly after the *zazen* experience my family and I were in Kyoto, Japan, where we visited many ancient temples. Some filled us with awe because of their exquisite beauty and harmonious peace. It is good just to know that such places exist in the world! I saw my own wonder reflected in my children's eyes and sensed all of our questions about how another religion could mediate such a great aesthetic, spiritual experience.

A missionary who spent twenty-eight years in Sri Lanka said that when he went to the mission field he believed Christian faith was unique and other religions were false. All that changed when he visited a Buddhist holy place, Anuradhapura. There he experienced such a sense of peace that he felt he was truly in the presence of God. The difference in faiths no longer mattered. The missionary became convinced that all religions include love and compassion. From then on he saw his ministry not as "creed" but rather as "need." Because of the great beauty and depth he experienced in another religious context, he lost his faith in the unique truth of the Christian gospel.

Hinduism. Only the most insensitive fail to see spiritual and aesthetic excellence in the people and practices of other religions. In a Hindu temple the use of flowers, food, incense, dance, music and art as vehicles of praise proclaims a rich tradition which makes Christian worship sometimes appear shallow, cold and overintellectual. In Hindu Bali I was totally unprepared for the artistic beauty, playfulness and joy that seem inherent to Balinese religion.

One evening in a Balinese village we saw a long procession of beautifully dressed women carrying magnificent flower and fruit offerings on their heads to the temple. Donning appropriate Balinese dress, we followed and were treated to a wonderful evening of entertainment. Dances, dramas, laughing children, chanting adults, serious priests—the whole village was there. This was no show put on for tourists. Nor was it a major festival. It was just ordinary life. Extraordinary!

Islam. Spiritual practices often strike us at a deeper level than doctrines. At a World Council of Churches consultation on Christian education in a Muslim context, I led a worship session using the forms of Muslim ritual prayer. Having announced my plan several days before the service, I was amazed at the anxiety it generated. Liberals who would think nothing at sacrificing Christology for the sake of interreligious dialogue were noticeably nervous about participating in a Muslim form of ritual prayer.

The only thing in the entire *sholat* that might be rejected on doctrinal grounds is the affirmation "Muhammad is the Prophet of God." This phrase was changed to "Jesus is the Son of God." The service began with the wonderfully chanted Arabic call to prayer and included removal of shoes, ritual washings accompanied by prayers of repentance, affirmations of the mercy and greatness of God, and prayers of praise accompanied by various prostrations.

As in the *zazen,* I found that a foreign act of worship gave me a new experience of God. As I repeatedly prostrated myself, forehead to the ground, and extolled the greatness of God, I was profoundly impressed with my own unworthiness before the almighty and holy God. Even more amazing was my imagination of what it must be like to structure your life around prayers like that, five times a day, for as long as you live! It's easy to see why *Islam* means submission. Now I can better appreciate the frequent calls to prayer blasted over loudspeakers from mosques near our home. They remind me of God's greatness and the goodness of worship. As the 4:00 a.m. call puts it, "Prayer is better than sleep!"

The challenge of virtue in other religions is not just intellectual. We feel in our senses and emotions the goodness of a foreign faith. This may weaken our confidence in the universal truth of Christian faith even while our mind continues to believe orthodox Christian doctrine. The ethical imperative of mission may lose its urgency.

Other religions have a great deal to teach Christians about beauty and worship. Religions are vehicles of the highest aspirations and longings of the human spirit. They provide basic foundations to whole cultures. Christians believe all people are made in the image of God. The Word of God is at work in everyone who comes into the world (Jn 1:9). The kingdom of God cannot be equated with the church; nor should we entirely discount evidence of God's work in non-Christian religions.

The dark side of religious experience. Unfortunately, this sanguine picture must be balanced with the dark side of aesthetic and spiritual experience. Religions are too often inane, tyrannical and demonic. First, religion is not only a vehicle of "the highest aspirations of the human spirit" but also a vehicle of narrow, petty, superstitious and inane sensibilities. Of course it is unwise to judge others, especially from strange cultures. What is inane to me may be deeply meaningful to you. Still, kitsch, sentimentality and superficiality are ubiquitous. The "worshiper" waving incense in front of a garish idol in hopes of good luck in her mahjong game is easier to pity than to admire.

It is more serious when religious experience is used as a weapon to oppress the weak. The Marxist critique of religion as the opiate of the people has a lot of truth to it. Buddhist monks pressure followers into hours of chanting when their needs would be better addressed by thought and work. Muslim mullahs enforce strict conformity to rigid rituals in spite of the hardship it places on people who are already dirt poor. Hindu mendicants live their lives in severe deprivation in search of release from suffering.

Third, religious experience is also a vehicle of the demonic. Contrary to my Western education, I believe there are real demons and evil spirits that use religion to subjugate and destroy people. Aesthetic and spiritual experience can be the channel of degradation and oppression. In Indonesia the line between "spiritual" and "material" is not so distinct as in the West. Converts to Christianity sometimes experience great release from fear and bondage to spiritual oppression.

One of my most profound spiritual/aesthetic experiences occurred in a Hindu temple in Calcutta when I was twelve years old. Having lived in Hong Kong, I was used to seeing temples and idols. But nothing had prepared me for the overwhelming sense of the presence of great evil as we entered this temple. I was terrified and experienced vivid nightmares for days afterward. Certainly there is no way to evaluate such an experience objectively. But I think I was in the presence of evil powers that had taken control of some of the worshipers.

The demonic may be seen at many different levels of spiritual experience. Religious art is often nightmare art that makes Hollywood horror movies appear tame in comparison. The gods appear not only crazy but horrible. When religious art combines kitsch with horror, as in the Tiger Balm Gardens in Hong Kong, the net effect is nauseating. The demonic, working through deep or shallow spiritual experience, is active at the individual level in personal oppression, in groups of people under the control of a cultic leader and in major social movements such as Nazism and the Serbo-Croatian-Muslim war, in which cruelty exceeds the limits of understanding.

The tendency in the overrationalized West is to treat "principalities and powers" as personal beings if you are Pentecostal, as structures of injustice if you are a social activist, as mythological representations of human experience if you are liberal and as doctrines if you are evangelical. I see no reason that they may not be all four.[3]

The Challenge of Goodness in Non-Christians

Most of us have been gifted with acquaintance with a few people whose sheer goodness is stunning. They are "salt of the earth" people. We may also know many more who, while not so outstanding in the saint department, are good, solid folks who show more than their fair share of the "fruit of the Spirit." More than a few Christians, including myself, owe their conversion to the witness of such people. Their faith, hope and love are a powerful attraction. They make us believe that all the rhetoric of faith may just possibly be true.

Are Christians better people than non-Christians? What happens, then, when you keep running into really good people who are not Christians but devout believers in another faith? The easiest way to avoid the ethical challenge of the virtuous pagan is to confine your relationships with non-Christians to "ministry." If you always are in the position of preacher, teacher or minister, you are much less likely to face a human being whose life may put yours to shame. As Wilfred Cantwell Smith pointed out, we are not confronted with other faiths but with other believers.

Just as the lack of goodness in fervent Christians may be the most powerful argument against Christianity, so the goodness in non-Christians is a powerful argument for a relativistic attitude to other religions. The many "ordinary," good non-Christians are more challenging than the occasional saint. We may view Mahatma Gandhi as an exception, as unique or even as a secret Christian (not likely). No such luck with your everyday virtuous Hindu. In light of the extravagant hospitality of a poor Muslim farmer, we may wonder who first taught us to love our enemies. In the face of the tranquillity and compassion of a Buddhist monk, we may wonder who knows more about the peace that passes understanding.

In Muslim Pakistan my family was repeatedly impressed with the devotion, goodness and honesty of some of the serious Muslims we met. As we rode up into the Himalayan mountains in an ancient bus, I sat next to a devout Muslim who was deathly carsick. This tended to limit the possibility of conversation, since he had his head out the window half the time and was white as a sheet (no mean feat for a Pakistani!). My first surprise was that in his excruciating nausea he seemed genuinely concerned that he might be disturbing me. As the poor man staggered from the bus at a prayer stop, before refreshing himself and attending to his prayers he guided us to a nearby restaurant, explained what there was to eat and gave the waitress instructions on our behalf.

During the eighteen hours we shared the bus, although he obviously felt awful he was unfailingly considerate, dignified and thoughtful of our needs. As we ascended the mountains and darkness covered the snowy peaks, we were sore, miserable and exhausted from the constant jostling. Freezing drafts of wind penetrated our tropical clothes, but our twelve-year-old son was too tired to care and fell asleep on the floor. I knew I was sitting by an angel when my Muslim neighbor quietly took off his own coat and laid it over my son. When we arrived in Gilgit at 3:00 a.m., all the passengers hurried off to find a bed. As we stood in the dark feeling lost, our sick benefactor came back to lead us to a decent hotel before disappearing forever into the night.

This is just one story out of dozens that could be told of kindness, gentleness and integrity coming from Buddhists, Jews, Muslims, Hindus and Christians—people who give without expecting a reward. Of course it would be easy enough to match the good stories with bad ones. There are thieves, hypocrites and cruelly arrogant followers of all the world's religions.

There are no statistics to determine whether a higher percentage of Christians are "brave, honest, loving, peaceful and true." But even if such a thing could be demonstrated, it would not vitiate the question: If Christianity is the only truth, why are there so many devoted religious people whose virtues outshine those of many Christians?

John Hick argues that there is essential parity between the world religions in terms of good and evil effects on people. He says,

> Each tradition has constituted its own unique mixture of good and evil . . . some of its aspects promoting human good and others damaging the human family. In face of these complexities it seems impossible to make the global judgment that any one religious tradition has contributed more good or less evil, or a more favorable balance of good and evil, than the others.[4]

Hick argues that the failure of Christianity to produce more good people or just societies leads to the conclusion that it should no longer be considered the one and only truth. This is a leap in logic that nevertheless retains some intuitive force. Simple modesty and a desire not to arrogantly assert that we have all the truth may make a Christian hesitant to claim that Christ is the only way, truth and life.

The real issue here is not salvation by grace as opposed to works. Knowing that all our righteousness is as filthy rags before a holy God and that only grace, appropriated by faith, can bring us new life does not answer this ethical challenge of pluralism. The question is, Where is the new life that should be mediated by faith in Christ? Jesus said, "You will know them by their fruits." Could it be that the Holy Spirit is failing the body of Christ?

A negative assessment of non-Christian practices. Often Christians deny that ethical excellence in non-Christians poses any threat to Christian faith. First, there *are* many Christians whose lives exemplify Christian virtues. Their stories help substantiate the goodness and truth of Christian faith but do not answer the questions posed by pluralism. Second, crime and evil in society are associated with people who are not committed Christians. But the law-abiding virtues seem to correlate with any disciplined religious devotion rather than specifically Christian commitment.

Third, evil sometimes reaches its zenith in religious leaders like the Ayatollah Khomeini, Rajneesh and Jim Jones, as well as quasi-religious tyrants like Hitler and Stalin. In religions there are vices and structures of oppression so dark that the existence of the demonic becomes a lived experience. I remember the horror of seeing little Hindu kids in Singapore pull great weights that were attached to their backs by hooks through their skin. These children had to placate the anger of their parent's gods. I remember villages in Sumba, a small Indonesian island, devoting all their wealth to be buried with their king while the people lived in miserable poverty and even slavery. All too commonly people face torture or death if they attempt to leave their religion. Women are treated like property and lower castes like dirt.

Comparative religious ethics usually focuses on similarities between the positive moral teachings of the world religions. But any serious consideration of religious ethics must also confront the doctrinal assumptions that are expressed in the dark practices of religion. Ultimately Hinduism knows no evil, Buddhism knows no sin, and Islam tolerates no dissent.

Unfortunately, Christianity is not exempt from the house of horrors. Some who led murderous crusades were even canonized as saints! Perhaps such people were not true Christians. Or at least they were horribly mistaken, victims of a fundamental perversion of Christian ideals.

Should we look at ideals rather than people? A standard freshman objection to Christianity is to point out the Crusades, or the Inquisition, or the hypocrites in the church down the street. In university I used to respond to criticisms of that sort by disassociating myself from the form of Christian religion indicated. I'd say, "Don't look at the church, look at Jesus. In Christ you will see the Truth."

But the same kind of argument can be made on behalf of other religions. In Islamabad, Pakistan, we were fortunate to stay with a devout Muslim innkeeper who was honest and friendly. All over Sharif's house there were pictures of Mecca and verses from the Qur'an. Late one night he tried his best to convert me, or at least to get me to read the Qur'an. It was a novel experience to be on the receiving end of what very much resembled a fundamentalist Christian style of evangelism.

Sharif argued that all truth is contained in God's revelation through Muhammad. The Qur'an is the most perfect book of instructions about how to live. If only the world obeyed God's commandments in the Qur'an, there would be peace and justice.

Perhaps Sharif was afraid I was thinking of all the war and injustice within the Muslim world, for suddenly he gripped my hand and said something very familiar. He said, "I know that Muslims fail to live up to the teaching of the Qur'an. The whole Muslim world is far from what it should be. *But don't look at Islam, look at the Qur'an. There you will find truth.*"

A positive view of good people in other religions. There is no conclusive answer to the challenge of goodness in other religions. It is better to regard the phenomenon from a positive standpoint. Ecclesiastes 3:11 says that God "has set eternity into the hearts of men" (NIV). Some of the finest people are drawn to religion in order to find expression for their own sense of transcendence. Others spend their entire lives seeking to fill Pascal's "God-shaped vacuum" in their heart.

Good people who bear the image of God are drawn to religion in part because of a hunger and thirst for righteousness. All of the major world religions express high ethical ideals. As in Christianity, few people live up to these high ideals, but some come closer than others. As Aristotle recognized long ago, people learn virtue by practice. The quality of their home life may have as much to do with how far they succeed as which religion they follow. Religions offer the disciplined patterns of behavior that can provide a road to relative virtue.

The Challenge of Competing Religious Social Projects

Perhaps the most fundamental challenge to Christian confidence in a universal Christian truth stems from a major cultural paradigm shift. Western culture is no longer recognized as the center of the world, but rather stands accused of hundreds of years of oppression. Christians are confronted with massive *social* evils, both present and past, which are associated with Christianity.

We must live with a long history in which unimaginable cruelty and oppression have been justified by "the true faith." Even now, racism, environmental exploitation, war and sexism are given a Christian warrant in places like the United States, Europe and Africa. In contrast, the nonviolent simplicity of the Hindu Gandhi, the peace and tranquillity promoted by Buddhism, the nature reverence evident in Native American religions and the rejection of Western sexual decadence in many Muslim countries may appear very attractive.

The accusing finger pointed at Christian religion is a sign of the decline of the Western empire. For four hundred years it seemed to Europeans and North Americans that their "civilization" was superior in every way: politically, militarily, economically, socially, scientifically, morally and religiously. Indeed, not only the colonialists but also their subjects seldom questioned English, Dutch, French, Spanish or American superiority. A book like *A Passage to India* delicately shows the paradox of how colonial subjects experience a profoundly internalized inferiority married to repressed rage.[5]

When everyone assumed Western civilizations were more advanced than others, it was easy to assume that Christianity was also superior. Christianity was considered the foundation of Western leadership. Westerners believed Christianity was either the only truth (conservatives) or at least the most advanced religion (liberals).

But since World War II, Western superiority has come under increasing attack, and by now it is no longer assumed. In fact, at least morally and religiously, the opposite is often assumed. With the flourishing of Japan, even scientific superiority can no longer be assumed. But the most devastating attack is in the area of social ethics.

I still remember the time, in 1966, of my first vivid recognition of the evil of my own people. The land of the free and the home of the brave was also the land of systematic genocide of Native Americans, black slavery, exploitative capitalism and neocolonialism. The Vietnam War, the explosion of racial riots, the ecology crisis, the nuclear threat and the linking of world poverty with Western neocolonialism not only called into question the righteousness of Western political institutions but also cast grave doubts on their purported Christian roots.

Imperialism, colonialism and neocolonialism are historically linked with the mission of the church. Many people wonder whether another religion might provide a better basis for life on this planet. Many more question whether any religion can claim universality.

Religions as social projects. Religions are not primarily privatized systems of personal morality, belief and experience. They are also the basis of civilizations. Religions are social projects.[6]

The very word *religion* is problematic, since it groups together the ways diverse cultures understand and interact with "the real" as if such ways had certain common characteristics. In fact, different cultures construe what is real in radically different ways.

The category of religion reflects the dichotomizing tendency of Western thought to separate the spiritual from the material world. "Facts" and "values" are considered unrelated. The politically expedient (and necessary) division of church and state promotes the illusion that religion occupies the realm of values—aesthetics, personal ethics and spiritual experience. In this way of thinking, material life—that is, politics, economics and social order (facts)—must be regulated by reason and science. For thousands of years cultures have struggled to separate religious from political power. The particular way this is done in Western liberal democracies has many merits. But it should not confuse the fact that Christianity, like all the world religions, aims to bring about a certain kind of society.

The core of Jesus' teaching concerns the coming kingdom of God. The Bible conceives this kingdom as universal in scope and characterized by equality, justice and peace. In this kingdom all will bow before the one and only God as revealed in Jesus. History is in motion toward the coming kingdom. Just as Abraham set out for a land he did not know, so the exodus is a paradigmatic story in Hebrew-Christian religion with its image of a journey out of slavery toward freedom.[7] Similarly, Jesus defeated death and promised to return to usher in the kingdom. The dynamic of Christianity is the transformation of the world.

Though no less concerned about justice and equality (at least for males), Islam foresees both a different path and a different goal in the ideal society. God has dictated a single, universal sociocultural structure governed by the written, absolute commandments contained in the Qur'an. Not only the material precepts but also the assumed Arabic social structure are to be perfectly followed. Since the Qur'an contains the actual words of God, it may not be translated out of Arabic.

The ideal Muslim society is one that is faithful to Qur'anic law in every detail. The commandments of God are the basis for a just and righteous social order.

The dynamic of Islam is obedience and submission to God. A corollary of submission to God is a strong belief in fate. Consistent with an emphasis on the overwhelming power of God is the acceptance of whatever happens as the fated will of God.

The ideal social project of Hinduism is diverse, since Hinduism has no unified body of doctrines. The safest definition of Hinduism is "Indian religion." Therefore it is not surprising that Hinduism has not spread much beyond India. Nevertheless, certain social features of Indian and Balinese religion are well known and foundational. A clearly defined caste system is based on reincarnation and *karma* (the belief that your social situation results from merit or guilt built up in past lifetimes). Since all that is is God, the social dynamic of Hinduism is acceptance of all that is.

Hindu philosophy has an impact far beyond the shores of India. Joseph Campbell's popular writings on myth well illustrate the social dynamic of Hinduism. He writes:

> People ask me, "Do you have optimism about the world?" And I say, "Yes, it's great just the way it is. And you are not going to fix it up. Nobody has ever made it any better. It is never going to be any better. This is it, so take it or leave it. You are not going to correct or improve it." . . . James Joyce has a memorable line: "History is a nightmare from which I am trying to awake." And the way to awake from it is not to be afraid, and to recognize that all of this, as it is, is a manifestation of the horrendous power that is of all creation. . . . One of the problems of life is to live with the realization of both [good and evil], to say, "I know the center, and I know that good and evil are simply temporal aberrations and that in God's view there is no difference."[8]

Buddhism, as a reform movement built on Hinduism, has the same basic worldview. Nevertheless, the social project of Buddhism is changed by its greater emphasis on individual personal enlightenment. Caste, karma and reincarnation are less central. Anyone may escape the wheel of suffering. In theory the most individualistic of the world religions, Buddhism does promote a compassionate and tranquil society through the eightfold path of morality. But the goal remains individual release from a life characterized by suffering. Thus the Buddhist social dynamic that promotes enlightenment is tranquil detachment from an illusory world of pain.

While the preceding analysis is vastly oversimplified and inevitably includes a Western and Christian bias, it should be sufficient to show that the social projects of the various world religions may not be easily harmonized. Fundamentally different valuations of what is real issue in different social practices.

A standpoint for evaluating religious social projects. It is not possible to actively critique any of the social projects without starting from a particular "religious" standpoint. Without some particular notion of *what* is "real," we are reduced to silence. John Hick's latest solution of making "the Real" the unifying point of all religions is of little help. The meaning of the term (with or without a capital *R*) is radically different in each religion.

The social dynamic of each of the world religions contains strengths and weaknesses that give rise to both good and evil social practices. Naturally the social structures of cultures shaped by different social dynamics also reflect those strengths and weaknesses. The fact that Christians do not agree with the worldviews of the other religions or with the prioritized social dynamics that give expression to those worldviews does not mean there are not aspects of truth in the social projects of other religions.

Islam knows something about submission to the Almighty God of the universe which Christians may have forgotten. Moreover, the Muslim attempt to build a sociopolitical structure reflecting that submission has much to teach us, perhaps as much through its failures as through its successes.

Hindu acceptance of all that is also has much to teach us. Western Christian attempts to transform and therefore dominate reality have led to an arrogant triumphalism that bends everything to utilitarian ends. Imperialism, neocolonialism and the destruction of the environment may grow out of the transformational dynamic. From Hinduism we may learn to adapt to the natural order and seek harmony with it in the knowledge that our karma is to reap what we have sown.

The compassionate, tranquil detachment of Buddhism contains aspects of truth urgently needed by Westerners addicted to greed and power. While Christianity tries to curb the ego with the tools of love, repentance (guilt) and forgiveness, there are additional Buddhist tools (practices) needed for balance. Buddhist detachment may add depth to Christ's teaching about dying to the self. The Thai social structure, in which a large proportion of the population shave their heads and become penniless monks for at least a couple of years of their life, may have some important lessons for us. (Perhaps a mandatory two-year Peace Corps program is a better idea than universal conscription into the military.)

This chapter cannot embark on a full-fledged analysis of comparative religious social virtues. Here I can only suggest a few avenues for mutual ethical enrichment. The acknowledgment of rich values in non-Christian social practices does not require acceptance of the religious doctrines they express. I suspect that religious doctrines are abstractions from narratives that attempt (often mistakenly) to explain or rationalize the existence of social practices. The narratives and the practices are a seamless web that support each other. In any case there are aspects of truth, insights and mythic wisdom in most religious narratives, as well as in religiously based social practices.

There is no Archimedean point of objectivity from which the social practices of other religions can be evaluated. As a Christian, I am to take my critical standard for ethical analysis from the kingdom of God revealed in Jesus. My understanding of biblical Christianity is influenced by my American, white, middle-class, male, intellectual, experiential interpretation of biblical Christianity. Thus I would be wise to listen to other views, not in order to shed my own perspective but to enrich it.

The Christian critique of the Western empire. A particular moral standpoint is needed for an adequate critique of Western civilization. The declarations of the fall of the Western empire have been premature. Certainly assumptions of Western superiority have taken a beating since World War II. Nevertheless, neocolonialism is alive and well in the form of a Western- (and Japanese-) dominated international economic and cultural order. Viewed from Indonesia, America appears both more powerful and less just than it does to many Americans. The growing gap between the rich and poor of the world belies the powerful Western myth of economic development.

The irony is that the impetus for a critique of the old colonialist world order grew out of a Western, essentially Christian, world-transformative social dynamic. The same dynamic that led to an imperialist drive to make the world over in the image of the "Christian" West also provided the foundation for its critique. Nationalist leaders who led the drive for independence and freedom were almost invariably Western-educated. Marxist theory, which played a significant part in this process, is a Western product and arguably a Christian heresy.

Social movements aimed at overthrowing a powerful social order that had been dominant for hundreds of years were unlikely to stem from non-Christian social dynamics. Social projects that stress submission to God (and fate), acceptance of reality (and caste) as karma, or tranquil detachment from the illusory world of suffering could not provide a narrative capable of fomenting revolution. For that you must turn to the exodus. The tragic fact that "Christian" nations did not live up to their vision of a kingdom of righteousness should not be surprising, given a biblical perspective on sin.[9]

The best hope for a sustained critique of the current international order also stems from a Christian social dynamic. But it is unlikely to come from the West. The center of gravity for a vital Christian social critique has passed from Western Europe and North America to the Third World. The Bible and the West and God and society all look incredibly different when seen from Latin America, Asia or Africa. The social dynamic of Christianity is no longer primarily Western. The center of vital Christianity is in the Third World, and that is where the vision of the kingdom is best understood. Indeed, crosscultural social ethics may soon be the only ethics worth studying.

Shall we conclude that the Christian social project is the right one and the other religions are all wrong? By no means! Even if we believe a transformational Christian social project is best, there is still much to be learned from the social projects of other religions. The preceding analysis has been vastly oversimplified. The complexity and richness of an ideal Muslim, Hindu or Buddhist social project have hardly been treated justly in these few pages. I have given caricatures to make a point. In order to feel the power of other religious social visions, we must listen directly to the followers of another way.

I am convinced that the biblical narrative is true. The world needs to know Christ. But I am also anxious to hear other narratives that can enrich the practices that grow out of biblical faith. Not all Christians have a "world-transformative" faith.[10] Not all who do agree on what it entails. The massive injustices perpetuated in the name of world transformation should be sobering enough to induce us to listen to other ways of reading the world.[11]

Theological Perspectives on Religions

A common typology of approaches to the plurality of religions uses the categories "exclusivist," "inclusivist" and "pluralist." From a pluralist perspective these three categories represent a trajectory of enlightenment from infantile exclusivism through adolescent inclusivism to mature pluralism. For the exclusivist it is the slippery slope of apostasy.

I am unhappy with this definition of the debate. There are many different variations of each "type" which are not easily grouped. Moreover, the same person may inhabit different groupings depending on whether the focus is on doctrines, narratives, ultimate salvation or social praxis. *Pluralism* used to refer to the fact that one society contains multiple religions. Recently it has come to be used as a normative term for a particular theology of religions.

"Pluralism" and its variations. John Hick, Paul Knitter and others argue that we need a "Copernican revolution" in our concept of our faith such that "God" or "Ultimate Reality," rather than Christ, is the center. Because of differences in geography and culture, they say, the "One Real" is differently named in different places. The Incarnation of Christ is true only in the truth of the attitude it evokes in the believer. The result is a new theology of pluralism that denies the existence of absolute truth in other theologies. Similarly, Wilfred Cantwell Smith, Stanley J. Samartha and others suggest that mystical experience is the unifying core of all religions.

Langdon Gilkey suggests that the logical conclusion of pluralism is complete relativism. But he wants to retain ethical criteria for judgment. In contrast, Raimundo Panikkar affirms an ontological pluralism: there is no unifying principle between the religions, because ultimate reality is diverse. Different religions may all be ontologically true, because there is more than one ultimate reality.

These various versions of pluralism need to be recognized for what they are: not the enlightened toleration of all religions but the creation of various new (or old) theologies that are at least as competitive with the world religions as they are with each other. Some versions of pluralism have accepted an essentially Hindu perspective on reality. The view of different paths up the same mountain predates the Christian era. Hindus acknowledge different paths, but they believe only they know what the mountain is all about.

Ethical problems with pluralism. A critical appreciation of wisdom in the social practices of non-Christian religious cultures includes the recognition that from a Christian perspective there is much that must be rejected. Muslim intolerance, Hindu caste and Buddhist moral relativism are incompatible with a transformative Christian standpoint. This is deeply problematic for the moral relativism incipient in pluralism. If all religions are equal and truth is equally unknown by all, then there is no standpoint from which to condemn any religious practices.

This dilemma is vividly recognized by Langdon Gilkey. He comments,

> For in our century intolerable forms of religion and the religious have appeared: in a virulently nationalistic Shinto, in Nazism, in aspects of Stalinism and Maoism, in Khomeini—and in each of these situations an absolute religion sanctions an oppressive class, race, or national power. These represent

the "shadow side" of religion, and they are radically destructive. When faced with one of them, we *must* resist, and we must liberate ourselves and others from them.[12]

This is a problem for which Gilkey admits he has no rational answer, since he has already accepted a radical pluralism. He recognizes that

in order to resist . . . we must ourselves stand somewhere. That is, we must assert some sort of ultimate values . . . the values of persons and of their rights, and correspondingly, the value of the free, just, and equal community so deeply threatened by this theocratic tyranny. And to assert our ultimate value or values is to assert a "world," a view of all of reality. For each affirmed political, moral, or religious value presupposes a certain understanding of humankind, society, and history, and so a certain understanding of the whole in which they exist. Consequently any practical political action, in resistance to tyranny or in liberation from it, presupposes ultimate values and an ultimate vision of things, an ethic and so a theology. And it presupposes an absolute commitment to this understanding of things.[13]

Gilkey rather lamely proposes a "relative absoluteness" based in praxis, although he admits that such a solution "both stuns and silences the mind."

Can social praxis unify all religions? Other writers in Hick and Knitter's *The Myth of Christian Uniqueness* attempt to find in praxis a unifying point at which pluralists from various religious traditions can work together. The problem is, of course, that there is no unifying praxis that unifies radically different religious narratives. Praxis unifies theory and practice. But in fact neither the theories nor the practices of the different religions are the same. A karma praxis is unlikely to fight for the rights of "untouchables" in India. A Muslim praxis of obedience will probably not struggle for the human rights of non-Muslims in Iran.[14] A Buddhist praxis that expresses detachment is not the most likely source of opposition to torture and political oppression in Myanmar (Burma).

Pluralists also have a narrative that employs universal categories such as "the human community" and "the truth of us all." Such a narrative includes a social project (dialogue and harmony) and a social dynamic (acceptance of all that is as good). But a contradiction arises when someone like Paul Knitter moves from a pluralist conception of doctrine or ultimate salvation to a focus on praxis. When Knitter turns to social ethics, the pluralist turns into an exclusivist. Justice, equality, freedom and peace must exclude injustice, oppression, domination and war. No "rough parity" is acceptable.

Pluralism as a new form of colonialism? In a thoughtful and polemical essay Kenneth Surin (from Malaysia) suggests that the homogenizing thought of the global theorists of pluralism renders the various religions into a kind of McDonald's hamburger.[15] The specificity of the various religions, as well as their concrete location in particular sociopolitical contexts, is ironed out. Religion is turned into a commodity to be consumed. The choice of which one is "merely cultural." Surin comments, "This liberal subject ranges over the globe only to conclude that, although everything is different everywhere, in the end things are perhaps not all that different after all."[16]

Surin's most provocative thesis is that globetrotting pluralists are actually (though perhaps not consciously) part of "Western cultural hegemonism."[17] Pluralists are drawn from Western and Western-trained Third World elites. Their identity and power are linked to Western cultural and economic dominance. By erasing the deep divisions between different religious perceptions of reality, the pluralists promote their own, Western, "enlightened" view as the standard by which all others are judged. The real issues of conflict and domination are smoothed out. The essential "equality" of religions is demonstrated by how well they measure up to Western ideals of liberal, enlightened modernization. Surin suggests that there is no grit in pluralists to really fight Western domination because they are a part of it.

"Inclusivism." Inclusivists believe that Christian faith is uniquely true but the God of Jesus Christ also works through other religions. Other religions are true in a lesser way. Though pluralists believe they have decisively "crossed the Rubicon" away from the parochial ethnocentrism of inclusivist Christianity, which assigns second-class citizenship to other religions, pluralist perspectives actually shade into the inclusivist grouping. Some writers could appear in either category.

Some inclusivists maintain a respectful agnosticism regarding other religions. Charles F. Andrews, a highly respected missionary who worked closely with Gandhi for Indian independence, suggested that while for him Christ is the ultimate expression of God, he is unable to judge other religions. Andrews is often fulsome in his praise of Hinduism. In this he sounds just like a pluralist. But when engaged in polemics with Hindus he insisted that Vedantist *advaita* and Christian faith could never be reconciled. Andrews wrote that a Christian could "never accept as finally satisfying a philosophy which does not allow him to believe that love between human souls may be an eternal reality."[18] Thus for ethical reasons he slips into inclusivism.

Charles McCoy, the early Robert Bellah and others suggest we need a "second naiveté" that affirms Christianity as our tradition while remaining agnostic about other traditions.[19] This may sound close to pluralism, but both McCoy and Bellah are deeply attached to the basic assumptions of Christianity in their social thought, such that inclusivism is a better label for them.

Some inclusivists, such as J. N. Farquhar and Teilhard de Chardin, had an evolutionary view of religion with Christianity at the top. Their focus was the relativity and development of truth. Such thinking seems fatally linked to the ethos of the colonial era and finds few theological supporters today. It lives on, however, in some functional approaches to sociology of religion.[20]

More common is a focus on the efficacy of all religions as a means of ultimate salvation. Many writers seem to have a utilitarian view of religion—that different religions serve the same function. Bishop David Brown believes that many followers of other religions

> have a living relationship with God and know the power of his grace in their lives. . . . They worship God as he has been made known to them, in spirit and truth. . . . The God whom they worship is he whom Christians know as the Father of our Lord Jesus Christ, even though their understanding of his relationship with the created universe differs from that of Christians.[21]

Brown is an inclusivist in that he believes a true knowledge of God only comes through Christ. Other religions may, however, be a means through which God in Christ saves the followers of other paths.

Panikkar, who speaks out in *The Myth of Christian Uniqueness* as the most radical of pluralists, sounds just like an inclusivist in some of his writings. He argues that God uses all religions as *instruments* of Christian salvation. All religious practitioners may be saved by Christ through the practices of their own religion. Panikkar writes, "The good and bona fide Hindu is saved by Christ and not by Hinduism, but it is through the sacraments of Hinduism, through the message of morality and the good life, through the Mysterion that comes down from him through Hinduism, that Christ saves the Hindu normally."[22]

Most inclusivists are primarily concerned about how to get non-Christians into heaven. Hans Küng has suggested that the non-Christian religions are an ordinary way of salvation, whereas Christianity is a "very special and extraordinary" way to salvation. Paul Tillich and the Niebuhr brothers represent "liberal" and "neo-orthodox" writers who affirm the finality and uniqueness of Christian revelation but believe that God might also work through other religions. Perhaps Karl Rahner is the most cautious example in the inclusivist grouping. Rahner is well known for his acknowledgment of the possibility of "anonymous Christians" in other religions.

Even C. S. Lewis may be grouped among the inclusivists, if his fictional portrayals of the good atheist in *That Hideous Strength* and the good follower of Tash in *The Last Battle* are taken seriously. Of course all universalists—including Karl Barth, whose polemic against "religion" is well known—must be considered inclusivist if belief in ultimate salvation is the defining criterion of the position.

Recently, several evangelical theologians have argued for an inclusivist approach to the fate of the unevangelized. While rejecting the term "anonymous Christians," Clark Pinnock suggests that followers of other religions may include "pre-Christian" believers in God who are already saved by grace through faith.[23] Similarly, John Sanders rejects both "restrictivism" and universalism and provides a carefully nuanced biblical, theological and historical argument for a hopeful view of the destiny of the unevangelized.[24]

"Exclusivism." The so-called exclusivists also occupy a range of positions. Usually exclusivists concentrate on doctrine and truth issues. They argue that there is an absolute contradiction between Christian faith and other religions. Non-Christian religions are not only inadequate but indeed false. They are going in the wrong direction. If you want to go to New York but set off in the opposite direction, you are not merely taking a different path. It won't help to go faster or find a nicer car. You need to turn around and find the right road.

Fundamentalists frequently see non-Christian religions as vehicles of damnation. Demonic forces use non-Christian religions as a means of holding people in darkness. Religions are just so many roads to hell.

Barth is often identified with the exclusivist position because he saw a radical contradiction between the revelation of God and religion. Barth was keenly aware of the idolatrous tendency of all religions, including Christianity. Religion is the human attempt to grasp and control God. Through religion, according to Barth, "we lock the door against God, we alienate ourselves from him, we come into direct opposition to him."[25] Barth's rejection of all natural theology is well known. What is puzzling to many is the dialectical tension in his thought which led him to an inclusivist position in regard to the ultimate salvation of all.

One of the most outstanding followers of Barth's negative assessment of religion was Hendrick Kraemer. Kraemer's theology avoids Barth's dialectical extremes. He neither followed Barth's total rejection of natural theology nor accepted his universalism. While the harshness of his condemnation of all religion moderated as he got older, Kraemer maintained the sharp Barthian division between God's grace and all human efforts.

> The cross and its real meaning—reconciliation as God's initiative and act— is antagonistic to all human religious aspirations and ends, for the tendency of all human religious striving is to possess and conquer God, to realize our divine nature (*theosis*). Christ is not the fulfillment of this but the uncovering of its self-assertive nature, and at the same time the rebirth to a completely opposite condition, the fellowship of reconciliation with God.[26]

An Indian evangelical, Ken Gnanakan, is critical of the Barthian exclusivist position for its confusion of the absolute claims of the Bible with a Christian's relative relation to a non-Christian.[27] Such absolutism, according to Gnanakan, leads to a colonial Christian mentality. Exclusivism projects an attitude that is hard to square with the example of Christ. The harshest criticisms of Christ were directed at the exclusivist Pharisees. Barth's style of exclusivism, perhaps in reaction to optimistic evolutionary liberal theology, posits too extreme a discontinuity between the Word of God and natural human understanding. To see *no* continuity between the revelation in Christ and human religious strivings betrays a peculiar kind of blindness.

Regarding eternal salvation, some evangelicals and fundamentalists argue that any compromise with the stark fact that only in Christ is there escape from eternal damnation undermines the imperative for evangelism. It is a capitulation to creeping relativism. But some prominent evangelical leaders have warned that while the Bible is clear that forgiveness and redemption come only through the blood of Christ, it is less clear regarding how God will judge those who do not know Christ.

There is much we don't know. Clark Pinnock reminds us that according to Jesus, on Judgment Day there will be some major surprises (Mt 25:31-46). While rejecting the suggestion that some do not need to repent and believe the gospel, Pinnock speculates on the basis of 1 Peter 3:19 that those who have never had the opportunity to know Christ may be given a second chance after death.[28]

John Stott also urges caution against Christians' usurping God's prerogative of judgment. Stott reminds Christians of the incredible mercy of God revealed on the cross and that we are never definitively told how God will judge those who do not know Christ. Stott even cherishes "the hope that the majority of the human race will be saved." He says,

> But we need to remember that God is the Creator of all humankind, and remains infinitely loving, patient and compassionate towards all whom he has made. Yes, and he is also everybody's "Father," both in the sense that they live and move and have their being in him, deriving the richness of their human life from his generosity (Acts 17:25-28), and in the sense that he continues to yearn for his lost children, as in the parable of the prodigal son.[29]

This chapter is not intended to explore the complex theological and ethical issues involved in an understanding of judgment, heaven and hell. Suffice it to say that along with Pinnock and Stott, I am happy to acknowledge my ignorance of exactly who will be saved through the death of Christ. I trust in the mercy and justice of God. The New Testament is clear that only through the death and resurrection of Christ is there forgiveness of sins and reconciliation with God. There is no other way to earn salvation. If this were not so, the incarnation and crucifixion would be unnecessary. Evangelization would lose all urgency. But nowhere in the Bible are we given definitive information on who will be saved and who will be damned. In our ignorance (and hope) we may leave the last judgment to God.

Dialectic: Good and Evil in All Religions

In this chapter I have tried to maintain a dialectical stance toward other religions. On the one hand, non-Christian religions are good and filled with truth and beauty. Many of the greatest achievements of humankind have come through religious devotion. Religions also mediate many of the ordinary everyday virtues that sustain a decent society. On the other hand, they are idolatrous vehicles of demonic oppression and darkness. Not only do religions lack truth, but they're also the source of some of the greatest evils in history. On the everyday level, religions constrict and tyrannize life in petty and large ways.

Pluralistic appreciation. In one sense I am a pluralist. I am not comfortable with the idea of a "rough parity" in the achievements of religions, because it suggests the comparing of apples and potatoes. But in regard to cultural and social achievements I am unable to claim Christian, much less Western, superiority.

An Indonesian pastor asked me if Western culture, because of its Christian foundations, was superior to Javanese culture. I found it a very complex question. But it was clear to me that the answer was no. Not only the great social evils associated with Western culture but also the current quality of life in Western countries make it difficult to affirm the superiority of Western culture. I am not at all sure that an inhabitant of a small fundamentalist Christian town in America has a better life than a Muslim inhabitant of a village in Java.

The two cannot be objectively compared. But it is safe to say that each setting has some great advantages over the other. There are villages in Indonesia where locks and burglary are unknown, police do not exist and crime is negligible. Families are very tightly connected, the weak are cared for, and the whole village works together for survival. People are poor, but they have time for each other and live in close contact with nature.

Western culture, including that fundamentalist town, is far from being primarily structured in ways consistent with biblical faith. There are many other streams of influence that often overpower Christian ideals. But even if Christianity were the only major influence, human beings have a way of twisting power structures to their own personal benefit. In contrast, it is one of the mysteries of the human spirit that people with very few resources and very little freedom sometimes construct very rich lives.

There are many wonderful aspects of Western social life that systematically structure Christian social morality. The rule of law, social equality, individual human rights, democratic institutions and a decent telephone system (just kidding) are things to be treasured. Writers as diverse as Max Weber, Basel Matthews and Francis Schaeffer have argued that Christianity is the basis of most of the world's greatest cultural achievements. Such claims may be true, but they are no easier to prove than the pluralist assumption of a "rough parity" in religious achievements. More troubling is the equally unprovable claim that Christianity is the source of all the greatest evils of the modern world.[30] It seems quite likely to me that Christian ideas are *one* of the sources of both the greatest evils and the greatest goods of the modern world. It is very unlikely that Christianity is the only source of either.

In my ultimate epistemology I am a pluralist. Christians do not have a greater natural capacity to know the truth than anyone else. Faith is a gift not based on intellectual ability.[31] We believe God's Spirit illuminates the understanding of those with faith. But we cannot prove that this spiritual illumination is truer than that of a Zen master in his cell. If I know the God of the universe and others believe in radically mistaken narratives about "life, the universe and everything," in a sense it is an accident of geography. They were born in Hindu India while my parents are Christians. Ultimately we cannot prove beyond the possibility of reasonable doubt that Jesus was God incarnate. Only on the "last day" will our faith become sight.

But I *believe* Christianity is true. Through intellect and experience I have many reasons to *think* it is true. When I live by its premises I *experience* its truth. I am *committed* to the God of Jesus Christ, before whom I bow. My whole life is structured by the central convictions of my faith. Through the eyes of my faith I *see many evidences* of its truth (Heb 11:1). Faith is the substance that ties me to the community into which I was born. Our decision to be loyal to God in Christ is not just an individual decision based on an exhaustive examination of evidence. It is a personal and communal response to the concrete actions of God in history. Our faith does not rest on individual judgment alone, but on our acceptance of a "great cloud of witnesses" recorded in the Bible and in the past and present history of the church.

Nevertheless, by my own premises we are all finite sinners. Both our limited wisdom and our sin make us poor judges of the ultimate meaning of life. There is no proof that all Christians are not living a dream. Such a position is different from simply affirming one's tradition from a stance of basic agnosticism. I cannot prove justice or love exist. I cannot prove that my wife and children love me. I cannot prove any of the things I would stake my life on. That does not make them any less true.

But if I cannot prove the truth of what I believe, still less can I prove the falsehood of what millions of others believe. Nor do I have to. I am not their judge. I am just a fellow sinner on the way.

Inclusive acknowledgment of the mystery of grace. There is a sense in which I am an inclusivist. Christianity is the lens through which I view other religions. Neither the primary narratives of the major religions nor the pluralist narrative gives an adequate account of human life. The incarnation of God in Christ is the key for understanding both God and history. It is also the definitive event through which God offers forgiveness and new life to humankind. The social project of Christianity, which anticipates the coming kingdom, is the only hope for all humanity.

Nevertheless, I believe God works through other religions. Other religions may be vehicles of grace, both for individuals and for societies. Wherever Buddhists succeed in restraining evil through promoting detachment from egoistic impulse and the result is a tranquil society, God may be at work. Wherever Hindus promote a celebration of the goodness of all created life and the result is a society that reverences all creation, God is glorified. Wherever Muslim law results in a society structured by worship and moral discipline, we may see hints of the kingdom.

Exclusivist focus on truth. Different religions contain aspects of truth that render them capable of becoming means of grace. But taken as a whole, they are not merely incomplete but indeed false. They point in the wrong direction. Therefore there is a sense in which I am an exclusivist. All human beings need Christ, not just for personal and ultimate salvation but because their societies need to be transformed by the values of the kingdom of God. Evangelism is morally imperative. Opposition to slavery, sexism, poverty, human-rights abuses and racism is a fundamentally Christian value needed by all cultures.

At issue is not just different cultural ways of relating to an unknowable ultimate reality. The issue of truth is fundamental. It is self-deluding, flabby thinking to suppose that all religions are equally true. Material and social reality are radically different if there is a loving, just and personal God rather than an impersonal ultimate reality that contains both good and evil. If evil is a reality hated by God, a reality that must be combated, it implies a very different society from one in which evil is illusory and suffering is fated by karma or God. False narratives give rise to unjust social institutions.

The most basic truth question of all is whether the God of the universe was uniquely incarnated in Christ. If Jesus is the Son of God who died for the world, then any conception of a "rough parity" of religions is literally nonsense. It is simply a fancy way of saying no religions are true. If the Christian story is the revelation of God's actual action in history, then the kingdom of God is really coming and we had better get ready.

Dialogue, Humility and Conviction

Interreligious dialogue. Of the many good reasons for relating to believers in other religions, the most compelling is necessity. Most countries of the world are multireligious. Believers in different traditions have to get along with each other for everyone's benefit. Formal interreligious dialogue sponsored by multinational ecumenical groups is only a small part of the interchange that is taking place every day. Dialogue is necessary for survival.

Living in the largest Muslim country in the world, I can well understand the Marxist who remarked in the context of a Marxist-Christian dialogue, "If we do not speak with one another now, we will shoot one another later."[32] In many parts of the world relations between Muslims and Christians are very tense.

Violence lies just under the surface.

Religions do not actually dialogue, people do. The interchange is more often in an office, in the street or at a school function for the kids than in an impressive conference room. When you cross cultures, everyone you meet may be the follower of a strange tradition. Each meeting is an opportunity to increase mutual understanding, defuse potential conflict, enrich perceptions and, of course, pass on the good news.

Certainly evangelism and conversion are one of the goals of dialogue. How primary they are depends on the situation. There are two (or more) parties in a dialogue, and both of them influence why they are talking to each other. It may be because they like each other. Or because one is lonely. Or because they work together. Or because they are curious about each other. What each party wants from the relationship will, through negotiation (usually unconscious), determine what happens. Evangelism should not be a unilateral activity. Nor should good news be withheld from those who are ready to hear it.

When I started going to San Quentin Prison once a week to visit with prisoners, I had no intention of doing evangelism. I wanted to learn from the prisoners how they saw the world. And I wanted to be friends with people, some of whom have not had a visitor or a letter for years. But something about the situation turned me into an evangelist. It's pretty hard not to talk about the good news with men who are so used to bad news. The love of God and the possibility of forgiveness were like water in the desert to some of my new friends. Some wanted badly to be converted.

Often dialogue may take place because Christians share goals with people in other religions. In September 1993 we held a conference cosponsored by Christian, Muslim and Buddhist universities on religion and the environment. Papers with different religious perspectives on the same problems were presented. The purpose was not dialogue per se, but to find ways to work together on a problem bigger than any of our communities.

In relating creatively to people from other religions, praxis is crucial. By our actions people have a chance to see what we mean. Relationships with people in other religions is a part of praxis.

Two dispositions toward knowledge and truth make interreligious friendships possible. Dispositions are settled attitudes or orientations. The two are epistemological humility and ontological conviction.

Epistemological humility. Epistemological humility means a humble attitude toward what we know and do not know. Everything we know, including the story of our faith, we know through the particular eyes of our culture, age, sex, social position and so on. Much that we think we know we actually misunderstand, are confused about or know imperfectly. "Now we see in a mirror, dimly" (1 Cor 13:12). We can see only a little bit of reality, and none of it perfectly. All that we do know is a gift.

Much that we know best about our faith we know through our experience. That provides a starting point for dialogue with someone from another religion. We can tell him or her our story. But my experience is finite and "peculiar," even if I happen to be the most experienced person in the world. Anyway, I happen *not* to be the most experienced person. We need to be humble toward someone from another religion because we don't actually know much about infinite reality. And our vision of what we have been given (revelation) is distorted by sin.

Epistemological humility is also necessary because we do not know what the other person knows. One thing is sure: followers of another religion know many things of which their Christian friends have no idea. They have narratives, practices and experiences that will remain a mystery to us until they are willing to share them. There is no doubt that the Holy Spirit has been working in their lives. I believe the Holy Spirit is actively seeking every person on earth.

Epistemological humility means an openness to the other, a willingness to learn and a respect for the other's right to speak or remain silent. It means a willingness to listen and not rush in with a prerecorded answer before we understand the other's question. It may be that God wishes to speak *to you* through the other, rather than vice versa. In the stranger we may meet the face of Christ. If Christ should address you, it would be a shame if you didn't listen because you were too busy doing evangelism!

Epistemological humility makes possible true dialogue between committed followers of different faiths. It allows you to accept the other as strange and not require her or him to be like you before you speak with each other. A Muslim student who studied in our program was a great example to me of this. His ears were open and his senses wide to understand a Christian perspective on social reality.

Epistemological humility is not to be confused with theological pluralism. Some pluralists have it and some don't. Some only want dialogue with other pluralists. If only people who agree that all religions are equally valid talk to each other, it may be questionable if real interreligious dialogue has taken place.

With sufficient epistemological humility, people with extreme differences in opinion can learn from each other. In fact, the greater the differences, the greater the potential benefits of dialogue. Those about to pick up stones against their enemies most need to talk with them. One of my most fruitful academic friendships is with an agnostic Jewish scholar of religious phenomenology who blames Christianity for most of the evils of the world. We have great arguments! We both find each other's views fascinating, in part because they are so strange to us.

Ontological conviction. The necessary dialectical partner to humility is ontological conviction. Without conviction about what you believe, humility regarding the limitations of knowledge easily degenerates into intellectual flabbiness. Epistemological humility can become an excuse not to be committed to anything at all controversial. Humility by itself can be cheap. It requires no commitment to that which is costly. Ontological conviction requires the courage to commit yourself on issues that really matter.

There is something disturbingly weak about some liberal Christianity. Epistemological humility has been taken to such an extreme that good Christians are afraid to admit they believe anything for fear of being seen as arrogant! What they *do* believe about ultimate questions (such as the Incarnation) is categorized as personal, purely subjective religious truth. Such truth is difficult to talk about and hardly worth dying for.

Often epistemological humility is assumed to *require* lack of conviction about ultimate reality. After all, who are we to say we know the Truth and everyone else is wrong? It is much safer to simply say, "According to my tradition there is a loving God." This avoids any public appraisal of the truth of the claim. Whether there really is a loving God of the universe becomes incidental. It is "religious truth" and therefore beyond rational discussion. It is a matter of belief, not reason.

But why believe it at all if you do not think it is true? Despite "Pascal's wager,"[33] I think it is better not to believe in that which is not true. If there is no ultimate reality, or if ultimate reality is radically different from the one portrayed in the Christian narrative, I would prefer to know it and deal with the consequences. I doubt that in the eyes of God a purely utilitarian "faith" would appear preferable to an honest atheism.[32]

Some people are content to have little conviction but simply to "follow their tradition" because of its emotional, aesthetic or social value. Such religion is just waiting to be buried. A living faith capable of inspiring the costly struggle to see

God's will done on earth must be based on deep convictions about the nature of reality. Jesus urged his followers to daily face the possibility of death by torture (Lk 9:23). They were urged to care not for their lives in comparison to seeking first the kingdom of God (Mt 6:33). You have to believe something is true in the real world before you will die for it.

Real convictions, if accompanied by humility, make dialogue possible. Because I really believe in Christ, I can respect someone who really believes in Buddha. I do not reduce her beliefs to cultural, symbolic categories but am willing to address them as real, legitimate claims about the nature of the world. I also have convictions about the ultimate.

Convictions also make dialogue *desirable*. I want to talk to someone in a strange tradition because I believe truth matters. Christian convictions impel the believer to care enough about the other to tell him the truth. Humility requires that I respect him enough to listen to his convictions and openly consider their truth claims.

Convictions are not based on logical or empirical proof. No knowledge is based on such proof. All knowledge must begin with assumptions or beliefs. Christian convictions are rooted in God's self-revelation. Like all other important matters, they are subject to reasoned discussion. They are not private. They have been publicly debated, defended, preserved, developed and interpreted by a continuous community for thousands of years. They are part of a narrative that makes sense of life. Christian convictions entail participation in the social project of the community that is formed by the Christian story.

NINE

WOMEN AND MEN
AS STRANGERS:
GENDER CONFLICT
ACROSS CULTURES

Women who visit or live in other cultures, whether within their own country or abroad, face particular problems of crosscultural ethics. In all cultures there are assumptions about what is proper and good in the relations between the sexes. Sexual role divisions are universal. Differences in cultural perception easily lead to stereotypes and hostility toward those who are different.

In practically all cultures, power and prestige are ascribed more often to the activities of men than to those of women. But the actual conventions for the behavior of men and women differ widely. This creates a dilemma for a stranger in a new context who may not know what is acceptable behavior. Moreover, even when different conventions are understood, they may be ethically and emotionally unacceptable. This chapter examines some of the commonly faced moral problems of women and men who experience gender-role conflict in a strange culture

The Power of Images in Sexual Relations

Any attempt to understand another person or another culture begins with categories.[1] Knowledge begins with categorization and discrimination. We say that a person is "this" and not "that." She is white and not black, rich and not poor, Christian and not Muslim, woman and not man, foreigner and not fellow citizen, young and not old, enemy and not family, "out-group" and not "in-group."

Categorization and stereotypes. Categories, or names of classes of people, enable us to know how we should act toward them. When we classify a person as police officer rather than thief, we have some conception of what is expected of us and what is safe. "Women" and "men" are universally recognized categories. In every culture or subculture, people assume a range of appropriate behaviors based on the sex of another person. Unfortunately for crosscultural contact, the behaviors and characteristics assumed differ dramatically from culture to culture.

When we meet strangers, we assume that we know something about them based on the category we use to name them. Our categories are deeply influenced by personal experience, especially experience that is dramatic or emotionally charged.[2] If one white kid beats up a black kid, the black kid may fear all whites for a long time to come. Everyone characterizes a stranger based on their own limited experience.

Anyone who enters another culture encounters stereotypes. An Indonesian may admire a white American as rich, educated, self-reliant and free. The same person may also assume all Americans are arrogant, sexually immoral, racist, neocolonialist and anti-Islam. Stereotypes are generalizations about large classes of people based on limited information. When walking through villages in Indonesia, I am often referred to as "Belanda" (Dutch). For some Indonesians the distinction between Dutch and Americans is less significant than the difference between Javanese and Balinese Indonesians.[3] Most Asians know far more about America than most Americans know about Asia. But their knowledge of Westerners in general is understandably laden with stereotypes. This is especially true when it comes to perceptions of white Western women.

Stereotypes of white women. Many people of color have a stereotype of white women that includes a sexual element. Most of the world derives powerful images of Western women from a highly sexualized global media. Western movies image women as available sex objects. Multinational advertisements and American television are beamed all over the world via satellite. Even sexual behavior that is mild by Western standards is shocking to many foreign eyes.[4]

The behavior of white tourists seems to confirm the common assumption that many white women are promiscuous. In response to tropical temperatures, and because they are on vacation, many women tourists wear very few clothes. They seem unaware that even a sleeveless blouse is considered immodest in many Asian, Latin American, Middle Eastern and southern European cultures.[5]

Before arriving in Pakistan, an experienced traveler advised our family to wear Pakistani dress. If we did so, we would be less conspicuous and would be treated with greater respect. Accordingly, the first thing we did on arrival in Islamabad was visit a tailor and order full Pakistani outfits for all five of us. The extremely baggy clothes cover all flesh from neck to toe and conceal every bodily contour. They were topped with head scarves for the women and rolled-up hats for my son and me.

Having already experienced various forms of sexual harassment in several countries we had visited, my wife, Frances, and our daughters, Jen Marion and Rina, were happy to have the relatively easy change in dress as a means of escaping unwanted attention. We had heard horror stories of how Western-dressed single women are sometimes subjected to intense sexual harassment in this strongly Muslim society.

Pakistani men and women treated my wife and daughters with great respect throughout our stay. Both our dress and our family togetherness positively influenced our Pakistani hosts. We fit into their category of "respectable" people rather than imaging their stereotype of immoral Westerners.

Stereotypes and sexual harassment. Unfortunately, a change of clothes does not always protect a woman from harassment. White women receive a great deal of sexually motivated attention in many cultures. Every country in the world includes many males who would love to make the "conquest" of a sexually available female.

Women have many culturally specific behaviors both to attract and to discourage male attention. These include clothing, posture, ways of moving, use of the eyes (or nonuse), scent, bodily distance, tone of voice, group behavior, age and status signals, times and places where it is acceptable for a woman to be alone, makeup or body paint, and a host of other symbolic behaviors. Women visitors to another culture often don't know how to give the right signals. A foreign visitor lacks social location and may not even have the language to complain effectively. As one rural development worker commented, "It's amazing how much better I'm treated when they discover I speak 'human.' "

When we first arrived in Indonesia, village people often greeted us with the few English words they knew. They followed us with cries of "Hey, mister!" and "Good morning, miss!" at all times of day. Frances, Jen Marion and Rina were also regaled with phrases like "I love you!" "I want to kiss you!" "You are so beautiful!" Crowds of high-school boys were the worst offenders. They assumed we could not understand their unprintable comments.

The problem of sexual harassment is worldwide and knows no cultural boundaries. With catcalls in the United States, pinches in Italy, staring in China and whispered propositions in almost every country of the world, women are objectified as targets of masculine conquest. Some women shrug off or even enjoy such attention. But for most it is a mild irritant and sometimes a source of fear and rage.

Harassment has few age limitations. Both my wife and our twenty-one-year-old daughter may be pursued, wooed and insulted by males ranging in age from ten to eighty. Once in Jerusalem, after a day of mild flirtations, our elderly taxi driver tried to convince my wife to give him a kiss. I was upset and frustrated by his brazenness, but the man was so old that my wife was merely amused. It takes too much emotional energy to react to *every* sexual come-on.

For a woman in a foreign culture, sexual harassment can increase insecurity and alienation. She may lack the nuanced understanding and the cultural skills necessary to defuse or escape the situation. This can lead to loss of self-confidence and feelings of helplessness. In her own culture, sexual harassment is also disturbing and may be more dangerous. Violent crimes against women have reached alarming proportions in the United States. But at least most Americans can recognize the complex meanings of sexual communication in their own context and know how to avoid situations that are unpleasant or dangerous.

In some countries where verbal and indirect harassment is notorious, the probabilities of assault or rape may be very low. Nevertheless, the stress may be greater in a foreign context than in a more dangerous setting that is better understood. When my daughter lived in Yogyakarta, Indonesia, she could go almost anywhere, day or night, without fear of assault. But the unsolicited attention of young men often made her prefer to remain a prisoner in her own room. Going out alone just wasn't worth the hassle.

The experience of consistently being treated as an object of sexual attention easily gives rise to sexual stereotypes regarding foreign men. In the United States there is a common stereotype of Latin, Middle Eastern and Indian men as sexual predators. The aggressive few are taken as representative of their whole cultures. These men are easy to meet because they are looking for opportunities to get to know white women.

One tall, handsome Middle Eastern man found that his stereotype of "loose American women" was confirmed during the first part of his stay in America.[6] After a number of relatively easy sexual conquests, however, he realized that his experience applied only to a certain type of women. He called them "foreign student groupies." They were insecure, socially marginal women who apparently could not form satisfactory relationships with American men. The American women he wanted to know were not nearly as sexually available. In the process of learning that his own stereotypes were invalid, he contributed to the negative stereotypes of Middle Eastern men.

In Indonesia many Western women have a negative stereotype of young Indonesian men. Some men congregate in tourist areas and try to make serious sexual contact. Others have no serious sexual intent but are curious about white people. For a man, this curiosity can become annoying. Tourists are asked the same few questions dozens of times in a single day. Superficial conversations with strangers are emotionally exhausting.

For women the constant attention afforded to strangers is more disturbing, especially since the line between sexual attention and curiosity is rather vague. When we were traveling by ship between some Indonesian islands, groups of Indonesian men gathered to stare at any white woman who ventured alone on deck. In the West staring for long periods of time at someone of the opposite sex is impolite and even threatening. In highly communal cultures there are no such inhibitions to curiosity. Personal privacy is not a particularly important value. People may come and look through your window to see what you're doing or enter your room without knocking.[7]

Staring doesn't always indicate curiosity or sexual interest. Sometimes it is intended as a threat. A white person in an all-black or all-Latino neighborhood in Los Angeles would be naive to interpret prolonged staring as a neutral gesture. Where staring is known to be rude, prolonged staring is seldom friendly. But in many cultures the personal privacy Americans assume as their natural right does not exist. In China almost everyone stares at strange white people!

Sexual harassment is a fact of life everywhere, though it is more extreme in some places than others. Still, many adventurous women travel alone and live with great pleasure in almost every country of the world. Others find it more enjoyable to travel with a friend or group. Whether alone or together, many women find that the value of experiencing the richness of another culture far outweighs the occasional discomfort brought on by crude men. You cannot escape harassment just by staying at home!

Recently one of my Indonesian students had the opportunity to attend a conference in Oxford, England. She asked me if it was safe for a woman to travel alone in England or if she should go directly to and from the conference. (America is also widely perceived as a wild and dangerous place.) I advised her to go for as long as she could and travel as much as possible. The educational and cultural treasures to be gained from travel in another country far outweigh the dangers of sexual harassment. That doesn't mean it is safe, but neither is crossing the street. In either case you have to be careful.

Combating sexual stereotypes. Women are not just passive victims of the corrupt practices of evil men. They are active agents who can resist sexual harassment in a number of ways.

First of all, it is important to recognize the reality of the problem. Naiveté can lead to unpleasant results, not least of which is the confused perception that the victim of harassment is somehow to blame or that harassment is just a local custom. Sometimes ignorance of local conventions encourages sexual harassment. But even if that is true, it does not justify the harassment.

The critical factors in sexual harassment are lack of respect, an aggressive, insistent manner and/or an element of threat. Sexual harassment is wrong, no matter what cultural mistakes were made by the visitor. Many decent men in all cultures will not harass a visiting woman even if they are sexually tempted by her "strange" behavior. A few men in all cultures will harass *any* woman if they think they can get away with it.

Sexually motivated attention is not necessarily harassment. Communication between men and women often includes a sexual element. People from different cultures differ on the acceptability of mild flirtation in social situations. Signals of sexual interest are given in many ways. Such signals, even if inappropriate or immoral, may not qualify as harassment if they are polite and noncoercive.

Women should not accept sexual harassment in the name of cultural sensitivity, either as their fault or as something that can't be helped. Sometimes ignoring the insult is the best or only defense. But sometimes men (or boys) need to know their actions are offensive. A polite greeting in good Indonesian often brings order to an unruly group of students who don't quite realize you are a real person. At other times more direct action seems necessary. One Western woman confronted some crude Javanese boys with the question "Belum orang Jawa, kok?" (What? Are you not yet Javanese?), which is tantamount to suggesting that they are not yet fully human.

Sometimes nonverbal signs of displeasure are effective. While I would not recommend this as a normal strategy, I can understand the feelings of an American woman who had reached her frustration limit after being stared at through a car window from less than a foot away. To the consternation of her admirers, she suddenly turned to face them and stuck out her tongue!

The most effective nonverbal communication is to conform to local conventions of modesty. A visitor is a guest on another's turf, whether it is across town or across the ocean. Consideration for the values and sensibilities of the host is not only polite but also safe. The easiest (though often ignored) way to follow local conventions of politeness and modesty is in clothing.[8] Travelers who aspire to know people and not just sights should wear clothes that are appropriate in the eyes of their hosts.

This does not usually require buying a whole new outfit, as we did in Pakistan (though it might provide a good excuse). Western styles are now common in most countries. But attention to what local women of one's own age and status wear in different social situations can provide a rough guide to standards of modesty.[9] My daughter, who enjoys sleeveless shirts, wide necklines and short skirts, found that in Indonesia she was not comfortable wearing most of her American clothes. In spite of the heat, she soon learned that sleeves, high necklines and long skirts brought more respect and less unwanted attention.

Nonverbal signals may be given in other ways as well. In many cultures certain times, places and types of behavior are considered inappropriate for women but not for men. Women who do the wrong thing in the wrong place at the wrong time of day are likely to be misunderstood. This is tricky, because sometimes it's a good idea to flout practices that are oppressive to women. At other times it's not worth it.

One night soon after our arrival in Indonesia in 1989, my wife heard the sounds of an outdoor dramatic performance in our village. Since everyone else was busy, she went by herself to see what was happening. I was surprised when she returned after less than half an hour. There were other women at the performance, but she didn't like the kind of attention she received. We soon learned that Indonesian women don't usually go out alone at night. To be without friends or family in a social setting at night invites all kinds of speculations. It sends the wrong signals, especially if you happen to be blond!

Nevertheless, women and men who sojourn in another culture have the important ethical task of resisting and breaking common sexual stereotypes. Stereotypes are based on oversimplified images of whole classes of people. Truth destroys false stereotypes. Women of integrity undermine images that trivialize, objectify and degrade them. Patterns of masculine behavior that assume male superiority are undermined by men who relate to women with respect and justice.

No one can overturn entrenched prejudices in a short time. But the cumulative effect of strong examples of integrity in gender relations can both enlighten individual men and give hope to women. At the very least, stereotypes of all Western women as sexually promiscuous cannot survive sustained contact with Western women who show dignity and chastity in sexual relations. Married couples can show an example of healthy married love and friendship between equals. Though far from perfect, our marriage has elicited comments from young Indonesians who see hope for women in an example of equal partnership, mutual respect and genuine love.

There will always be Western men and women who propagate ugly stereotypes by fulfilling negative expectations. "Sexual tourism" involving extreme forms of sexual exploitation of poor and powerless women and children is a continuing, serious problem in many Asian countries. It is not always ignorance that causes suspicion of white (and Japanese) males. People of color in many countries of the world remember a long history of imperialist arrogance in which male conquerors treated powerless women and children as objects of sexual pleasure. Sexual exploitation of the poor by rich foreigners is still widespread.

Western women also contribute to negative stereotypes. In spite of AIDS, there continue to be white women who initiate or accept casual sexual relations with a variety of local men, thus reinforcing images propagated by third-rate movies. The stereotype of pleasure-seeking, helpless rich women is also unfortunately exemplified by too many tourists.

In China a communist government recruitment agency specifically requested *Christian* teachers from the West. A significant factor in the unusual invitation was the agency's experience of Christians as sexually responsible and dedicated to their work. In contrast, other foreign teachers were described (stereotyped!) as sexually immoral and undisciplined. Christians, by their character and lifestyle, had broken the negative stereotypes that underlie sexual harassment.

Structural Patterns in Gender Conflict

Crosscultural ethical problems faced by women and men include more than stereotypes and prejudices held by individuals. Institutions, practices and structures of whole societies systematically differentiate between the rights of men and those of women.

The cultural universality of sexism. Every society recorded in history or present today is structured to give men more recognized prestige and power than women.[10] Almost everything done by men is also done by women. In one culture men weave baskets and women build houses, while in another women weave baskets and men build houses. But whichever work is done by men is considered more important. The culture where men weave baskets may even despise the other group because its men do "women's work."[11]

In Russia the majority of physicians are women. But there doctors receive low wages and very little status. Their status and power are analogous to those of nurses in the United States. Until recently physicians in the United States wielded enormous social and economic power. Most of them were men. Today the prestige of the American medical profession is in sharp decline. Perhaps it is only coincidence that finally women are entering medical schools in significant numbers.[12]

The only gender roles that are always differentiated in all cultures are those to do with childbirth and lactation for women and warfare for men.[13] Every other task is performed by some men and some women in some cultures. Why then is women's work so universally devalued? Women do two-thirds of the world's work, earn a tenth of its income and own less than a hundredth of its property.[14] Rough statistics like this conceal the true power of women in the world, but they do illustrate a worldwide pattern.

As Mao Zedong stated in 1940,

> Women are subjugated by four thick ropes. A man in China is usually subjected to the domination of three systems of authority: political authority, clan authority and religious authority. As for women, in addition to being dominated by these three systems, they are also dominated by men. But women hold up half the sky.[15]

The *way* men dominate women differs in every culture. There are an infinite variety of structures and rationalizations for oppression. But in every case, ideological or psychological assumptions of male superiority are reinforced by practices and institutions controlled by men. All of this has been extensively documented.

In her profound study of women Simone de Beauvoir wrote,

But it will be asked at once: how did all this begin? It is easy to see that the duality of the sexes, like any duality, gives rise to conflict. And doubtless the winner will assume the status of absolute. But why should man have won from the start? It seems possible that women could have won the victory; or that the outcome of the conflict might never have been decided. How is it that this world has always belonged to the men and that things have begun to change only recently? Is this change a good thing? Will it bring about an equal sharing of the world between men and women?[16]

Feminism in the United States. The modern feminist movement was a reaction to the declining importance of the family as a social institution. World War II required the active participation of American women in economic life to support the war effort. After the war women were expected to return to the domestic sphere and achieve all their fulfillment in caring for their husbands and children. As Betty Friedan vividly showed in *The Feminine Mystique,* "the problem that has no name" involved the trivializaton of women through their limitation to a sphere of activity no longer vital to the nation.[17]

Traditional societies also radically limit women to the sphere of home and family. But in traditional societies the family is vital to educational, economic, social and political life. In the modern West, large institutions (schools, hospitals, corporations, social welfare, old age homes, the entertainment industry, clubs, the media, the military and even the church) have replaced the former functions of the family. The family is considered a place of emotional security with little connection to public life.[18] A traditional American housewife may be economically secure but have far less power than women in more traditional societies. Women who "have everything" are sometimes intensely unhappy. Feminism did not create this social reality but rather responded to it.

There is no uniform "Western" view of the role of women. Theories abound as to the original causes of the radical inequality of women all over the world. Biological, hormonal and evolutionary theories are highly unconvincing.[19] Since all the social, economic and political roles of men are duplicated by women in various cultures, it is likely that culture and socialization are the primary cause of the differences.

Christians differ greatly on what is implied by biblical teaching. In America there are wide differences of interpretation between white, black and Hispanic women, between "traditionalists" and "feminists," and even between different kinds of feminists. Different cultural, social and economic contexts produce different perceptions of gender and different readings of the Bible. Our convictions of what is right for a woman or man spring from different patterns of family, ethnic and class structure.

Nevertheless, women and men in the West experience the status and role of women within a broadly common culture. Using categories borrowed from John Condon and Fathi Yousef, we can broadly describe North American culture as *individualistic* in its relational orientation, *democratic* in its view of authority, *open* in its approach to role behavior and *highly mobile* in its sense of openness to movement and change.[20] Commonly held assumptions about the foundations of our social relationships may cause Western women to appear all alike in a foreign context. An Iranian might see very little difference in the overt gender behaviors of a radical lesbian feminist from New York and a fundamentalist housewife from Iowa.

Ever since the Fall and the subsequent "curse" in Genesis 3, there have been conflict, domination and subservience in the relations between men and women. Some women and men have always transcended the structural inequalities of their cultures. Some cultures have come close to structural gender equality. But even the most conservative "traditionalists" would concede the term *oppression* to describe some cultural practices of men toward women. The rapidly growing literature of women's studies vividly documents the suffering of women at the hands of men in virtually every historical period and culture.

The problem for crosscultural ethics is not whether sexual oppression exists but how to understand and respond to it. When a woman enters another culture, she cannot remain neutral to sexual oppression. It affects her identity in deep and significant ways. The definition of sexual oppression is controversial and complex, even in our own culture.[21] In another culture misunderstandings and misinterpretations are inevitable. Some of the structures of gender behavior in the non-Western world are morally repugnant and almost incomprehensible to most Westerners. The best known and most widespread of these structures is the systematic segregation of women from men.

The segregation of women from the public realm. Sexual segregation is most obvious in the Muslim world but is common in many other non-Western countries. The limitation of women, in varying degrees, to the sphere of home and family is common in Catholic, Protestant, Jewish, Hindu, Buddhist and Confucianist cultures. The most extreme structures of female segregation are symbolized by the *purdah,* a full-length veil or curtain used in some Muslim and Hindu societies for screening women from contact with all strange men.

During my family's travels in Pakistan, despite the gracious behavior of many Pakistanis we soon experienced a severe sense of cultural dislocation that was related to the treatment of women. The whole country seemed to have banned women from the public sphere. While staying in Islamabad I never saw the wife or daughters of our innkeeper, although we all lived in the same house. Hardly any women appeared on the streets or in public places. The ones we saw often wore veils from head to foot, with only their (heavily made-up) eyes showing. One day I spent an hour counting the men and women in the center of the capital city and arrived at the (unscientific) estimate that 90 percent of all people were male. I christened Pakistan "the land without women."

At times the segregation was humorous. One day I followed my wife and daughters onto a public bus, only to discover that I was surrounded by giggling, veiled women. Quickly I ascertained that the iron grating from ceiling to floor in the middle of the bus was intended to separate the women in the front of the bus from the men in the rear. I scrambled through a small hole in the partition to arrive with relief in the male section. Of course most buses do not have such a partition. Most vehicles are for males only, and modest women must wait for less frequent all-female or partitioned vehicles.

While the absence of women in public seemed tragic to me, it posed a more serious problem to Frances, Jen Marion and Rina. Relationships with other women were very hard to establish, as women in public did not talk to strangers. Women came out only for absolutely necessary tasks. Even the shopkeepers, market people and street sellers were all men. Unlike the men, women did not sit around in public discussing politics, religion and culture. No doubt there was a private sphere in which women related to other women and to trusted males, but as foreign tourists we had no access to that sphere.

Since Frances and our daughters could not talk to unrelated men, they were cut off from the normal, everyday interactions that make travel interesting. While I engaged in deep conversations about Islam and Christianity, Pakistani culture, Western imperialism, colonialism and even English literature with literate Pakistanis, my wife and daughters were isolated to their rooms or to silence unless accompanied by me.

While traveling we spent most of our time in public places. The whole structure of public life was tailored to the needs of men. Frances had to express her needs through me, or they went unmet. During a two-day bus trip into the mountains, the simple matter of going to the bathroom became a serious and embarrassing problem. Even though we were on a general public bus, Frances, Jen Marion and Rina were the only women passengers. The bus stopped at least five times a day for the mandatory Muslim prayer times. In addition to prayer, these were times when men wandered off to relieve themselves in the bushes. This was considerably more difficult for women in a semidesert terrain! The frustration reached its peak when one of our party, who had desperately waited for nightfall, tried to wander away from the party in the dark, only to be followed by a solicitous Pakistani man who wanted to make sure that she was "all right"! His concern may have been sincere, since we heard gunfire and the mountainous area included many fierce-looking armed Afghan refugees. But such concern only exacerbated the problem. Our whole family wanted to see the world. Pakistanis seemed to think that women should stay at home.[22]

Men are confronted with crosscultural gender segregation in a different way. Men are affected by abusive or unjust treatment of women who are close to them. They also face pressures to conform to the male gender-role expectations of the culture. Gender expectations for men range from the assumption that they will spend all their waking hours with male colleagues to the common practice of being served by women who may eat the leftovers only when the men are finished. These moral dilemmas are often the flip side of problems faced by women.

Sexual segregation enhances the freedom of men and curtails women's activities. One woman told me that as a male I would never understand the frustration of being a prisoner in my own home. Though a woman may need solitude— time away from her family or friends—she cannot go out at night. Understanding the cultural forms of discrimination may not lessen the sense of injustice experienced. In many countries, at night the world belongs to men.

A knowledgeable observer from the Middle East estimated that a high percentage of Western families in the Middle East left because of the wife's dissatisfaction.[23] He noted that the women's task of adjustment was much more difficult than that of men. While men found a respected place in the life of the community, their wives were confined to the home. Even women who saw their primary role as supporting their family found it very difficult. Few families lasted more than a year or two. Some returned home with serious emotional trauma.

One American woman apparently adapted well to life in Lebanon by abandoning her career and concentrating her attention on raising a family. Yet small everyday events left bitter memories. One day she walked through an outdoor market, traditionally a male preserve. There she spotted a Lebanese pastor who was a close friend of the family. When she called out to him in greeting, he averted his eyes and hurried past her. Later he apologized in private. He explained that it was not proper for him to greet a woman in public. But for his American friend, understanding the cultural conventions did not remove the sting of rejection.[24]

Paternalism and patriarchy. In many countries paternalism is the underlying rationale for sexual segregation. The restriction of women to the home does not necessarily imply that men consider them less intellectually competent. Women may even earn high educational and professional standing. But their achievements do not end paternalism. One Algerian woman is a respected ophthalmologist (eye specialist), with full freedom in her career. In the office, men obey her. But she lives with her brother-in-law, and in the private sphere she must obey him. She must return home by 7:00 p.m. every day and may not go out at night.

Paternalism assumes that men must protect women from a dangerous world. Women are sometimes considered not only weaker physically but also weaker morally and spiritually. Therefore patriarchy is necessary. Men are the rulers of women. In an ancient Chinese proverb, the common pattern is explicit: "A woman follows her father before marriage, her husband after marriage, and her son after her husband's death."[25] Similarly, the Laws of Manu (Hindu scriptures) state:

> Her father protects her in childhood; her husband protects her in youth; and her sons protect her in old age; a woman is never fit for independence. . . . Day and night women must be kept in dependence by the males of their families and if they attach themselves to sensual enjoyments, they must be kept under control. . . . Through their passion for men, through their mutable temper, through their natural heartlessness, they become disloyal toward their husbands, however carefully they may be guarded.[26]

A woman who lives in a paternalistic culture faces a series of crosscultural ethical problems. As a Western woman, she is offended by conventional behavior. First, she must interpret the meaning and intent of the behavior. A single American woman in Java learned that her boarding house had an 8:00 p.m. curfew. Before hearing this rule she had already moved in and paid a year's rent. In this case what appeared a major problem evaporated when she discovered all she had to do was ask for a key if she expected to be out late. If she forgot, there was always someone up who would let her in with no questions asked. So the rule was merely a nod to traditional conventions of proper behavior that were no longer followed.

Second, Western women abroad must sometimes adjust to conventional patterns of behavior. The woman in the above case soon discovered that her real dilemma was not the curfew but the fact that hardly any of her housemates ever *wanted* to be out later than 8:00 p.m.! She was forced to adjust to this reality. Going out alone at night was too emotionally draining. Another woman living in North Africa also chose to follow local conventions. When Algerian men asked her out for a date, she refused, even though she missed the experience of dating. She knew that in that culture "good" women did not go out alone with men, and she did not want to borrow trouble or ruin her reputation.

Third, a woman should know when she cannot conform to expected patterns of behavior and be prepared to pay the consequences. Far more subtle than curfews or veils are the assumptions of what constitutes modest feminine behavior in a paternalistic society. It has been noted that in America if a man is aggressive in his job he is called a "go-getter," while if a woman acts the same way she is considered pushy. A Thai professor told me that in Asia women are expected to act feminine. They should move slowly, use a soft voice, and be gentle in manner and delicate in dress. He commented that an ethics professor from Yale was not appreciated in Thailand because she was so aggressive. She got a reputation as pushy, argumentative, domineering and insensitive.

The Thai professor told of another American woman who was equally unconventional by Thai standards of femininity. Unlike her Yale compatriot, however, this woman won the respect and love of the Thais with whom she worked. The difference seemed to be that they could see that she really loved and respected them. Moreover, in spite of a busy schedule she took time to reach out to poor people. Her crass American ways (by Thai standards) may have been beyond her ability (or wish) to change. But it did not to matter to those who saw her integrity and love.

Sometimes the very qualities we consider desirable in an educated person are misunderstood in another context. They may not be things a woman is willing to change. A missionary in Ethiopia was informed that her behavior was scandalous for a woman. Her crime was that she looked people in the eye, walked "like a man" with her head up and expressed her opinions clearly. An African commented, "Only a prostitute would act as bold as she did!" Another American woman in Africa soon became known by the name "She Who Works like a Man."

In order to understand foreign assumptions of "proper" feminine behavior, it is helpful to see how Western behavior appears to others. The following story begins with the statement of an American teacher in Ethiopia who despaired of ever teaching her girls "simple human dignity."

"For three years, I've tried to get those dear little girls to behave like normal human beings, to have some pride, to hold up their heads, look me in the face, and answer a question in a voice I can hear without straining. They're so bright; they learn as fast as the children back home, but they're hopeless, absolutely hopeless. . . ."

The school day ended. Kebedetch walked stiffly home. She felt rigid, brave and frightened. Entering the *gojo* (small hut), Kebedetch was greeted warmly. Father asked the usual daily question: "What did you learn today?" Kebedetch threw back her head, looked her father in the eye, and proclaimed in a loud, clear voice, "Ethiopia is composed of twelve provinces plus the Federated State of Eritrea. . . ."

Momma and Poppa talked late that night. What had happened to Kebedetch? She was no longer behaving as a normal human being. "Did you notice how she threw back her head like a man?" asked Poppa; "what has happened to her shyness as a woman?" "And her voice," added Momma. "How happy I am that our parents were not present to hear a daughter of ours speak with the voice of a foreigner. She showed no modesty; she seemed to feel no pride." "If she were normal, she would be ashamed to raise her head like that, being a girl-child, and to speak so loud as that," Poppa added with a deep sigh. "Kebedetch has learned so much," said Momma. "She knows more than I, and this has given me great joy. But if her learnings are making of her a strange, ungentle, beast-like person, I do not want her to learn more; she is my only daughter." Poppa pondered. Finally he shook his head and spoke. . . . "The frightening behavior of hers tonight has convinced me. She has lost her sense of pride, lost her sense of shame, lost her dignity. She must never return to the school."[27]

The manner of feminine behavior considered proper in many paternalistic cultures stems from complex cultural values. To reduce it all to sexist or patriarchal motivations is too simple and easily becomes ethnocentric. Westerners often consider individualistic, democratic, open and socially mobile patterns of behavior as norms against which all other cultures are measured. But women in some cultures may be more "advanced" than we think.

The Power of Women in Cultural Perspective

Many Westerners believe women in the "Third World" lag far behind their more advanced Western counterparts in the struggle for equality. But the reality is much more complex. Different cultures measure the meaning of relationships in different ways. In Java the richest young businessman must speak with deference to the old woman who sells fruit in the marketplace, while her counterpart in the West is consigned to powerlessness in a retirement home. In Pakistan women cover their heads, but men are expected to treat them with great respect.

The meaning of power cannot be measured in economic or legal terms. The feminist movement in the West has significantly improved the economic and legal rights of women, but many women still suffer injustice and live on the edge of crisis.[28] The widely documented "feminization of poverty" in America indicates that the percentage of the poor who are women and children is steadily growing. Many are the victims of family breakdown and have no regular means of support.

Power and the family. The actual power of women in some overtly patriarchal societies compares favorably with women's power in Western society. While the existence of matriarchal societies is largely a myth, *matrifocal* societies are quite widespread. In a matrifocal society the mother plays the central role in the family. She is structurally, culturally and affectively central. In matrifocal societies both men and women have economic and ritual power.[29]

In Java, Indonesia, an island of over a hundred million people, there are many indications of a patriarchal society. Javanese women traditionally show deference to men. At a local celebration of Independence Day I attended a ceremonial dinner for the heads of a number of villages and neighborhoods, all of whom were men. The food was all prepared by wives who stayed in the back room except when serving the men. Since we were seated on mats on the floor, the women served us on their hands and knees, keeping their heads well down to ensure that they were lower than those of the seated men.

Nevertheless, official appearances are deceiving. In many cases the wives were the ones who ran the local affairs, managed all the finances and made all important decisions for the community. Family economics is also controlled by the women. Traditionally a Javanese man turns over all income to his wife to take care of. True to the rule that women's work is considered less important than men's work, traditional Javanese consider real power to be spiritual rather than economic. Managing finances is a worldly affair best left to women.

In her study of the family in a Central Javanese town, Hildred Geertz concluded that both the family and the kindred system are matrifocal. She writes,

> For the nuclear family to be matrifocal means that the woman has more authority, influence and responsibility than her husband, and at the same time receives more affection and loyalty. The concentration of both of these features on the female role leaves the male role relatively functionless in regard to the internal affairs of the nuclear family. In such circumstances it is unimportant whether or not the male role in the family is actually filled, or whether or not it is always occupied by the same man. For the kindred to be matrifocal means that the persons of greatest influence are women, and that the relationships of greatest solidarity are those between women or between persons related through women. Correspondingly, the relationships with the least amount of influence and solidarity are those between men or persons related through men.[30]

Although Indonesia is the largest Muslim country in the world, it is unlike Pakistan and many Middle Eastern countries, where women are segregated from the public sphere. In Indonesia most occupations are open to women. Most Indonesians are rural agricultural workers, and women not only work in the fields with men but also dominate the small-scale agricultural trade in indigenous markets. At least in traditional sectors of the society, men have the titles of authority, but it is questionable whether they have more power.

Women and modernization. Modernization does not necessarily bring increased power to women. An ideology of equality is not the same as actual equality. For example, the Indonesian government makes strong statements in support of gender equality and the participation of women in all areas of national development. But Indonesian integration in a global, capitalist economy may not be accompanied by improvements in the relative power of women.

During the process of modernization, a growth of materialism seems to accompany the rise in prosperity. Prestige is increasingly identified with wealth rather than other kinds of power. Formal political power, dominated by men, is wedded to economic interests, and large institutions take over more and more of the functions traditionally served by the family. A traditional ideology of female subservience is replaced by modern notions of equality, but the family as an institutional vehicle for influencing all areas of life becomes relatively weak. As a result, the relative position of women in public life becomes progressively more marginal.

Alongside its official message of the equality of the sexes, the government emphasizes the primary, natural function of women as mothers and wives. But modernization brings about a decline in the social and economic function of the family. Women are encouraged to participate in all areas of public life. But those who do are at a distinct disadvantage. In addition to the demands of a paid profession, they must also do all their traditional homemaking functions. Both the family and the profession are shortchanged, and women become very overworked.

This pattern is emerging in Indonesia but is visible all over the world.[31] It is particularly vivid in China. After two thousand years of patriarchal subjugation, the communist revolution brought guarantees of equal rights for women in the workplace. This included the requirement that they do an equal share of the work assigned to them. But equality in the workplace was not accompanied by equality in the home or family. Women are still expected to do all the housework. In a Chinese government survey taken in 1986 of fifteen hundred women scientists and technicians, 75 percent said that they were obliged to work a "double day."[32] Modern ideology may increase a women's options in the workplace while actually decreasing her power in society.

The ideology and appearance of patriarchy are not *necessarily* signs that women are powerless, and its removal does not necessarily lead to an increase in women's power. Even in societies where the public realm is reserved for men, women may be central figures who hold the community together. Nancy Tanner argues that this is the case in the American black family. "There is a clear conception of what a woman should be: a strong, resourceful mother with a structurally central position. Girls are socialized for such roles."[33] Black males may be "macho," but everyone depends on the mother.

Indirect channels of power. One of my students in Berkeley expressed anxiety about her role as a woman in the "macho" culture of Mexico. She was going to spend several months working with a church near Mexico City. When she returned she was not only relieved at the freedom she had experienced but overjoyed at the strength and leadership of the Mexican women with whom she worked—even though men occupied all the formal positions of leadership in the church. The women were not only "permitted" to work behind the scenes; the church depended on them to run things. They exercised power and responsibility. Women did the real ministry of the church.

Western women who have lived in most parts of the world report similar experiences. A North American woman confided that she had a much harder time coping with the condescending attitude of some male American evangelical leaders than she did with Muslim men and women in North Africa! North African women defer to the overt rule of men, but men depend on women in many areas of life, and the women know it.

After several years in Kenya, one woman found adjustment to life in the States much harder than her life in Kenya. She acknowledged that Kenyan sexism was infuriating. Kenyan women often dropped their own plans to wait on the needs of men. Sometimes men ignored her wishes simply because she was "only a woman." Kenyan women always served the men first and expected to eat what was left.

Nevertheless, she saw African women not as weak but as strong. African women had ways of adjusting to male demands. By the time the men had been served their food, the women were often too full to eat anyway, because they had tasted everything on the way! To her, the trivialization of American women living in the suburbs was much more demoralizing than the obvious patriarchy in Kenya.

Cultures that honor women. Some paternalistic cultures that segregate women to the spheres of home and family honor women more deeply than liberal societies that conceal misogynous practices behind a veneer of equality. I will never forget the shock I felt when a Pakistani man took me to task for the oppression of women in America. It seemed self-evident to me that Pakistan was a barbarous country that kept half its population in virtual prison. But he didn't see it that way.

He said that according to the Qur'an, women are the most precious treasure on earth. They are far more noble than men and should be guarded from oppression and defilement. He pointed out that many women hold high positions in Pakistan, including that of prime minister. Pakistani women excel as scientists, executives, doctors, professors and so on. Women are equal in ability to men and should pursue their educational and professional opportunities to as high a level as possible. But women are vulnerable to the crude and vulgar lust of men. "Therefore," he continued, "the veil that shields a woman from violating eyes is a mark of the honor we hold for women."

This gentle Muslim could not understand why we in the West permit such gross exploitation and degradation of women in our societies. The treatment of women as trivial sex objects in advertisements, movies and television, not to mention their dehumanization in pornography and prostitution, is criminal. His only daughter is attending university in the United States, and his greatest fear is for her safety in our lawless society!

This analysis of sexual oppression was a revelation to me. I realized there was some truth to his perspective and that I had made the characteristic American error of confusing freedom with equality and justice. Since women in America are relatively free to do and be whatever they like, while women in Pakistan are restricted and confined by veils and taboos, I thought it followed that America was the land of equality and justice while Pakistan was not only patriarchal but indeed feudal.

My knowledge of Pakistan is impressionistic and superficial. Certainly I am in no position to judge the position of women there relative to that of women in the United States. In Pakistan there are forms of restriction and oppression that I find appalling. But I must confess that the same applies to America. Muslim polemics against the West are sometimes extreme caricatures. Decadent Western society is portrayed as depriving women of family solidarity, marital faithfulness and economic security.[34] In contrast, Muslim women are portrayed as fully equal, protected by law and honored in the community. But women who excel in Pakistan do so against the odds. Illiteracy is high in Pakistan, and if you are a boy you are more than twice as likely to be sent to school than if you are a girl.[35] Women may be honored, but they are also chained. They may be a treasure, but they are a treasure owned by men.

A Muslim critique of Western oppression of women is important. Many Americans have a stereotyped, simplistic perception of the status of Muslim women. A Muslim magazine chose a kind of superwoman as its model woman. She has nine successful, highly educated children, teaches in the university, holds office in several Islamic institutions, lectures on Muslim teaching, is a board member of several schools, hospitals and orphanages, is fluent in Arabic and practices her religion with great devotion.[36] Perhaps this idealized picture of overwork explains why women's life expectancy in Muslim countries is so low![37]

The fact that women exercise power and are respected in patriarchal countries should neither surprise us nor lead to the conclusion that patriarchy is morally acceptable. A Chinese woman from Hong Kong commented that Asian women have more power than is apparent. Older women are especially powerful. Women cloak their power behind a gentle and meek exterior in order to protect male egos. But even in the male bastions of Korea and Japan, women have great influence.

But that does not excuse the injustice of more work for less pay, less prestige and less recognition. It does not excuse the lies of male superiority that conceal the many ways in which "women hold up half the sky."

The Crosscultural Task of Gender Justice

Biblical perspectives on power and evil. According to the biblical story of human relations, gender conflict began in the Garden of Eden. Man and woman were both created in the image of God and together given dominion over the earth. The primal sin that separated humanity from God also separated man and woman. The temptation was not to sex but rather to power. Both woman and man wanted to be like God.

The results of the curse in Genesis 3 led to male tendencies to exchange dominion over nature for domination over women. The flip side of male domination is a female tendency to exchange dominion over nature for dependence on men. As Mary Stewart Van Leeuwen puts it, the characteristic male sin is domination while women are tempted to sacrifice responsibility for sociability.[38] Both sexes are sinners who seek their own power in ways that are destructive of true human community.

The reconciliation brought about by the life, death and resurrection of Christ not only bridges the gap between human beings and God but also breaks down the power barriers between ethnic groups, between rich and poor, and between men and women. "There is no longer Jew nor Greek, there is no longer slave or free, there is no longer male and female; for all of you are one in Christ Jesus" (Gal 3:28). This ideal is worth struggling for today. It is the characteristic pattern of relationships in the coming kingdom of God.

From this brief sketch a number of biblical assumptions may be drawn about men and women in different cultures. First, men and women are equal in value, responsibility and overall ability in all human cultures. Their roles may differ for cultural, biological and contextual reasons. But every culture should honor a woman's equal dignity and provide her with opportunities to exercise her gifts and responsibilities.

The essential equality of men and women explains why even in cultures that systematically discriminate against women there is ample evidence that women still "hold up half the sky." That is, they are never mere adjuncts of men but are just as vital for the health (*shalom*) of society. Thus it is not surprising that women often exercise substantial power even in societies that conceal their importance behind an ideology of male superiority.

Second, men and women are equally sinners. Women are not morally superior to men, nor men to women. The characteristic patterns taken by the sins of men and women may be different, but they are mutually reinforcing. Male domination is enabled by female dependency. Both men and women seek power, although they often seek it in different ways.

The characteristic patterns of male sin have led to the creation of patriarchal structures in most societies. Even though neither sex is morally superior to the other, it is safe to say that women are more often victims of male oppression than vice versa. Of course in individual cases the converse may be true. Since women often exercise power in more hidden ways, individual men may be oppressed by individual women. But structurally men have greater power to oppress women than vice versa. And according to the values of the kingdom of God, oppression is not only bad for the oppressed, it is bad for the oppressor and for the entire community.

Third, male domination and female overdependency are evils to be opposed in anticipation of the kingdom of God. The curse in Genesis 3 describes a characteristic pattern of sinful gender relations in all cultures. It should not be taken as normative. Patriarchy ("your desire shall be for your husband, and he shall rule over you," Gen 3:16) is a curse rather than a pattern of creation. The curse included evils like pain in childbearing, toil and sweat in work, thorns and thistles in agriculture, and death itself. Patriarchal gender relations fall into the same class of evils to be combated.

This implies that gender justice is not an area of cultural relativity. Sinful domination and dependency are evident in all cultures, and in all cultures they are wrong. Just as racism, oppression of the poor and wanton destruction of creation are wrong in all cultures, so sexism is evil in all cultures.

An Indonesian once commented to me that feminism was unnecessary in Indonesia because men and women have equal rights and there is harmony between the sexes. I thought to myself, "Not likely." If it were true (and it's not), Indonesia would be the first such Eden since the original Garden.

Learning from women and men in a strange context. It is hard to distinguish sexism from other forms of power relations, even in one's own culture. Feminism is a powerful interpretive tool for understanding sexual discrimination. But its overuse is dangerous. If all complex situations in which women experience suffering in their relations with men are interpreted through the lens of sexism, men and women are polarized and other factors are obscured.

The first task of a stranger in a foreign culture is to listen and learn. Women and men who live within a culture know far more than a stranger about the ways in which they sin against each other. A white middle-class American feminist interpretation may radically misconstrue the situation of women in another culture. Black womanist critiques of white feminism in America demonstrate how different women interpret and prioritize their experience differently.

Categories and terms (including *feminism, sexism* and *patriarchy*) illuminate reality in one context but may obscure it in another. For example, one intelligent Chinese career woman rejected the idea that women in Asia are ruled by men and need more power. She said, "We women in Asia already have a great deal of power. What we need is for that power to be recognized and acknowledged."

Some Asian feminists disagree with this perspective and welcome the interpretive tools forged by feminists in the West. They argue that "sexism," "oppression," "patriarchy" and other Western interpretive concepts are very helpful in casting light on their experience. Feminist ideas have spread throughout the world. An intercultural dialogue on gender relations is very valuable. Within this conversation, the stranger is a partner in dialogue who may freshly see what is hidden to an insider.

Transforming unequal structures of power. A woman from the West cannot change social structures that have been formed over centuries. Inequality is not just a matter of individual patriarchal attitudes. Social, political and economic structures systematically control what classes of people have access to power. Change is usually gradual and painful. As we have seen, ideological and even legal improvements in the status of women do not necessarily improve the lot of women. Real equality requires both changed attitudes and new structures that provide women with access to recognized power.

Sometimes Western women create subtle changes in structural assumptions simply because their whole manner of life contradicts "the way it has always been done." Such women do not internalize the inferiority promoted by conventional practices. Thus the practices and the structures underlying them are called into question. A foreign woman can be a catalyst for change in part because the particular patterns of patriarchy in a strange culture are not a part of her already-formed identity.

An American who lived in Algeria related that a foreign context made it much easier to deal with sexism than at home. Since the culture was so foreign, it took a long time for her to internalize any feelings of inferiority that might otherwise be prompted by belittling male behavior. She was so different from the Algerian conception of a woman that the patriarchal behavior she experienced seemed amusing, quaint or at least unrelated to who she really was.

Cultural distancing from conventional gender behavior may be practiced by both sides. Western women are occasionally treated as a separate category from local women. Sometimes this can be hurtful. A missionary in Africa was asked to join a board of elders that was all male. She pointed out that the board did not usually elect women. The male elders replied, "Oh, but we do not think of you as a woman!" The woman was deeply hurt, as she felt they did not recognize her essential humanness as a woman. Nevertheless, she is a woman. Her non-conformity to stereotypes broke open a traditionally all-male structure.

Unconscious assumptions often reveal unequal structures of power. In many cultures (including American evangelicalism) it is assumed that if possible men should always take the public role. If there is a choice between a qualified man and a qualified woman, the invitation to lead will automatically go to the man. The choice may not imply disrespect for the woman. But male leaders are more afraid of offending the man if they choose the woman, especially if the woman is his wife. Networks of male friendship also make male candidates more real to their associates.

Men in a foreign context can challenge this pattern by refusing invitations to lead and suggesting equally qualified women in their place.[39] This may appear costly, but it is necessary if women are to break into all-male circles of influence. A Christian executive suggested to me that worldly leaders step on a rival in the climb to the top. Humanistic leaders help another along. But Christian leaders step down in order to give room to the other.

Women sojourners can also bring change by confronting discrimination in a culturally sensitive manner. Often male colleagues are unaware that their unconscious assumptions of gender roles are hurtful. In the context of a positive relationship, one woman frankly discussed with her director her needs for respect and encouragement. Her sensitive openness cleared the air and opened the way for a healthier partnership.

In some cultures an unmarried older Western woman, or even a wife without children, may have difficulty finding entrance or acceptance. In many groups a woman's status takes a huge leap at the birth of her first child. A mother from the West may be enfolded into the community because her children form a natural bridge to the other women. An unmarried woman lacks access to the natural structures of power located in family institutions.

In other contexts a single older woman may find it easier to break out of gender stereotypes because she is not in the normal category of wife and mother. She is neither an adjunct to her husband nor "the mother of José." If she has valued skills, she may be regarded as an individual in her own right.

Many cultures have a special category for women who are strong leaders. The recorded history of most cultures includes accounts of strong women who transcended stereotyped gender roles. Sometimes the most rigidly patriarchal cultures made room for outstanding women leaders. From Queen Victoria, who ruled over the largest empire in history, to Cory Aquino, who mobilized a nation against impossible odds, there have been women who inspired the loyalty of even the most sexist and macho males.

Unfortunately, the exceptional woman who transcends all cultural and social barriers does not often pave the way for her more ordinary sisters. The normal patriarchal structures remain in place. Nevertheless, a foreign woman who refuses to follow the expectations of a paternalistic male leadership may be tolerated by those who value her presence. This is all the more true if behind her "unfeminine" manners can be seen a person of humble integrity who truly cares about the people she serves.

Some of the most effective crosscultural women I have known were unconventional personalities of great moral character. One of them, Pauline Hamilton, did not conform to any culture's stereotype of a missionary or a woman. She was short and overweight, smoked a pipe for her asthma, slept during the day, stayed up all night and managed to change the lives (and social structures) of hundreds of gang members throughout Taiwan.[40] Perhaps because she *was* a woman, she dared many things that no man had ever tried.

Most of us are not larger-than-life personalities who can change the world by sheer force of character. Nevertheless, the example of such people is instructive. Virtue and character are more important than conformity to conventional cultural expectations. Someone whose life is a True Story can transform the unequal structures of power.

Recognizing and empowering women. Effective crosscultural Christians recognize and empower others. Patriarchal assumptions repress the abilities of half the human family. Women learn they can succeed only within certain narrow boundaries. Someone from outside a culture can often recognize the special gifts of women who play second fiddle to less talented men. These women need the catalyst of an example. Everyone, regardless of sex, needs the support of people who believe in them.

Foreign women who adapt sensitively to a patriarchal context are pioneers who swim against the stream without being defeated. By their example they give hope to gifted women who may play a crucial role in the life of their church and nation. By encouraging women from a different ethnic community to excel, they participate in a worldwide movement for justice.

Men also must recognize and empower women. In some cases Western men can open or close the doors of opportunity for women in the Two-Thirds World. The recognition of women by respected men, whether in a business, an urban development project, a hospital, a school or a church, may determine the future of a woman, and of the many others who will follow her.

Encouraging women within a strange social structure requires delicacy and tact. An American teacher in a Muslim country explained that she was cautious about radicalizing women beyond what they could handle. She felt it was crucial not to push a person beyond his or her ability to face the consequences of the new ideas or actions. Within a strict Muslim context, Western ideas of liberation could easily lead to rejection, shame, divorce or even death.

This perceptive teacher was also careful about her relation to the men and institutions that trusted her. When the director of her department suggested that she spend regular times with his wife, she was grateful for the opportunity and did not abuse his trust in her. The wife was a strict, conservative Muslim in a very traditional marriage. In honoring the husband's trust, the teacher could not directly talk to his wife about the role of women in a conservative Muslim marriage. If she had done so, the woman might have moved out! Yet the teacher's long visits did provide the wife with a radical example of a different way of being a woman.

On the other hand, when other Muslim women took the initiative to confide in this teacher their frustrations and hopes, she tended to share their anger. She saw the world through their eyes and shared with them her own hopes and dreams. Thus she walked a tightrope between respecting the religious and social world in which she was a visitor and letting in the light of the gospel for those who had eyes to see and ears to hear. Certainly her most effective communication to Muslim women was through her example and empathy for those who became her friends.

Partnership in a movement for gender justice and peace. We are all the products of our culture and time. Therefore we need one another, the community of faith, the Bible and the Holy Spirit if we are to understand ourselves. No one culture can be said to have achieved justice and peace between the sexes. Therefore no one culture can be held up as the model for all others. The cultural oppression of women is well captured by Paulo Freire's definition of oppression in general. He writes,

> Any situation in which "A" objectively exploits "B" or hinders [the] pursuit of self-affirmation as a responsible person is one of oppression. Such a situation in itself constitutes violence, even when sweetened by false generosity, because it interferes with [a person's] ontological and historical vocation to be more fully human.[41]

Even a minimal and negative definition of oppression such as this points to the existence of gender injustice wherever men and women live together. The biblical concept of *shalom,* however, reveals a positive ideal for gender relations. Augustine defines *shalom* as "the perfectly ordered, harmonious enjoyment of God and one another in God."[42] This is an ideal for all people in all cultures. Women and men from all cultures need one another in our imperfect search for *shalom.*

The ancient rift between Adam and Eve continues to be played out all over the world. The healing of this rift is one of the great promises of the coming kingdom of God. In the meantime, the work of the kingdom is crosscultural. Each culture has its own perverse methods of encouraging dominance in men and subservience in women. Each culture has also invented creative ways in which women transcend cultural discrimination. In each culture there are men and women who live in relative peace and justice with one another. The task for Christians in a strange culture is not to solve all the problems of that culture. Rather, it is to see what God is already doing. By humble listening we may be honored to participate with local women and men who are seeking the kingdom.

TEN

THE UNITY
OF PERSONAL AND
SOCIAL ETHICS

C hapter eight suggested that Christianity is not only a set of beliefs and practices but also a social project. Chapter nine examined that project in relation to gender conflict in a crosscultural context. This concluding chapter considers how a crosscultural Christian can contribute to that project in a strange community. Grandly stated, the Christian social project is the kingdom of God. This chapter explores ways in which personal behavior contributes to the kingdom.

Personal Behavior and the Social Project of Christianity

Anyone who enters a new community makes a social and political impact. Strangers make a bigger than usual impact because of their strangeness. Some of their impact is good and some is bad. Even the very best of early missionaries reinforced the structures of colonialism by their behavior. Uncritical identification with the interests and values of their own country led them to provide moral and sometimes physical support to Western imperialism.

Similar charges are still levied today against white middle-class members of business, development and mission organizations who enter ethnic or Two-Thirds World communities with notoriously mixed motives. Strangers are often perceived in terms of their social, educational and class position, their race, their economic power and their lifestyle choices. These factors provide the medium of their message.

Very "personal" issues of lifestyle and very "private" matters of finance, family relations and personal integrity affect the social impact of strangers in a new culture. Personal actions have social consequences because everything we do is linked with other people's lives. I will not play golf in Indonesia, not because there is anything wrong with golf but because many golf courses in Indonesia are on rich land that was taken from poor farmers who had farmed it for centuries. I didn't steal the land, but if I use it I identify with the rich people who did. By playing on the farmers' land, I enrich their oppressors. My personal leisure time cannot be divorced from the economic structure of my context.

This chapter examines the dynamics of responsible Christian life in the midst of suffering and injustice by means of a story. An American couple living in Africa fought a costly war against evil that was personal, structural and spiritual. Evil men created structures of social, physical and spiritual oppression. This couple could not coexist with this evil for one simple reason: they are Christians. They were not professional "political activists," but their compassion for suffering people led them to political action.

Case Study: A Christian Response to Torture

Linda Adams is an American who lived in a town in "Mabuk," West Africa.[1] Her husband, Frank, was an engineer who worked for a local airline. They lived in a nice part of town, and their neighbor to the north was the Internal Police Department (IPD, or secret police). The head of the IPD was a large, powerful man named Kofi who often traveled with Frank. Kofi was a tribal "brother" to the president of the country and reputedly close to him. People said he practiced witchcraft. He had a frightening reputation.

Kofi and other leaders of the IPD frequently dropped in at the Adams house to ask for small favors or just hang around. The second in command came for pointers on how to play the guitar. Kofi liked to joke about how hard Linda worked and about their relatively simple lifestyle.

Men frequently came to Linda's house, sometimes directly from the IPD, to sell smuggled items, gold or even hashish. Linda and her husband repeatedly refused to buy. After this had happened many times, Linda practically threw one insistent seller of hashish out of the house. She suspected a setup.

Occasionally IPD officials called in the Adamses' workers and questioned them about the Adamses' activities. Linda felt they were just trying to show who was in control. She told the workers not to worry but just tell the truth.

After about four years the trouble began. Linda writes,

I began to hear screams coming from the secret police offices, especially at night. We had electricity only three hours in the evening and during this time I would hear screams as the lights would flicker. Frank was often gone for days and even as much as two weeks at a time and he could not believe that I was hearing people tortured. I doubted my own senses and discreetly asked a neighbor who was married to a Mabukian government official if she was hearing these noises. She looked at me very long and said, "Yes, sometimes there are bad things in this country." "Does your husband know?" I asked her. "One does well to pretend not to hear," she replied.

I prayed about it and asked our Bible-study group to pray about it. In general they did not seem to want to know about this but promised they would pray.

The screams became worse and now there was the sound of moaning and screaming, sometimes even in the day. Then I saw IPD men beating an old man on the steps. They beat him almost senseless in broad daylight. I started to go over and try to intervene. The gardener stopped me, "Please Madame, it won't help and you will get hurt."

When Frank returned from his trip I told him I could not live there and continue to do nothing. The very next day he saw them beating an old man on his bare feet. One of the men involved was the third in command, [whom we called] "Dark Glasses." Frank went over and asked to speak to Kofi. Kofi laughed and assured him the man being beaten was a thief and, "in this country, unlike yours, we must sometimes resort to distasteful measures." When we told the workers this explanation they snorted, "That's a lie, they wanted to extort money from him and he refused."

Not long after this the IPD soldiers began to harass our night guard and on two occasions fined him for not having certain papers. Our gardener also complained of harassment. The screams began anew and got worse until it was almost a daily happening. Then one night I heard a woman screaming against our fence. The IPD were raping her. I ran out of the house and threatened the soldiers with everything I could think of. They waved a rifle at me and told me to mind my own business. Frank was on a trip and the night guard, an elderly man, ran after me. He begged me to come back into the house. He was very upset about the woman but begged me, "Madame, there is nothing you can do. Please, you are my responsibility." He was very frightened.

When Frank returned I told him the story and we sat down to pray and think what we should do. It was now obvious that none of our Western friends were willing to get involved. To involve any of our regular African workers or friends would be very dangerous to them and we did not have the right to do that.

Frank went to our boss, an African Christian man living in another town. He is a man of some status and wealth. He said we could move (we were living in one of his homes); he could build a very high, soundproof fence around our present house; or we could press the matter and he would do what he could to help us. After prayer we chose the latter. Really we felt we had no choice.

Our boss began to feel out the matter. He found that we were giving an accurate picture of the conditions but ran into a dead end. He was not big enough. Frank often did repairs for the Governor of the province and decided to take a chance and tell him. The Governor listened and seemed interested and concerned. He promised to do something.

In the meantime our boss suggested we contact the Catholic Bishop who had great prestige and often used the airline. Most of the government officials, including the IPD officials, are Catholic and might listen to the Bishop.

Frank contacted the Bishop, an imposing man in purple silk with a huge ring on his finger that everybody kissed. He was very receptive, asked intelligent questions, and promised he would do all in his power to stop the torture.

And it stopped. The IPD still treated people roughly but the screams and beatings stopped and the neighborhood settled down to its usual hum.

A few months later Frank and I stepped innocently into the middle of an IPD action while strolling near our home. We were arrested. "Dark Glasses" held a gun to our heads and told us he could kill us any time he liked. After taking us to IPD headquarters he released me. Frank was tortured for a short time, threatened with the gun again and thrown into the detention room.

During the course of the threats "Dark Glasses" said, "You drive right by me in your car and I eat your dust but I can kill you any time I like."

I got the immediate help of our boss and after several hours of hassle, he was able to get Frank released. We were under house arrest for some weeks and gradually everything returned to normal. Kofi would wave and joke and call me "the woman who works like a man" and "sister." The second in command, who had not been present during our trouble, disappeared. Some said he had moved, others that he had had a mental breakdown.

During the time of our troubles one single missionary friend and several Mabukian Christians came by to "sit with us," as they say. Other missionary friends said they couldn't afford to get mixed up with the IPD or their work would come to an end. One Christian Canadian in our Bible study felt that we had asked for trouble by meddling in things that didn't concern us and caused danger to our friends. I felt shamed somehow as though we had committed some big social *faux pas* but I didn't know what it was.

Some months later while driving the wife of a worker to a mission hospital, I saw "Dark Glasses" trudging down the road towards the hospital. I knew I should pick him up, but I did not do it. Instead I wished that he would find he had cancer and that I could see his eyes, without the sunglasses, when he heard the news. . . .

There is no question that I should have picked up "Dark Glasses" on the way to the hospital (Luke 6:27-28). Also my hatred of him was an act akin to his mistreatment of other human beings. Although I probably injured only myself, it is possible I did him a greater wrong than I know.

In this story most people who knew of the torture avoided doing anything about it. Whether Christian or non-Christian, most felt it was none of their business. Fear was no doubt a major factor. Involvement was costly. Not only could involvement put their own lives at risk, but it also threatened other values. The government could terminate mission work, national Christians might "disappear," friends and family could be hurt.

Like good Christians in Germany, who looked the other way when Nazis arrested their Jewish neighbors, many people find it easier to ignore social problems that do not directly affect them. Unless their own daughter or spouse is being tortured, it's best to "pretend not to hear."

Costly action for social justice is not just dangerous but also lonely. The Adamses felt alienated from friends who distanced themselves from their dangerous action. Prayer by friends unwilling to help is cheap. Those who stood with them were unlikely allies: household workers, a Catholic bishop, a distant colleague, one single missionary and African Christians who came to "sit with them." All but one were Africans who had more to fear than their Western friends.

Linda and Frank's wisdom and courage are instructive for Christians who work for justice. In order to do what they did, they had to be certain kinds of people first. The primary virtues of faith, hope and love (1 Cor 13) gave definition to their lives. They did not know it, but they were ready to be used by God because the story they were living gave them "no other choice." Someone else would have just moved out or, more likely, never have gone to Mabuk.

The option of building a soundproof wall around the house is a parable of our times. The cries of the oppressed assault us. We all find ways to stop our ears. We turn off the TV, close the book, look the other way, pass by on the other side. We must, to preserve our sanity. Linda and Frank did not. Against the pleading of an elderly night watchman, Linda went into the garden and wept drops of blood. There was "nothing she could do," but she did it anyway.

The Story as a Paradigm for Christian Social Involvement

This is a true story, not just because it really happened but in the sense that it tells the truth about life in the real world. It tells the truth about good and evil, sin and redemption, death and resurrection. Linda's account is truer than the nightly news. There are many ambiguities in her story, because that is the way life is. But hers is a gospel story. In it we see the love and suffering of Christ for a lost world.

The sequence and structure of events in this story are very important. The story provides a paradigm with which to interpret many aspects of the search for justice in a crosscultural context. The following twenty points use this story as a framework for unpacking essential elements in Christian social and personal ethics.

1. *Social location and commitment.* Linda and Frank chose to live in "Mabuk" with the express purpose of serving the people as Christians. Social location and commitment to the people are basic to the story. None of this would have happened if they had stayed in an American suburb and worked in a "normal" job appropriate to their education. While they did not consciously choose to live with the poor, their neighbors turned out to be powerless victims in a house of

torture. One response would have been to move. But they chose to stay. The Adamses did not have answers or an ideology to solve the problems of the world. But they lived close to the questions.

People who live close to the poor experience their suffering. Their experience of others' suffering is painful. Pain is a powerful stimulus to action, not just for the sake of the other but also to remove the cause of one's own suffering. Personal experience of others' oppression is a far greater stimulus to action than the evening news. Politically correct ideas or a theology of liberation may hinder real compassion if a person's social location is premised on living as comfortably as possible. Proximity to poverty makes direct action for justice possible and necessary.

In a course on crosscultural ethics one of my students was a conservative missionary who had spent many years in Africa. She was an independent thinker and refused to be swayed by my emphasis on social justice. Throughout the course she aggressively argued that verbal evangelism was primary. Social ethics was not an integral part of the gospel, she said, but an optional byproduct. I thought her ideas were simplistic, but as the course progressed I admired her more and more.

She had spent her whole life living with the poor and working for their welfare. For many years she had lived in a grass hut with a mud floor. She gave away her possessions, helped the people obtain clean water, organized them to resist government attempts to take their land, taught them to read and affirmed their pride in their traditional culture. She had not gone to Africa to do these things, but she loved the people. The Christian social project was part of who she was, irrespective of her theology. Her location among poor people made her actions possible and necessary.

A Christian Marxist was in the same course. He was passionately concerned for justice. He had a comfortable apartment in a prosperous community and worked for the Bank of America. He was still young, so it is impossible to judge the trajectory of his life. But it is safe to guess that unless he changes his social location, his rhetoric will fade into a more self-justifying ideology.

The first three rules of real estate are said to be "location, location, location." Perhaps these should also be the first three words of the Christian social project.[2] One need not cross national borders to be located among neighbors who need the light of God's justice and love. Just get out of the suburbs and take a stroll downtown. The first step for anyone concerned about social justice may be to move house.

2. Integrity in everyday life. The Adamses' integrity during the four years prior to the crisis provided the foundation for their action. They lived in relatively simple comfort and were hospitable to whoever came to their door. They practiced regular spiritual disciplines and lived transparently. In his business Frank was known for his honesty, precision and incorruptibility. Both of them worked hard and served with humility. They refused to profit from minor acts of injustice (smuggling). If they had compromised with questionable activities in everyday life, they would have been vulnerable to blackmail. Their honesty allowed them to live openly and without fear.

The Adamses are not professional social activists, but their lives are focused on the kingdom. Prayer was not cheap for them but an urgent necessity in time of crisis. Prayer and Bible study were regular practices that shaped their experience. Their marriage evidenced love, mutual respect and fidelity. This is not to say they were perfect saints. My impression is that they are both stubborn, strong-willed people.

Activism for justice cannot be isolated from the fabric of life. The Christian social project is not something to seek in leisure time, after we come home from work, or when a crisis occurs. It is rooted in a lifestyle that enfleshes the values of the kingdom. Everyday life demonstrates the substance of our faith. A crisis just dramatizes or magnifies what we're already made of. If we ever do something really *good,* it's probably the fruit of what we do every day—the "habits of the heart."

3. Getting at the truth through research and social analysis. When the crisis occurred, Linda made sure of the facts. She neither trusted her own immediate perceptions nor avoided ugly realities, but checked her suspicions with several different sources. Even though her husband initially doubted the substance of her fears, Linda set out to find independent confirmations of the truth. Throughout this story Linda and Frank continued to build an ever-stronger case against the practices next door.

This is very wise. Especially in a strange context, fears can blow things out of proportion. In Indonesia we often hear terrible screams and moaning at night. But we just grin (or scowl) and bear it. The humanlike sounds let us know that the alley cats are mating again!

In this case, as the empirical evidence mounted the facts became clear, grotesque and insistent. Often social injustice is more hidden or ambiguous. A human tendency is to half know and half not want to know what is really going on.

Once we suspected that Lucy, a very bright little girl from a poor neighborhood near us, was being abused by her parents. She was always very dirty, dressed in rags, and twice she appeared at our door with scrapes on her face and body. While cleaning the cuts, Frances asked how she got hurt. Both she and her friends appeared very embarrassed by this question as well as by any reference to Lucy's parents. It seemed odd.

I basically ignored the situation. I probably didn't want to know. But Frances went to visit Lucy's home. In the hovel where the little girl lived, Frances met her parents and discovered that they are both blind. They have no running water, electricity or plumbing, and no regular source of income. They make their living by begging. Suddenly Lucy's unkempt appearance and the embarrassment the girls exhibited at the mention of her parents were explainable.

Lucy is a scrappy, rebellious little kid, and her wounds are likely the result of fights with other rough children. Since she denies any mistreatment, it seems quite likely that she is not abused. Her condition can be explained by other factors. At least we know that her parents send her to school and are trying to cope with a very difficult reality. We can help her a little, but her suffering is primarily rooted in structures of poverty, not individual malice.

Sometimes the reality of injustice can be discovered only through social scientific research. When our first daughter was born in Singapore (1972), Frances had to insist on breastfeeding her. White-coated representatives of the Nestlé Corporation gave her free samples of baby formula and told her she could not and should not breastfeed her baby. Formula feeding was the "modern" way. Nurses refused to wake her for the night feeding. If she had not been insistent, by the time she left the hospital her milk would have begun to dry up and she would have had to buy formula.

Since we knew breast milk is best, we thought this was just an isolated occurrence of misguided ignorance. But others looked more deeply into the facts and discovered our experience was a worldwide phenomenon. The Nestlé Corporation was pushing its products on poor and uneducated women all over the world. Research showed that child mortality rose dramatically in poor contexts where Nestlé was successful. Poor mothers watered down the formula to save money and used unsafe water supplies. The tragedy is that it was so unnecessary. Medical research shows that mother's milk is healthier, even in the best of conditions, let alone in conditions of poverty.

The result of this research was a worldwide boycott of Nestlé products which finally succeeded in pressuring the corporation to give up its aggressive "marketing" tactics and conform to UNESCO guidelines. None of this could have happened if there were not people who, like Linda, checked the facts. Research was needed to discover a structured economic practice that was directly causing the death of thousands of infants.

Ethics needs social science to find out the facts and interpret the moral questions that arise from them. Social science can never be completely value-free, because the moral commitments (or lack thereof) of the researcher influence the direction of the investigation. Linda could have investigated soundproofing when she was bothered by noises. Instead she investigated the causes. The facts are interpreted and valued in relation to the commitments of the investigator. The sounds next door were not just facts to Linda. She evaluated them through the lens of her commitment to the Mabukian people.

A further step in the relation between ethics and social science is social analysis. According to Joe Holland and Peter Henriot, "Social analysis is the effort to obtain a more complete picture of a social situation by exploring its historical and structural relationships."[3] Social analysis in this situation would ask questions like, How did the IPD come into being and why? What is its relation to other structures of power, such as the president, the courts, the legislature, the regular police, the military, the business community, religious institutions, nongovernmental organizations, the international community, organized crime and racial or tribal groups? Are there any laws to which it must conform—in theory or in practice? Who benefits from its activities? What kind of people are arrested by the IPD and why? What kinds of people work for the IPD and why? Why do they torture people? What is the IPD's source of funding? What are its positive functions? Does it have any powerful enemies? Are there any democratic structures capable of challenging its activities? Where is it vulnerable?

If Linda and Frank, or any other group, wanted to make a permanent impact on the practices of the IPD, these are the kind of questions they would need to ask. They would need to do social analysis. Frank and Linda's protest was apparently effective in curbing the practices of the secret police. But there is no guarantee that the torture did not just move to another location or go underground. The IPD could also build soundproof walls.

4. *Community and racism.* When sufficient evidence was gathered, Linda shared everything with Frank. Together they sought strength and wisdom in prayer and with a few close friends. The community they initially depended on

proved less helpful than the one that gathered around them later. But even a weak community is better than none. The small group promised to pray for them and provided an outlet for their thoughts and feelings.

These Western friends did not really want to hear about torture next door and later deserted Frank and Linda. This should not surprise us too much. The twelve apostles did the same to Jesus. Later they came back, and most were martyred for their faith. We should not judge too harshly those who cannot go the distance. People are at different stages of faith. All of us will lack courage and fail our friends sometimes.

Nevertheless, it is helpful to speculate about a likely cause of the friends' faintheartedness: racism. The written account of this story is too sparse to allow us to know for sure, but racism is a common reality in affluent white communities. If white people were being tortured by blacks in the house next door, it is unlikely that the white Bible study group would just want to "mind their own business." They might feel their kinship with the raped and battered and find courage to go to their defense. If the tortured happened to be white missionaries, it's hard to imagine the white community pretending not to hear.

Racism shuts out compassion by drawing a sharp line between our own humanity and that of another race. In contexts where whites are rich, educated and powerful while those who suffer oppression are black, poor, uneducated and powerless, racism lies at the door. Racism is a cancer that undermines a community's ability to love its neighbors. Racism also becomes a social location. It puts a great gulf between "us and them," whatever the physical geography.

There is a social structure to racism. A white community of privilege needs the black elite in an African country to defend the social order. The masses of poor are a threat to the wealthy whites. Repression prevents rebellion that could threaten the security of the status quo. That does not mean the whites approve of torture. But if it occurs, it is better not to know. In any case, it can be tolerated as long as it is only blacks who suffer. The apparatus of repression has to be strong in an unjust society. It is dangerous to threaten it, not only because it could turn its instruments on the whites but also because it defends a social order favorable to the whites.

A similar structure of racism underlies police brutality toward people of color in North American cities. Blacks and other people of color can be safely brutalized, both because they are relatively powerless and because the white majority does not challenge the practice. Whites just don't want to know about it. The apparatus of repression (police) is necessary to protect public order. As long as whites are not assaulted by the police, "certain excesses" are tolerated for the sake of security. Fear of crime and media that glorify violence against the "bad guys" reinforce the structure. "Dirty Harry" is a hero.

Racism also structures the U.S. prison system. America incarcerates a higher percentage of its own population than any other country in the world, except South Africa. But the prison population does not match demographics. Most prisoners are nonwhite. It is likely that crime occurs in fairly even proportions in every racial group and economic stratum. But white-collar crime, white-people crime and economic crime by people with power goes unpunished. It's easier to lock up an angry black teenager who threatens the public order.[4]

White missionaries, "tentmakers" and Christians in any nonwhite community are not immune from racism. Even if they came for "ministry," paternalistic racism is quite compatible with a desire to serve. Sometimes effective Christians are aware of their racism and fight a lifelong battle against it. In any case, no matter how subtle, racism is a deadly foe of the kingdom of God. In Christ there are no Jews or Greeks, slaves or free. The dividing wall has been broken down. Those who try to rebuild it are enemies of justice.

The community that finally came alongside the Adamses in their need was largely black. Blacks could appreciate the risk the Adamses took because they could identify with the victims in the house of torture. They or their families might easily be next. The black Christians who confronted the apparatus of repression or "came to sit" with the Adamses were unencumbered with racism. Thus they were free to love both their white neighbors and the victims of torture.

Those who live in a strange culture must find their own balance between meeting valid needs through a culturally similar support group and finding community with the local people. It is easier to relate deeply to people from the same cultural background, especially if there is a language barrier with the foreign culture. But white people can easily become "ghettoized" and "liminoid," or alienated from the dominant culture. Racism is a constant danger. As Frank and Linda discovered, closeness to the local community is usually a better route to evangelism and social justice than the comfort of a Western subculture.

5. *Prayer and the struggle against evil.* When Linda and Frank gathered with their friends, the first thing they did was pray. Prayer is a practice of dependence. Prayer is an acknowledgment of our own weakness.

No one can solve the major social problems of our day. As in this situation, the powers arrayed against those who oppose oppression seem far too strong to fight. Prayer clarified to Linda and Frank that God is higher in power and authority than the secret police. Insofar as the Adamses recognized in prayer that their lives were in God's hands, they were freed from the power of the IPD.

Prayer was a lifeline for the Adamses because it was a part of their struggle against evil. Those Christians who promised to pray but refused to struggle in a real social context were alienated from true prayer. Prayer without involvement is like faith without works. It's dead (Jas 2:17). True prayer is not prior to or separate from struggle against evil, it's part of the struggle. Prayer is another form of action.

The spiritual world is not separated from the empirical world of evil. Spiritual good and evil are incarnated in real historical events. In prayer we struggle against evil in ourselves and in the world. If we pray as a substitute for acting to oppose what is evil, we have ceased to struggle and our prayer is hollow. Such prayer is not only useless, it is an abomination to God. It is a pious mask for evil (Is 1:11-17).

I do not mean that we should cease to pray when we are powerless to act. Sometimes prayer is the only way we can struggle against evil. But prayer may be part of the evil if it is a religious form of disobedience to God.[5]

In prayer Linda and Frank sought wisdom, strength, safety and power from God. They also prayed for the victims and asked God to intervene on their behalf. In prayer their will was united with God's to oppose the powers of oppression. Social action often involves confrontation with "principalities and powers." Prayer is an essential part of this confrontation on a spiritual level.

In many Two-Thirds World countries, most people, whether or not they are Christians, assume the existence of demonic power. The likelihood that Kofi practiced witchcraft underlines the probability that those who tortured their victims were influenced by the demonic. The demonic may be conceptualized as personal evil beings or as social structures that incarnate an evil will.[6] In either case, evil is a force greater than the perversity of an individual person or group. It is a spiritual power that must be opposed spiritually.

If Paul is to be believed, our struggle against evil is always a spiritual battle (Eph 6:12). Prayer is not just a psychological practice or a form of communication with God. It is a weapon and a defense against evil. Linda and Frank needed God's strength and protection if they were to confront the principalities and powers next door. Prayer is an integral part of the Christian social project.

6. *Confronting the problem directly.* When no doubt remained, Frank went straight to the source of the violence to complain. The director of the secret police responded with jokes and lies. This is a typical response to confrontation and exposure of evil.

Sometimes confrontation is enough to stop an unjust practice, even if it is not acknowledged. Those who deny the problem are anxious not to get caught again. In this case the secret police (with the possible exception of the second in command) were invulnerable to shame and addicted to violence.

Directly confronting those responsible for injustice may be the first step in bringing pressure against them. It lets them know that their deeds are noticed and opposed. It also gives them a chance to explain or justify facets of the problem that you have not seen. Usually there's more than one side to an issue.

When student activists opposed the building of a new university campus on the shores of an environmentally threatened lake, they went straight to confront the president of the university. He showed them careful research that suggested that irrigation and farming practices around the lake were far more damaging to the lake than the campus. A political battle had been waged for the use of the land, and the university had narrowly won, partly because it was less damaging to the environment than the other options. The students thought a park around the lake was a better solution, but they went home from the meeting with a lot to ponder about lesser evils in an imperfect world.

Face-to-face confrontation may be more or less effective depending on the cultural context (see chapter five). In some cases sending an intermediary is more effective. But face-to-face encounter is always stark. It puts the person on the spot and may make him lose face. The results are unpredictable. Personal confrontation is an act of courage. It allows the guilty party to plan measures and mobilize resources to destroy or neutralize the confronter. Whether confrontation is right, wise or justified depends on the situation.

A foreigner is sometimes better situated to confront evil in this way than a local citizen. A foreigner cannot "disappear" without an international incident. But a white stranger is vulnerable in other ways. He or she may be resented as a neocolonialist meddler who has no right to criticize. The white person represents the hated colonialists—white racists who exploited and oppressed the people for hundreds of years. What right do white guests have to criticize their hosts? (See chapter six.) White people with powerful enemies may soon find themselves without a visa.

Sensitivity to criticism from former colonial powers runs very deep and can prompt drastic responses. Not long ago Holland threatened to withhold aid to Indonesia in protest over human-rights abuses in East Timor, an island ruled by Indonesia. Holland was the chair of a group of nations that provided substantial funds for Indonesian development. Indonesia responded by unilaterally rejecting all future aid from Holland and dissolving the group Holland chaired. Many Indonesians, including some human-rights activists, cheered the decision. Even if they don't like what their own government does, Indonesians hate criticism and pressure from their former colonial masters.

7. *Harassment, intimidation and hope.* The immediate result of Frank's open complaint against the IPD was harassment of the least powerful in his household, the workers. Soon there was also a flagrant increase in violent oppression. The screams came to be heard daily. This was a clear message meant to intimidate the Adamses. Kofi was rejecting any curb on the activities of the IPD. He was saying, "If you oppose me, you'll be sorry. And it won't do any good anyway."

Action for social justice often seems futile and may even make things worse in the short term. Even in the long term the situation may deteriorate. The Adamses' deeds were not guaranteed success. They were not premised on effectiveness. Usually action intended to bring about justice must be carefully planned to bring about the most good for the most people. Heroic moral deeds that just make the situation worse are usually unwise no matter how good the motives. We must be "wise as serpents and gentle as doves."

But sometimes we have no choice. As in the case of Linda and Frank, if the situation is morally intolerable it should not be physically tolerated.[7] Resisting gross injustice against all odds is a moral duty that cannot be escaped. Some actions are optional and dependent on their probability of producing positive results. But an ethic of calculation cannot be the last word. Hope for the kingdom of God sees further than the eye of reason dares look.

The early Reinhold Niebuhr wrote,

Without the ultra-rational hopes and passions of religion, no society will have the courage to conquer despair and attempt the impossible; for the vision of a just society is an impossible one which can be approximated only by those who do not regard it as impossible. The truest visions of religion are illusions which may be partially realized by being resolutely believed. For what religion believes to be true is not wholly true but ought to be true; and may become true if its truth is not doubted.[8]

The paradox of this statement leaves the impression that the necessary tool of social idealism is an irrational passion that is somewhat out of touch with reality. What this view lacks is an eschatological perspective of the coming kingdom of God. Actions that are "futile" or even make things worse may be important as signs of the presence of the kingdom. They are premised on hope not just in the effectiveness of the act but in the ultimate reality of God's kingdom. The forces of evil are to be opposed not because we know we will defeat them in our lifetime but because we believe God has already defeated them in Christ. Even if they win in the present, their days are numbered. The kingdom of God is coming.

At this point in their story, Linda and Frank were a good example of this. The likelihood that a conservative Christian American couple could influence the practices of the secret police were not very great. Their protest seemed to make things worse. Their friends thought they were just endangering themselves and those around them. But they had hopes and commitments to a power greater than the IPD. They could not back down, because they were living the gospel story. They were a light in a dark place.

The few Christians who opposed the arrest of their Jewish neighbors in Nazi Germany were also involved in futile acts. Their protests did little or nothing to halt the murder of Jews. All they seemingly accomplished was to increase their own suffering and that of their families. But their protest was a witness that has lasted until today. They served a different kingdom from the Nazis, and their presence was a sign of hope that their kingdom was not extinguished.

During the 1970s, when most of the United States was into "self-realization" and was "drowning in a sea of luke-warm yogurt,"[9] my wife and I were part of a small group who regularly protested the U.S. nuclear arms policy. Hardly anyone in the country seemed to care. It was not on the agenda of a country exhausted from the turmoil of the sixties and the pain of the Vietnam War. Our pitiful little protests outside Lockheed Missile Corporation seemed hopelessly idealistic and futile.

We were protesting the manufacture of nuclear missiles, some of which were over one hundred times as powerful as the bomb dropped on Hiroshima. These weapons were targeted on millions of Soviet citizens, many of whom hated their own government. Our country was seriously threatening the "evil empire" with a holocaust that would make World War II look like child's play.

As far as I could see, our protests did very little good. They just made the

Lockheed workers mad. The president didn't hear. We had been producing nuclear warheads at a rate of three a day since World War II. When President Reagan was elected in 1981, he poured in billions of new dollars to speed up the process. When Daniel Berrigan broke into a missile plant and personally destroyed a nuclear warhead, he seriously joked that it was the world's first act of nuclear disarmament. None had ever been destroyed before. For his efforts he was sentenced to years in prison. Only in the mid-1980s did the morality of nuclear targeting get on the national agenda.

The little group continued its protests year after year, not because they seemed to be effective but because, like Linda and Frank, we *had* to say something.[10]

8. Costly presence at the side of the afflicted. Linda took immediate action when it was necessary. She did not plug her ears, stay weeping in the house or plead feminine helplessness. When the time came, she risked her life to stop a brutal rape in progress. She could not call the police; the rapists *were* the police! The weapons she used were her presence, her anger, her social status and whatever verbal threats she could think of on the spot.

Being on the side of the poor means being *at* their side physically when they have no other ally. It's obviously dangerous. The crazed soldier, intent on sexual violence, could have easily killed Linda. But she was not alone. God was in her as she was next to the victim of rape. She was the presence of God, pleading on behalf of the oppressed. Does this mean she could not have been killed? No indeed. Jesus was killed; most of the apostles were killed.

Others were tortured, refusing to accept release, in order to obtain a better resurrection. Others suffered mocking and flogging, and even chains and imprisonment. They were stoned to death, they were sawn in two, they were killed by the sword; they went about in skins of sheep and goats, destitute, persecuted, tormented—of whom the world was not worthy. (Heb 11:35-38)

The young Reinhold Niebuhr was right. Only those with "ultra-rational hopes and passions" dare to put their lives in danger for tormented strangers. One of the reasons liberal Christianity is so anemic is that it often preaches a social ethic without the resurrection. Paul said, "If Christ has not been raised, your faith is futile" (1 Cor 15:17). If Christ is not raised and his kingdom is not coming, who would dare to sacrifice themselves for an anonymous victim of the secret police? In the gospel story Linda was living, the resurrection was central.

In some countries the very presence of American citizens can stop people from being killed. White skin has many negative associations. But one advantage

Americans have is that in most countries they are not lightly killed. The international ramifications are too serious.

This principle was dramatically demonstrated over a period of years by the Christian organization Witness for Peace. In 1985 my wife, Frances, joined a women's delegation from Witness for Peace to go to Nicaragua. They intended to travel to the most dangerous part of the country, where guerrilla attacks by the contras were most likely. Frequently contras used U.S. weapons to massacre whole settlements: men, women and children. Frances and her group went to a dangerous border area and worked in the fields with the people of a village. Experience had shown that wherever there were North Americans present, the contras would not attack. So peasants' lives were protected when there were white people by their side. (Ironically, Witness for Peace tactics would be of little value against the violence in North American cities. White skin is no protection in the ghetto.)

When Linda confronted the soldier in the garden, she did not only go as a white American, she also went as a woman. The presence of an angry, fearless woman is very different from the presence of a man. Soldiers are trained to fight and kill other men and dominate weak women. A strong, unarmed woman poses no physical threat to a soldier, but her moral authority may be stronger than that of a man, especially if the culture is matrifocal. Men do not expect to be opposed by an unarmed woman and may not know how to respond. If her anger is righteous and she is filled with the Holy Spirit, she a formidable presence indeed.

Pauline Hamilton, a missionary in Taiwan who was my local guardian when I was a teenager at boarding school, was a spectacular example of the power of Christian presence. It was not just her white skin, her Ph.D. in physiology and her American passport that made her presence powerful. Part of it was her robust laugh, her intense integrity, her uncompromising bravery and her subtle, loving wisdom. These virtues showed the presence of Christ in her. Both police and gang members stood in awe of her.

For years Pauline worked with gang members, some of whom stayed in her home. She was physically weak, and there were several attempts on her life, but somehow no one could bring her down. Whenever she came around, the most brutal Mafia-like criminals would cease their violent and illegal activities. Thus she could go where the police did not dare. On a number of occasions authorities received a tipoff regarding a major war between rival gangs. The police did not want to intervene, because they were afraid of the danger. But they called "Grandma Han" and let her know. She would go to the pool hall or apartment block where the confrontation was to take place and would hang around all night talking to gang leaders. As long as she was there, nothing would happen. Her presence brought the presence of Christ. And everyone could recognize it.

9. *Reflection, prayer and planning.* After the violence in the garden, the Adamses did not rush into further action or flee the danger. They sat down together for further reflection on their experience, more prayer and careful planning. They realistically counted their true friends and decided not to involve those who were most vulnerable.

Those concerned about justice in another culture must be *very* careful about the impact of their actions on national colleagues and friends. One activist missionary, after leaving a delicate situation, wrote a scathing report about the government. The report was internationally publicized. As a result, national Christians associated with his denomination experienced intense pressure from the government. The report made a fragile situation much worse and created severe tensions between American and local Christians in that denomination. The report satisfied the righteous indignation of the missionary, but the local Christians had to bear the fallout after he was long gone from the situation.

Linda and Frank's careful reflection, prayer and planning are a familiar sequence to those acquainted with the "hermeneutical circle." The hermeneutical circle is a model of how to do moral and theological interpretation. Experience in a context of commitment leads to communal reflection on the experience in light of the Word of God. Social analysis making use of the appropriate social sciences clarifies the nature of the ethical problems and possible responses. Pastoral planning devises strategies for change and gives rise to appropriate action. Action to bring positive change is a new experience to be reflected upon, and the circle continues (see diagram).

Interpretation is a process, not a once-for-all decision. Moral activity is constantly tested in prayer, reflection on experience, Bible study, discussion in community, social analysis, planning and renewed activity. It is a circle without beginning or end.

Linda and Frank were already committed. They were already acting. They were already struggling to know the truth. Their theological and ethical reflection was based on actual experience and always open to new understanding. Their prayer was engaged. Therefore their planning was realistic.

10. *Dependence on local leadership versus neocolonialism.* The most critically

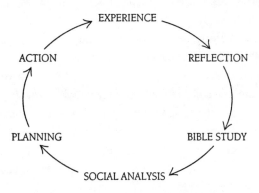

The hermeneutical circle

---

important decision the Adamses made was not the decision to protest against the torture. Rather, it was the way they went about it. They decided to ask advice from their African colleagues. The plan that took shape relied on African leadership and worked through local channels of power. The Adamses turned to Africans for guidance.

Westerners like to solve problems by themselves. If they have to work through institutions and power structures, they prefer Western institutions and power structures, or at least local ones that are under Western control. This gives an illusion of control. A mission board, a foreign-dominated denomination, a multinational corporation, a Western human-rights organization and even the U.S. embassy are all safe channels of influence. These are rule-governed, law-oriented institutions that have set procedures comprehensible to a Westerner. They are "rational."

Many non-Western cultures do things differently. Law may be less important than who you know. Relationships are more significant than rights. Things get done in a roundabout manner. Obligations and honor take precedence over predetermined procedures and principles. The facts are less important than the feelings of the parties involved. Boundaries and lines of authority are vague and intuitive. Truth-telling is subordinate to harmony. What's "right" is what makes all parties happy.

One reason the Adamses' friends did not want to be involved may have been a perception that the IPD was beyond the pale of rational (Western-style) control.

How do you tackle an African director of secret police who is related to the president, practices witchcraft and tortures people in broad daylight? If the U.S. embassy can't do anything, there must be nothing any Westerner can do.

Western cultural procedures are absolutized as right. Abstract principles of rational organization derived from universal reason were a cardinal faith of the Enlightenment and are still assumed by many people today. But this is a typical neocolonialist attitude. Neocolonialism operates wherever national institutions are formally independent but actually controlled by a foreign power. In many countries the church is still a neocolonialist institution. On paper it is independent, but missionaries have the money, education, resources and plans necessary to maintain the church's programs.

National Christians are grateful. They certainly don't want to shut off the aid. But they are also resentful, sometimes without knowing why. Local leaders measure themselves by the standards of Western conceptual patterns, forms of organization, theology and lifestyle. They don't measure up to their Western "partners." So they try harder, import more missionaries, feel inferior and nurse a burning resentment. If possible they go to the West for more education.[11]

The church is not unique in its neocolonialist characteristics. Businesses, universities, nongovernmental organizations and even governments have the same neocolonialist structure. Of course this analysis is oversimplified. There are many universally valid aspects of Western modernization. National institutions need advice and resources from the West in order to develop in the modern or postmodern world. International partnerships are valuable. But partnerships must be equal, and national leadership is imperative. Culturally appropriate social institutions cannot be imported. They must be locally grown. The search for justice must come from the inside rather than being imposed.

When the Adamses decided to rely on African leadership, they acted as a catalyst to prod African Christians to challenge unjust practices in an African way. First they went to their African superior. He suggested several safe ways they could avoid the problem. This was appropriate. They were embarked on a dangerous path, and he was concerned with their safety. Throughout these events he showed considerable courage and promised to stand with them if they went ahead. They were no longer standing alone.

11. The decision to go ahead. After more prayer, Linda and Frank realized what they had to do. They would continue their campaign to stop the torture. They were not trying to be heroic. Like Paul, who said, "Woe to me if I do not proclaim the gospel!" the Adamses had no choice but to fight for the victims who lived and died next door. Their response was less a decision than a compulsion. As Linda said, "Really we felt we had no choice." Nevertheless, their response took courage. Compulsions *can* be resisted.

The moral compulsion to tackle a particular social problem comes from the Spirit of God, the conscience of the individual and the consensus of the community. No doubt there were other social problems close by which the Adamses felt no such compulsion to tackle. Perhaps there were people in dire poverty just down the road. "Not everything that should be done, can be done, and not everything that can be done, should be done by you."[12] The choice of which aspects of the Christian social project a person chooses to address is a matter of social location, prayer, competence, opportunity, individual conscience and the leading of the Holy Spirit.

Every Christian has a responsibility to love their neighbor and struggle for the kingdom in one way or another. In a cash economy, putting money in an envelope for a good organization is an important means of reaching out. But if our path directly passes that of a suffering neighbor or a pattern of oppression, it is dangerous to the soul to cross to the other side.

12. On not giving up. The Adamses' first attempt to work through the power structure was a failure. Their African superior was not big enough. He ran into a dead end. We are not told exactly what this meant. Perhaps he was told to "shut up or else." Perhaps he could not even get an appointment with a key person. Perhaps lower officials confirmed the Adamses' story but higher officials responded with jokes and denials.

A dead end is seldom absolute. There is usually something more that can be done if you are brave and persistent. But perhaps Frank's superior had reached the point where if he pushed any harder, he would get seriously hurt.

This is the point at which many Christians would quit and pull out. Linda and Frank had tried their best. They had done their duty. But they were not trying to do their duty. They were trying to stop the torture. The cries of suffering next door were etched in their minds. It was real people they cared about, not a social issue.

Most forms of oppression will not yield to the first attempts to stop them. Real social change only comes from people with "ultra-rational hopes and passions." The Adamses just kept looking for a bigger handle on the situation.

13. Trying the most important political contact they had. The Adamses tried the governor, with uncertain results. We do not know if this contact was helpful. The governor may or may not have been a significant factor in their final success. A governor may be small potatoes compared to the head of the secret police who is close to the president. The governor may not have really cared. On the other hand, even if he had little power over the situation and didn't care, addressing him with the problem made it official and public. A governor is a symbolic political figure who must at least appear to care about his subjects. Contacting the governor upped the ante.

Progressive exposure of evil at ever higher levels has a cumulative impact. Paul writes, "Take no part in the unfruitful works of darkness, but instead expose them. For it is shameful even to mention what such people do secretly; but everything exposed to the light becomes visible" (Eph 5:11-13).

Perhaps 90 percent of work for social justice consists of interpreting and exposing social evil. Evil likes darkness and cannot stand exposure. The story does not mention the possibility of using the media. Perhaps the media were controlled by those in power. If not, taking the problem to the press would be a logical next step in the exposure of evil.

14. The religious leader as a key political figure. It was Frank's African boss who identified the key person: the Catholic bishop. In white middle-class Protestant culture, religion and politics are sharply divided. A white American does not go to a pastor to get something done politically. That division is not nearly so sharp in black and Latin American cultures. Martin Luther King Jr., Jesse Jackson, Bishop Oscar Romero and Dom Helder Camara were (or are) political figures who brought more profound social change than most politicians. In most of the world (not only Iran) religious leaders have great political power. Mahatma Gandhi brought down the British empire. Bishop Desmond Tutu is in the forefront of the current demise of apartheid in South Africa.

Recently the Indonesian National Lottery was eliminated by the government after mounting nationwide demonstrations. The campaign against the lottery as oppressive to the poor was spearheaded by Muslim leaders who are relatively immune from political coercion. Hardly any "secular" political figure could have achieved the same results, because the governmental elite benefited from the lottery. Politicians are subject to many kinds of pressure, but religious leaders with a wide popular base of support have power. In the "People Power" movement that overthrew Ferdinand Marcos in the Philippines, it is possible that the most significant political leader was not Cory Aquino but Jaime Cardinal Sin.

The Mabukian bishop was culturally and religiously strange to the evangelical Adamses. They were unlikely to think of him as a political figure. But the Adamses were fortunate to have good advice from an African. The bishop proved sympathetic, intelligent and powerful.

In recent years Christian Catholics and Protestants have frequently worked together for justice. They are natural allies with a common agenda: the kingdom of God. Christians can also cooperate with leaders from other religious faiths. The key role played by the bishop in Linda's story might be played by a Muslim mullah in another context. Even where ultimate goals and basic theology differ, Christians and other religious or political communities are often "cobelligerents" against social and environmental evil. Cobelligerents are not the same as allies.[13] While Protestants and Catholics are natural allies, Christians and Buddhists are more likely to be cobelligerents, because the ultimate goals of their social projects are different. Christians have often worked with Marxists in Latin America for common goals of social justice, even while differing on ultimate aims and intermediate tactics.

In one context Jesus said, "Whoever is not against us is for us" (Mk 9:40). Jesus was giving his approval to someone who was fighting evil and casting out demons. The person was not one of Jesus' followers, but he was in the same battle against evil. In another context Jesus said, "Whoever is not with me is against me, and whoever does not gather with me scatters" (Mt 12:30). In this context, he was referring to those who opposed his struggle against evil and criticized him for healing a blind and mute demoniac. This is a good example of the contextual nature of truth. There is no contradiction in these opposite statements. One is talking about uniting with others to fight evil. The other is talking about apparently neutral people who in fact oppose the kingdom of God.

15. The apparent victory. The result of the Mabukian bishop's efforts was dramatic: the torture stopped. The moral authority of the Catholic bishop was more effective than the efforts of a rich businessman and a governor. We do not know what he said or did. We can be sure he did not sue in a court of law or threaten Kofi with physical violence. Kofi would have laughed at "rational" or physical Western tactics. It is unlikely that the bishop suggested an economic boycott of Kofi's business enterprises. Nor would he have appealed to Kofi's humanitarianism or feelings of goodwill. It's more likely that he threatened to shame Kofi and the president of the whole country with a sermon the next Sunday. And it's just possible that he threatened to exorcise the IPD headquarters!

Whatever he did succeeded in a way that surprised Linda and Frank. At least the torture in the house next door stopped. Perhaps the bishop's efforts caused the president to rein in the powers of the IPD.

Westerners sometimes discount the significance of nonviolent moral protest. We are all too aware of the great power of large institutions. Words and moral convictions seem no match for big money, weapons and all the trappings of power. Ethics and moral argument are on a different plane from the "real world." Idealism is no match for tanks. Beliefs are private matters that are best kept separate from the necessities of power and competition. Even the name for the ancient and noble science of rhetoric has come to connote empty words without power.

To be sure, ideas divorced from action are vain words. But moral and religious convictions, especially if combined with the willingness to suffer, can change the world. This is not just a theory but a reality that has been demonstrated over and over throughout history. Ideas that are effective usually combine with material conditions that lend them support. The "Protestant ethic" did not create capitalism by itself.[14] But material conditions without someone to interpret them mean nothing.

There is a tradition in Javanese culture called "drying oneself in the sun." It is the last resort of an oppressed person who has no other means of recourse. "Drying oneself in the sun" means to sit or stand in the heat of the sun, perhaps for hours, days or even weeks on end. It is an appeal to the powerful for justice. Indonesia is right on the equator. Anyone who has lived in the tropics knows that standing in the sun is no joke. On a hot day I've seen a dozen Indonesian teenagers faint from standing at attention from 8:00 to 9:00 a.m. for an outdoor school ceremony. Real "drying oneself in the sun" can result in death.

A few years ago the Indonesian government built a dam that created a large lake. The farmers who lost their land because of the project received practically no compensation. For generations they had worked the land, but now for the sake of "development" they had to be sacrificed. The farmers tried all the means of conventional and legal appeal, but to no avail. They were penniless peasants fighting millionaires, generals and politicians. Finally they resorted to "drying themselves in the sun." As the water from the dam rose, they slowly kept moving to higher ground. They would not leave the edge of the lake or stop "drying themselves in the sun." Finally the government gave in and gave them new land to farm near the lake.[15]

Moral protest is powerful when it is combined with a willingness to suffer. Linda and Frank won in their protest against the secret police. But that wasn't the end. There was a further price to pay.

16. The cost of righteousness. Linda and Frank were arrested, threatened with death, imprisoned and kept under house arrest. Frank was tortured. Only their friendship with influential Mabukians kept them from experiencing a worse fate. They were abandoned by all but one of their Western friends and felt alienated and shamed by those who ostracized them. Like Job's friends, the Western Christian community, with the exception of one missionary, made the Adamses feel as if their suffering was somehow their own fault.

Frank and Linda were following the way of the cross. Their suffering was part of a long and noble tradition. Jesus said,

Blessed are those who are persecuted for righteousness' sake, for theirs is the kingdom of heaven.

Blessed are you when people revile you and persecute you and utter all kinds of evil against you falsely on my account. Rejoice and be glad, for your reward is great in heaven, for in the same way they persecuted the prophets who were before you. (Mt 5:10-12)

Suffering is a normal fact of life. Everyone suffers, from the richest to the poorest. One multimillionaire once said to me, "Bernie, why is life so hard? No one ever told me that it would be so hard." She had everything—a good husband and family, a palatial home and everything money could buy. But she still experienced life as suffering.

Buddhism teaches that suffering is the definition of life. Life is suffering. There is profound truth to the observation, though it is not the whole truth. Only Americans think that suffering is abnormal.

Normal suffering comes from natural causes, from our own sin and from the sin of others. It is not the same as suffering for righteousness or justice.[16] Normal suffering, in itself, is not good. Suffering and death are a result of the curse. They will be finally defeated in the kingdom of God.

Normal suffering is not good, but it need not be evil. Normal suffering helps us to understand what is going on in the real world. James says that all kinds of suffering can produce endurance and lead to maturity (Jas 1:2-4). Those who do not suffer when suffering is appropriate are to be pitied, not envied. Like lepers who have lost physical sensation, they cannot feel pain. When thinking about the suffering caused by warfare, Augustine wrote: "Let everyone who thinks with pain on these great evils, so horrible, so ruthless, acknowledge that this is misery. And if anyone either endures or thinks of them without mental pain, this is a more miserable plight still, for he thinks himself happy because he has lost human feeling."[17]

Suffering for righteousness and justice is different from normal suffering because it is redemptive. That is, it is *potent* for redeeming or liberating people from evil. Suffering for righteousness and justice is a powerful means of bringing in the kingdom. Justice cannot be achieved without suffering. Some of this is mystery. But some of the process is clear. Suffering for justice is a means of uncovering the reality of evil that loves to remain hidden. When the poor farmers "dried themselves in the sun," they brought shame on those who had stolen their land for personal gain. When oppression was revealed, it opened the way for justice to be done.

Suffering for justice is also a sign that goodness and truth are not gone from the world. It is a sign that the kingdom is already among us (Mk 1:14). Even if the physical evil is not immediately overcome, the presence of righteous suffering in response to the evil demonstrates that evil has not triumphed. Thus suffering for the kingdom is revelatory both of evil and of the good that opposes it.

Suffering for justice is participation in the suffering of Christ (2 Cor 1:7; Phil 3:10; 1 Pet 4:13). It is a mystery of Christian faith that the sufferings of Christ were potent for the redemption of the whole world. The cross revealed the full sinfulness of humankind and the unfathomable love of God. The cross changed the world. It became the door through which suffering sinners enter the kingdom. The sufferings of Linda and Frank were part of Christ's suffering. Their pain was the pain of the body of Christ, who died for the oppressed. Many years later, as you read this book, Linda and Frank's sufferings can still reveal the goodness of God.

17. Unexpected friends. Brief mention must be made of the fact that Linda and Frank were not deserted in their suffering. Their natural, cultural community might have left them, but it was replaced by a community of African Christians who risked their lives to identify with their white friends.

One of the great rewards of crosscultural life is the experience of solidarity with people who are so culturally different from oneself. It is almost a rule that when there is costly social action, some of those who are most relied on, like the disciples, will cut and run. But they are often replaced by the most amazing and motley crew of new friends.

When we had only been in Indonesia for a few months, we received the devastating news that Frances's father had died. I'm not sure our suffering would qualify as suffering for righteousness, but it was nevertheless very deep. The amazing thing was that we were surrounded by Indonesians, virtual strangers, who dropped everything to come to our house and express their solidarity with us in sorrow. For the first few days after we received the news, our house was crowded with people all day long. They didn't know Frances's father, but they arranged a memorial service to coincide with the funeral in the States. Christian communal solidarity may be one of the many gifts that some Third World communities can teach the Western church.

18. Suffering and hatred. The conclusion of Linda's account is startling. Linda felt hatred, burning and horrible, toward those who had become her enemies. Her feelings toward "Dark Glasses" on the way to the hospital were involuntary and searing. Perhaps the pain of that hatred will last as long as the pain of what was done to her.

Linda's passion reminds me of the cursing psalms. Near the end of one of the most beautiful poems in literature, the psalmist suddenly startles us by writing,

O that you would kill the wicked, O God. . . .

Do I not hate those who hate you, O LORD?

And do I not loathe those who rise up against you?

I hate them with perfect hatred;

I count them my enemies. (Ps 139:19, 21-22)

Linda could certainly understand the poet's feelings!

But Linda does not feel justified in her feelings. On the contrary, she feels her hatred for Dark Glasses was "an act akin to his mistreatment of other human beings." Linda saw herself in the same camp as the torturers. In a sense she is right. The cruelty of her wish for Dark Glasses to suffer shows her solidarity with him in sin. Christ tells us to love our enemies, not wish they had cancer. Dark Glasses was not only "out there," he was also in her own heart. If she had given Dark Glasses a lift and shown him love, it would have been a wonderful end to the story. Who knows what impact such a miraculous act could have had on such a man? No one is beyond the reach of Christ.

Although Linda's hatred of the man was evil, in another sense it is revelatory. Linda's vivid expression of honest, involuntary feelings gives us a glimpse of the depth of the wrong she had experienced. To hate the source of such evil is not evil but good. Her hatred was not only for her own suffering, it was for her husband, for the old man on the steps, for the woman at the fence, for the hundreds of screams and moans she had heard and the countless others she had imagined. Her hatred was God's hatred of evil. Dark Glasses was the symbol of that evil.

Hatred is an occupational hazard in the struggle for justice. Even when hatred is involuntary and focused on real evil, it is still painful. Only God can judge if it is sinful. It may be one more form of suffering for righteousness. Linda's hatred may simply have been a natural human outworking of the evil that was done to her. But even if such was the case, it is a destructive emotion. Freedom and healing for Linda required that she experience the process of forgiveness.

19. Forgiveness and the persistence of evil. Forgiveness of those who torture is a miracle and a gift of God. It is a process, not an immediate achievement. One person cannot command another to forgive. Apparent forgiveness is sometimes accompanied by a psychic rewriting of experience to lessen the emotional impact of the evil: We imagine that things were not so bad, and in any case they couldn't happen again. Things are different now, much better no doubt. This is not forgiveness. It is self-deception.

Certainly a human tendency is to exaggerate the fault of our opponents. But whether our enemies were better or worse than our imagination really has very little to do with forgiveness. Forgiveness does not imply the other was really not so bad. Rather, it suspends judgment and places the other in the hands of a merciful and just God. Because we are finite sinners, we are unable to judge another justly. Forgiveness does not declare the other innocent. Instead it frees the forgiver from the heavy burden of having to be an ignorant, powerless and sinful judge. Forgiveness is not just for the sake of the person who did evil. It is also for the sake of the forgiver. It is liberation from having to play God.

Forgiveness separates persons from the evil they have done. Even the most evil person is better than the sum of evil he or she has done. Kofi may be a wonderful father or a loyal friend. We do not know. In any case it is not relevant to whether Linda and Frank should forgive him. When they forgive him they do not thereby minimize the evil he has done. The one who forgives a fellow human being should not forgive the evil that person has done or is doing. *People* should be forgiven. *Evil* should not be forgiven. Forgiving Kofi seventy-seven times does not imply that he is getting any better (Mt 18:22).

Years after the events of our story, there was a large massacre of students in Mabuk who had been rightfully protesting intolerable conditions in their university. News reports indicated that Kofi was responsible for the massacre. Hundreds of students died as a result of his commands. So even if torture had been stopped as a result of Linda and Frank's earlier actions, Kofi had not been stopped.

Kofi represents the persistence of evil. If you win a battle in one place, he pops up in another. If he is permanently stopped, his brother or cousin pops up. Kofi has to be fought over and over again.

There are seldom permanent victories. If slavery is abolished, racism is quite capable of creating conditions even worse. But even temporary victories are worth fighting for. We will never know how many people were saved horrible treatment or even death as a result of pressure on Kofi. When structures of oppression are changed, not just one act is stopped. A whole pattern or system of oppression is stopped. If it pops up in another form, that just means it must be fought again.

The flip side of "no permanent victories" is "no permanent defeats." One of the very few prisoners to survive in a certain concentration camp during World War II used to repeat to herself her mother's wise advice when she faced disappointments as a girl: "This too shall pass." Every day, no matter how dark things were, she repeated this sentence and thus retained hope in the future. With hope she could survive when others lay down and died.

20. Return to the struggle. If Kofi has to be fought over and over in different ways, it is because he lives in our own hearts. There are those who would react with horror to the actions of Kofi yet abuse their own wife or children. Some who are righteous in their own eyes think of AIDS victims as deserving their torture. The struggle for justice and righteousness in the world begins with repentance and humility. None of us are free of the very things we struggle against. Personal social ethics finally implies that social evil is personal because it is not "out there" but "in here." Like Linda, we are not that different from "Dark Glasses."

It is not enough to struggle against evil "in here." To do so we must also struggle against it "out there." Christians can keep on doing that over and over again, because of the gospel. Because of the good news, we can forgive ourselves and our enemies. Because of the good news, we know God loves the victims and the oppressors. Because of the good news, we believe in the resurrection and we know that the kingdom of God is coming.

When I was last in Berkeley, one day I was helping my daughter move to a new apartment. As we unloaded some furniture, a voice hailed me. As if it were an everyday occurrence, Linda and Frank stuck their heads out a neighboring window with a grin and asked what I was doing there. I said I was just back from Indonesia temporarily and asked what they were doing. "Oh," they said, "we're just about to leave for Mabuk." The next day I stopped by their apartment to have a chat, but they were already on their way.

APPENDIX

MAPS OR MODELS OF CULTURAL VALUE DIFFERENCES

I mpressive empirical work through international, multicultural surveys of values has been done to map out where various cultures stand in relation to each other's values. One of the earliest models was also the simplest. Ruth Benedict, on the basis of her studies of Japan, suggested that there are (1) *guilt cultures*, in which right and wrong are internalized and associated with personal sin, and (2) *shame cultures*, in which right and wrong are associated with disgrace or loss of face before the group.[1]

Benedict's model has been extensively discussed, elaborated and criticized. When evolutionary theories of culture were in vogue, it was suggested that guilt cultures were at a higher level of evolution than shame cultures. Studies in crosscultural psychology still make use of the distinctions between shame and guilt, even if they are not considered adequate terms for assessing whole cultures.

David Augsburger rejects the polarization between guilt cultures and shame cultures, arguing that all cultures have both and neither should be considered superior.[2] However, he accepts Erik Erikson's developmental model, which places shame before guilt in a person's experience. Augsburger observes that the Old Testament has more references to shame while the New Testament has more references to guilt. However, both put a strong emphasis on grace.

Augsburger does not propose a model to explain all the differences in cultural values. His focus is practically oriented to the needs of Christian counselors in crosscultural situations. Nevertheless, he organizes his reflections in two chapters in terms of two pairs that are continuums of value differences: (1) *inner controls* versus *outer controls* (his more neutral, and less interesting, terms for guilt and shame) and (2) *individualism* (the individual as the locus of identity and meaning) versus *solidarity* (the group as the locus of identity and meaning).[3]

Both of these pairs expand on Benedict's basic division between communal versus individualistic cultures. Augsburger makes the important observation that *individuality* is not the same as *individualism*. In fact, individuality is just as possible in a group-oriented society as in an individualistic one. Conversely, conformity can be just as pervasive in an individualistic society as in a communally oriented group. The common (and racist) stereotype of communal or collectivist societies as like colonies of ants where everyone looks, thinks and acts alike is far from accurate. Communalistic societies have their own share of characters who break the mold of shallow, conventional thought and action. And even the most individualistic, nonconventional groups have their share of shallow conformists.

Social scientists with more theoretical and universal interests than Augsburger have proposed categories to explain the source of all the differences in cultural values. Often the individual-group continuum is implicitly or explicitly included. One attempt to create a universal model of cultural value differences is offered by Talcott Parsons and Edward Shils, who try to describe all human activity in relation to five pattern variables that they conceptualized as choices between five pairs of alternatives:[4]

☐ *affectivity* (immediate gratification of felt needs and expression of emotions) versus *affective neutrality* (restraint of impulses and emotions)

☐ *self-orientation* versus *collectivity-orientation*

☐ *universalism* (applying general standards and universal principles) versus *particularism* (taking particular relationships and situations into account)

☐ *ascription* (judging others by who they are or by their status) versus *achievement* (judging them by what they do or by their accomplishments)

☐ *specificity* (relating to specific people only within certain specific roles and spheres) versus *diffuseness* (no prior limitations to the nature of relations)

Another study limits its model to a few specific communities and tries to allow more complexity by including three categories of response to each of a number of areas of human concern and activity. Florence Kluckhohn and Fred Strodtbeck published a study of five small communities and mapped out their value differences in terms of five variables evaluated in terms of three choices:[5]

☐ evaluation of human nature: (1) evil, (2) mixed or (3) good

☐ relationship of human beings to nature: (1) subjugation (nature as a lord to be served), (2) harmony (nature as a mother to be loved and respected) or (3) mastery (nature as a resource to be utilized)

☐ orientation in time: (1) toward the past, (2) in the present or (3) toward the future

☐ orientation toward activity: (1) being (enjoying the moment), (2) being in becoming (activity as a journey into the future) or (3) doing (changing reality through work)

☐ relationships among people: (1) lineality (hierarchically ordered positions), (2) collaterality (mutual relationships within a group) or (3) individualism

A. Inkeles and D. J. Levinson try to get away from the subjectivity of too many categories and choices (why not one more or one less?) and step up the level of abstraction another rung. They propose three standard analytic issues by which to evaluate value differences in all cultures[6]:

☐ relation to authority

☐ conception of self (including a person's concepts of masculinity and femininity)

☐ primary dilemmas of conflict and ways of dealing with it (including the control of aggression and the expression versus the inhibition of emotion)

Geert Hofstede narrows his field of purpose not by geography but by values of a certain kind, namely, values regarding work and the institutions, activities and relationships associated with work. Hofstede designed questionnaires in order to chart differences in work-related values across a large number of cultures. His categories, on which the questionnaires were based, posited four areas of cultural differences:[7]

☐ power distance (the differential in power and status between superiors and subordinates)

☐ uncertainty avoidance (the degree of desire for a highly defined, rule-governed, stable and stress-free work environment)

☐ individualism (a continuum between individual orientation and group orientation)

☐ masculinity (since most workers interviewed were men, this measures stereotypical "masculine values" such as independence, aggressiveness and so on against "feminine values" such as intuition, benevolence and cooperation)

In comparing different models of cultural values, I was struck by the small amount of overlap in categories as well as the similarities in themes. Out of thirty different categories proposed by different authors, there are sixteen distinct categories. This raises serious questions about the objectivity of any one of the models. The categories reflect the assumptions and interests of their authors, as well as their specific, limited experiences with different cultures. The questions different authors ask influence the answers they find. Nevertheless, the different models clearly share certain themes.

The attempt to be universal and objective is admirable and should not be abandoned just because it is a goal, not an achievement. But all theorists insert their conscious and unconscious assumptions into their research. As Hofstede remarked, "It has been said that the last thing the fish will discover is water; it only finds out about water when it has landed on the fishmonger's cart."[8] We are like the fish. It is hard for us to see the assumptions we live by. Crosscultural living is sometimes like being up on the fish cart where we are suddenly deprived of things we didn't even know we needed.

All of the above authors are aware that their models are not descriptions but rather simplified pictures of reality. Some are more cautious than others in claiming universal applicability, but all of the models are useful tools insofar as they help us see the differences between our assumptions and values and those of others. As tools, the models that are most helpful are the ones that are most clearly related to the goals of their authors. Their usefulness lies not in their theoretical completeness but in their application to specific contexts for specific purposes. In many cases the stories that are used to illustrate a model are of greater interest than the model, but the model helps us to understand the stories.

The chart on the following pages is my own attempt to construct a model of contrasting cultural value orientations. This model grew out of reflections on the above models as well as on my own experience and research. Needless to say, I make no claim to have found the universal key to map out cultural value differences. Like all models, this is an oversimplification that may serve as a useful tool of analysis.

Twelve categories of human thought and behavior are considered under three headings: "the individual," "the social" and "the cosmos." Each of the twelve categories are divided into two polar cultural value orientations. These should not be thought of as two different specific cultures but rather as the two ends of a continuum, with some cultures tending toward one extreme or the other. While "Western" culture tends toward the conceptions listed first (1), different cultures may be at different ends of the continuum for different categories.

My model focuses on the ethical implications of different value orientations. It is different from the other models in that it not only describes cultural value orientations but also evaluates them. It is both descriptive and normative. One category in the model focuses on different ethical priorities that seem to follow from different orientations. The last two categories suggest some moral strengths and weaknesses that may be inherent tendencies in particular orientations. The contrasting strengths and weaknesses reflect my assumption that no culture is free of moral weakness or devoid of moral strength. Often strengths and weaknesses or good and evil in a culture are flip sides of each other.

Continuum Model of Cultural Value Orientations
Individual

Issue/Area	Conception	Values	Priorities	Virtue/Skills Developed	Dangerous Vices/Results
inner and outer life, emotions	1. outer life controls inner and is the source of happiness 2. inner life controls outer and is the source of power	1. free expression, elimination of suffering, happiness 2. serenity, emotional control, asceticism	1. create conditions of life that will make you happy 2. develop a strong inner life impervious to suffering	1. openness, honesty, lack of inhibition, creativity 2. self-control, patience, good humor, discipline	1. lack of self-control, self-assertiveness, impatience 2. hypocrisy, repression and bitterness, dishonesty
motivation and repression	1. inner-directed, guilt-oriented 2. outer-directed, shame-oriented	1. live according to your own highest ideals 2. fulfill your duties to the group	1. authenticity, repentance, forgiveness 2. duty, respect, pride, absence of conflict	1. sincerity, integrity, responsibility, acceptance of criticism 2. discretion, dignity, consideration of others	1. conflict, self-centeredness, judgmentalism 2. hypocrisy, refusal of responsibility or criticism
thought process and learning	1. dichotomous, analytic, objective, inductive 2. holistic, intuitive, subjective, deductive	1. critical thinking, analysis of parts, facts 2. seeing the whole, sensing relationships, interpretation	1. perception of structure, objectivity, truth 2. subjective harmony, synthesis, contextual	1. accuracy, discrimination, constructive criticism 2. dialectical thought, holism, perspective	1. atomism, loss of perspective, positivism, reductionism 2. subjectivism, weak critical skills, prejudice
relational identity	1. core identity as an individual 2. core identity as member of a group	1. authenticity, independence, rights, equal opportunity, self-realization 2. group solidarity, harmony, the fitting	1. freedom, individuality, independence, procedural justice 2. group success, unity, harmony, conformity, distributive justice	1. initiative, respect for the individual, creativity, independent thought 2. social solidarity, care for weak, humility, security	1. selfish individualism, isolation, alienation, injustice 2. lack of initiative, dependency, abuse of human rights, conformity

Continuum Model of Cultural Value Orientations
Social

Issue/Area	Conception	Values	Priorities	Virtue/Skills Developed	Dangerous Vices/Results
family structure, authority	1. egalitarian, individualistic and democratic 2. hierarchical, lineal/collateral, authoritarian	1. equality, independence, self-determination 2. honor, filial piety, loyalty	1. individual rights, personal freedom, equal power, openness 2. "the fitting," duty, security, harmony	1. self-respect, articulateness, independence, competitiveness 2. other respect, obedience, self-control, loyalty	1. fragmentation, breakdown of authority, selfishness 2. tyranny, fear, inequality, oppression
sex and gender	1. gender equality 2. gender difference	1. equal rights and responsibilities for women and men 2. protection of women, male leadership	1. empowerment of women, eliminate inequality and exploitation 2. women's responsibility for family, stopping exploitation of women	1. personal freedom and independence for women, mutual respect between sexes 2. honor, submission, responsibility in your role	1. alienation, individualism, identity confusion, defensiveness 2. arrogance, oppressiveness, triviality, dependency, subservience
power and status	1. low power distance, status by achievement 2. high power distance, status by ascription	1. equality, achievement, competition, youth 2. honor, respect, duty, cooperation, obedience, age	1. equal opportunity, equal rights, success to the competent 2. social harmony, solidarity, respect	1. fairness, ambition, striving for excellence 2. humility, meekness, benevolence	1. survival of fittest, individualism, egocentrism 2. arrogance, resignation, oppression
activity goals	1. productivity, achievement, high mobility 2. relationality, social cohesion, low mobility	1. efficiency, material and intellectual results 2. relations, people, status	1. increasing productivity, results 2. strengthening relationships, maintaining harmony	1. efficiency, pragmatism, expertise 2. sensitivity, friendliness, flexibility	1. materialism, individualism, insensitivity, competitiveness 2. inefficiency, laziness, dependency

257

Continuum Model of Cultural Value Orientations
Cosmos

Issue/Area	Conception	Values	Priorities	Virtue/Skills Developed	Dangerous Vices/Results
spiritual and material	1. empirical and public existence entirely material 2. spiritual and material equally real and public	1. bring all life under material explanation and control 2. spiritual and physical conditions in harmony	1. mastery of nature, a just and prosperous society 2. spiritual power and safety, obedience to God	1. rationality, scientific expertise, practicality 2. spirituality, intuitiveness, piety, balance	1. materialism, reductionism, relativism 2. superstition, fear, bondage to spiritual power and rules
nature	1. nature as a resource to be used and enjoyed 2. nature as a power to be served or protected from	1. extract as much profit and pleasure as possible 2. appeasement and control of nature	1. exploitation and conservation 2. safety and survival	1. resourcefulness, respect, love for nature 2. reverence, fear, harmony with nature	1. greed, exploitation, lack of reverence or harmony with nature 2. fear, inhibition, antagonism or subjugation
time	1. linear, open, "monochronic," measured, limited 2. cyclical, "polychronic," immeasurable, determined	1. efficiency, productivity, planning, future 2. flexibility, spontaneity, submission, present and past	1. change, progress, transformation 2. harmony, the event, acceptance, peace, tranquillity, the fitting	1. discipline, hope, courage, initiative, commitment to tasks 2. long-suffering, patience, contentment, "apatheia," commitment to people	1. aggressiveness, ambition, selfishness 2. resignation, conservatism, corruption, apathy

Notes

Preface

[1]Caroline Armitage, *Reaching for the Goal: David H. Adeney, Ordinary Man, Extraordinary Vision* (Wheaton, Ill.: Harold Shaw/Singapore: Overseas Missionary Fellowship, 1994).

Chapter 1: Introduction to Crosscultural Ethics

[1]See Charles Taylor, "Interpretation and the Sciences of Man," in *Interpretive Social Science,* ed. Paul Rabinow and William M. Sullivan (Berkeley: University of California Press, 1979), pp. 25-71.

[2]Practices are similar to texts in their need for reinterpretation in different contexts. Hans-Georg Gadamer suggested that "if we are to say the same thing as an ancient text, we have to say it differently." See Hans-Georg Gadamer, *Truth and Method* (New York: Seabury, 1975), p. 256.

[3]*The Willowbank Report* (Wheaton, Ill.: Lausanne Committee for World Evangelization, 1978), as quoted in *Down to Earth: Studies in Christianity and Culture,* ed. John R. W. Stott and Robert Coote (London: Hodder & Stoughton, 1981), p. 313.

[4]Clifford Geertz, *The Interpretation of Culture* (New York: Basic Books, 1973), p. 89.

[5]The "modern" period in the West may be conceived as starting in the seventeenth century with the "Enlightenment." See Stephen Toulmin, *Cosmopolis: The Hidden Agenda of Modernity* (New York: Free Press, 1990).

[6]I have in mind here "tentmakers" living in Muslim or communist countries. However, America and Europe may also be characterized as hostile to real faith. This is neatly captured in the title of the book by Stanley Hauerwas and William H. Willimon, *Resident Aliens* (Nashville: Abingdon, 1989).

[7]Pierre Casse, *Training for the Cross-Cultural Mind,* 2nd ed. (Washington, D.C.: Society for Intercultural Education, Training and Research, 1981), p. xiii. Ironically, Casse's book is "dedicated to Christiane who knows that she knows." An interesting feature of this book is its heavy reliance on Jungian categories.

[8]"Errors of interpretation of meaning . . . are sustained by certain practices of which they are constitutive." Taylor, "Interpretation and the Sciences," p. 68. The same point was first made by Aristotle in *Nicomachean Ethics.*

[9]Clyde Kluckhohn, "Ethical Relativity: Sic et Non," *Journal of Philosophy* 52 (1955): 663-77.

[10]Clyde Kluckhohn, "Values and Value Orientations in the Theory of Action," in *Toward a General Theory of Action*, ed. Talcott Parsons, Edward Shils et al. (Cambridge, Mass.: Harvard University Press, 1951), pp. 409-10.

[11]I first heard this phrase in the class "Cross-Cultural Communication and Understanding" taught by Grace Dyrness and Patricia Benner at New College Berkeley, summer 1983.

[12]H. Richard Niebuhr, *The Kingdom of God in America* (New York: Willett, Clark, 1937), p. 242.

[13]For a discussion of the treasures of knowledge preserved in aboriginal groups, see Eugene Linden, "Lost Tribes, Lost Knowledge," *Time*, September 23, 1991, pp. 46-56. The popular film *Medicine Man* also explores this topic.

[14]An excellent survey of the differences between oral and literate cultures is found in Walter Ong, *Orality and Literacy* (New York: Methuen, 1981). Anthony Gittins also discusses orality in the context of Jesus' teaching style and modern missionary work in *Gifts and Strangers* (Mahwah, N.J.: Paulist, 1989), pp. 68-83.

[15]"Mission as Inter-Cultural Encounter: A Sociological Perspective," in *Down to Earth: Studies in Christianity and Culture*, ed. John R. W. Stott and Robert Coote (London: Hodder & Stoughton, 1981), p. 255.

[16]Edward T. Hall, *The Silent Language* (New York: Doubleday, 1959), p. 53.

[17]"The Problem of Historical Consciousness," in *Interpretive Social Science*, ed. Paul Rabinow and William M. Sullivan (Berkeley: University of California Press, 1979), p. 157.

[18]Hans-Georg Gadamer, *Philosophical Hermeneutics*, trans. and ed. David E. Linge (Berkeley: University of California Press, 1976).

[19]Aristotle, *Nicomachean Ethics*, Great Books of the Western World (Chicago: Encyclopaedia Britannica, 1957), pp. 367, 352.

[20]Ibid., p. 352.

[21]Hall, *Silent Language*, p. 51.

[22]L. Robert Kohls, *Survival Kit for Overseas Living* (Yarmouth, Maine: Intercultural, 1984), p. 1.

[23]E. M. Forster, *The Hill of Devi*, quoted in Craig Storti, *The Art of Crossing Cultures* (Yarmouth, Maine: Intercultural, 1990), p. xiii.

Chapter 2: Practicing Theology in Crosscultural Experience

[1]I also believe the Bible is foundational for Christian ethics. But an understanding of the Bible's moral teaching requires reason, tradition (theology) and experience. Just as the Bible addresses us with questions about our experience, so experience teaches us what questions we should address to Scripture. See chapter three for more on this "hermeneutical circle" in relation to culture. A naive approach to biblical ethics is illustrated by the fact that many conservative colleges and seminaries have many biblical scholars but no ethicists on their faculty.

[2]See, for example, Norman Geisler, *Options in Contemporary Christian Ethics* (Grand Rapids, Mich.: Baker Book House, 1981), and Walter C. Kaiser Jr., *Toward Old Testament Ethics* (Grand Rapids, Mich.: Zondervan, 1983). Perhaps the most comprehensive attempt to found ethics on biblical law is Greg L. Bahnsen, *Theonomy in Christian Ethics*

(Nutley, N.J.: Craig, 1979).

[3]The English is my translation of the following story by a student at Satya Wacana Christian University, Salatiga, Indonesia, March 1994: "Bolehkah Ikut Ambil Bagian Dalam Proses Perceraian?"

Bapak Diduk berusia 37 tahun. Ia bercerai dengan Mimi istrinya. Konon karena sikapnya sangat kasar: suka memkul istri (memukul istri telah dilakukan berulang kali). Suatu waktu Diduk memukul istrinya hingga babak belur. Ny. Tina (Janda-Ibu Diduk) melihat tindakan Diduk sudah sangat keterlaluan. Melihat keberingasan Diduk sangat membahayakan dan mengancam nyawa seisi rumah, Ny. Tina bersama Titi dan Netty (kakak Diduk) mengungsi ke rumah bapak Dodok (orang Kristen). Mimi dan anaknya (2 tahun) mengungsi ke rumah orang tuanya (bukan Kristen).

Dengan diam-diam Tante Netty berunding dengan kedua anaknya, Mimi, bapak Dodok dan bapak Didik (kristen) menghubungi seorang pengacara (kristen) untuk memprosesnya secara hukum dan melibatkan kepolisian. Untuk beberapa saat karena kasus ini Diduk di tahan di rumah tahanan kepolisian dan setelah deproses di pengadilan gugatan cerai diterima.

Beberapa bulan demudian seorang pendeta menemui Diduk. Diduk mencurahkan demarahannya tentang tingkah laku istrinya. Dan juga berkali-kali ia mengeluarkan unek-uneknya dan kemarahanya terhadap bapak Dodok dan bapak Didik yang berperan dalam proses perceraian. Dalam kemarahannya beberapa kali Diduk mengatakan kalau perlu adan membunuh bapak Dodok dan bapak Didi. Saat ini ia tinggal dengan anaknya. Pertanyaannya ialah bolehkah orang kristen ikut dalam proses gugatan perceraian?

[4]Even though it is forbidden, the divorce rate is high in Indonesia, even among Christians. Pastors usually lose their position if they divorce.

[5]Oliver O'Donovan, *Resurrection and Moral Order* (Grand Rapids, Mich.: Eerdmans, 1986), p. 190.

[6]See, for example, Thomas Keating, *Open Mind, Open Heart: The Contemplative Dimension of the Gospel* (Rockport, Mass.: Element Books, 1991). Swiss psychologist Hans Fillenz-Burke has developed the approach taken in this book through seminars that have deepened the spiritual lives of many evangelical leaders all over the world.

[7]Alasdair MacIntyre, *After Virtue: A Study in Moral Theology* (Notre Dame, Ind.: University of Notre Dame Press, 1981).

[8]Robert N. Bellah et al., *Habits of the Heart: Individualism and Commitment in American Life* (Berkeley: University of California Press, 1985).

[9]Ibid. Bellah considers utilitarian individualism and expressive individualism the two primary moral languages in the United States. They are moral languages in the sense that right and wrong are usually expressed or justified in individualistic language that appeals to utility (what works) or feeling. Bellah thinks Americans have better bases for moral judgments but they have forgotten how to express them. He and his associates would like Americans to recover biblical and republican moral language, since they believe these are better traditions for expressing good and evil.

[10]I am not suggesting that "John" really had no other values than individualistic utilitarianism, only that his language in one brief conversation provides a useful example of a common tendency in Western approaches to ethics. Bellah also believes that Americans have much deeper grounds for their moral commitments than are revealed in their

language.

[11]Joe Holland and Peter Henriot, *Social Analysis* (Maryknoll, N.Y.: Orbis, 1983), p. 14.

[12]These elements are all part of the well-known "hermeneutical circle." All the elements are integrally related to each other. None can stand alone. Traditionally Catholics were thought to emphasize reason and tradition while Protestants emphasized Word and Spirit or experience. Currently, however, this stereotype is misleading. Many Catholics are profoundly shaped by biblical study and spiritual experience, while Protestants have rediscovered the crucial role of reason and tradition in faith and practice.

[13]I use the term *well* in the Aristotelian sense of "with moral excellence." Living well means living with the skills and virtues necessary to achieve the highest ends of a human life. Unlike Aristotle, I think the highest end is not happiness but love of God and one's neighbor.

[14]Primrose Gigliesi, *The Effendi and the Pregnant Pot* (Beijing: New World, 1982), p. 28, as cited and adapted in David W. Augsburger, *Pastoral Counseling Across Cultures* (Philadelphia: Westminster Press, 1986), p. 244.

[15]E. Deutscher, *What We Say/What We Do: Sentiments and Acts* (Glenview, Ill.: Scott Foresman, 1973).

[16]Geert Hofstede, *Culture's Consequences: International Differences in Work Related Values* (Beverly Hills, Calif.: Sage, 1980), p. 18.

[17]Elizabeth Brewster and Thomas Brewster, *Bonding and the Missionary Task* (Dallas: Lingua House, 1982).

[18]Elizabeth Brewster and Thomas Brewster, *Language Learning Is Ministry!* (Dallas: Lingua House, 1982).

[19]Anthony J. Gittins, *Gifts and Strangers: Meeting the Challenge of Inculturation* (New York: Paulist, 1989), p. 115.

[20]Jesus affirmed this when he was confronted with the defensive question "Who is my neighbor?" (Lk 10:29). Instead of giving a theoretical answer he told the story of the good Samaritan. He then reversed the question by asking, "Which of these three, do you think, was a neighbor to the man who fell into the hands of the robbers?" (Lk 10:36). The question changed from an abstract one to a concrete inquiry about a specific context. The one who met the need of the stranger in a culturally sensitive way was a true neighbor. The question was transposed from "Who is my neighbor?" to "To whom am I a neighbor?"

Chapter 3: Knowledge, Friendship and Wisdom

[1]This story is related in Tim Stafford, *Friendship Across Cultures* (London: STL Books, 1986), pp. 22-23; originally published as *The Friendship Gap* (Downers Grove, Ill.: InterVarsity Press, 1984).

[2]Ibid., p. 23. My emphasis.

[3]Ibid., p. 22.

[4]George A. Lindbeck, *The Nature of Doctrine: Religion and Theology in a Postliberal Age* (Philadelphia: Westminster Press, 1984), p. 64.

[5]Lindbeck argues for an "ethno-linguistic" conception of doctrine that sees religious truth as a perspectival way of ordering reality. As a general approach it is agnostic on questions of ontological truth but remains open to its possibility. In Lindbeck's typology I might be classified as a "modified propositionalist." I believe some doctrinal and moral

propositions make truth claims about ontological reality. But I believe all propositions come from a finite perspective and may be expressed in diverse conceptualities or formulations that are rooted in the context of the speaker. (See ibid., p. 80.) I agree with Lindbeck that most Christian propositions "acquire enough referential specificity to have first-order or ontological truth or falsity only in determinate settings" (p. 68). That is, their meaning is ultimately clarified by the praxis to which they refer.

[6]John R. W. Stott and Robert Coote, eds., *Down to Earth: Studies in Christianity and Culture* (London: Hodder & Stoughton, 1981), p. 318.

[7]Bruce Olsen, *Bruchko* (Carol Stream, Ill.: Creation House, 1978).

[8]There are some theological questions embedded in this story. I do not suggest that it makes no difference if you call the causes of disease "spirits" or "bacteria." The word *spirits* brings with it a whole worldview, as does the word *bacteria.* I think that a scientific worldview is more potent for combating many kinds of disease than an animist worldview. But both worldviews are limited and tend to be reductionist. Neither is simply true. Worldview transformation is a process. In order to learn from science the shaman may need to begin by identifying bacteria with disease spirits. In order to learn from animism a doctor may need to begin by identifying spirits with psychosomatic illness.

[9]Even with inhuman activities such as these, a distinction should be made between clear repudiation of such practices for Christians and greater caution before going on a crusade to eliminate them in the broader society. A temporary toleration of culturally ingrained behavior that is a coherent, functional part of a total cultural context may be necessary. A foreign visitor may not have earned the right to confront practices that are so foreign to her cultural context. Deep knowledge and, if possible, partnership with local Christians are indispensable to moral confrontation.

[10]Stott and Coote, *Down to Earth,* p. 337.

[11]Both of these case studies, "Protest or Inaction?" by Stewart Willcuts and Helena Eversole, and "Onions and Wives" by Roger David Heeren, are related in Paul G. Hiebert and Frances F. Hiebert, *Case Studies in Mission* (Grand Rapids, Mich.: Baker Book House, 1987), pp. 215-19 and pp. 75-77.

[12]Cited by Augsburger, *Pastoral Counseling,* p. 32. Augsburger has an excellent chapter on "Possession, Shamanism and Healing Across Cultures." This case study was related to him in person by Pak Mesach in 1984. Augsburger comments, "The case of the Gold Talisman presents a public event that is beyond any explanations of a common scientific world view. Gold coins do not pass through skin without rupturing tissue, sleight-of-hand does not explain what is beyond reach. The inter-cultural counselor, working in a culture that accepts a rich variety of experiences from the mesocosmos, must be capable of interpathic entertainment of new possibilities and their emotional consequences." I have heard similar stories, both from Pak Mesach and from other reliable sources in Indonesia.

[13]Unfortunately, "quiet time" was often more in the category of the "desirable" than the "desired." "Q.T." always appeared on my personal schedules, but I followed my schedules only fitfully.

[14]Frances Screnock Adeney, *Citizenship Ethics: Contributions of Classical Virtue Theory and Responsibility Ethics* (Ann Arbor: University Microfilms International, 1988), pp. 60-61.

[15]G. W. F. Hegel, and Karl Marx after him, saw the same dialectic happening in material history. The dialectic between social and economic classes led to a new social order.

Marx, however, believed that the dialectic among material conditions determined the dialectic in the realm of ideas, whereas Hegel believed the reverse.

[16]Stanley Hauerwas, *Vision and Virtue* (Notre Dame, Ind.: Fides, 1974), p. 3.

[17]Edward T. Hall says, "Therefore the great gift that the members of the human race have for each other is not exotic experiences but an opportunity to achieve awareness of the structure of their own system, which can be accomplished only by interacting with others who do not share that system." *Beyond Culture* (New York: Anchor, 1977), p. 44.

[18]Richard W. Brislin, *Cross Cultural Encounters* (New York: Pergamon, 1981).

[19]Sherwood G. Lingenfelter and Marvin K. Mayers, *Ministering Cross-Culturally* (Grand Rapids, Mich.: Baker Book House, 1986), pp. 112-13.

[20]Aristotle, *Nicomachean Ethics,* Great Books of the Western World (Chicago: Encyclopaedia Britannica, 1957). See also Paul Wadell, *Friendship and the Moral Life* (Notre Dame, Ind.: University of Notre Dame Press, 1989).

[21]Compare Proverbs 27:6: "Well meant are the wounds a friend inflicts, but profuse are the kisses of an enemy."

[22]Augsburger, *Pastoral Counseling,* pp. 13-14.

[23]Hans-Georg Gadamer, "The Problem of Historical Consciousness," in *Interpretive Social Science,* ed. Paul Rabinow and William M. Sullivan (Berkeley: University of California Press, 1979), p. 108.

[24]Simone Weil as quoted by Iris Murdoch, "Against Dryness: A Polemical Sketch," in *Revisions,* ed. Stanley Hauerwas and Alasdair MacIntyre (Notre Dame, Ind.: University of Notre Dame Press, 1983), p. 49.

[25]Paul Tillich defined faith as ultimate concern, but unlike Tillich, I do not see faith as the existential product of individual consciousness but as a relational or "intersubjective" function of a community of tradition. See Charles Taylor, "Interpretation and the Sciences of Man," *The Review of Metaphysics* 25 (September 1971).

[26]José Míguez Bonino, *Doing Theology in a Revolutionary Situation* (Philadelphia: Fortress, 1975).

[27]Patricia Benner, *From Novice to Expert: Excellence and Power in Clinical Nursing Practice* (Menlo Park, Calif.: Addison-Wesley, 1984).

[28]Michael Polanyi, *Personal Knowledge* (Chicago: University of Chicago Press, 1962), p. 266.

[29]Donald Bloesch objects to the use of the term *virtues.* He says, "Speak more of graces than of virtues. Virtues indicate the unfolding of human potentialities, whereas graces are manifestations of the work of the Holy Spirit within us. It is not the fulfillment of human powers but the transformation of the human heart that is the emphasis in an authentically evangelical ethics" (*Freedom for Obedience: Evangelical Ethics in Contemporary Times* [San Francisco: Harper & Row, 1987]). But this is a false dichotomy between the natural and the spiritual. To separate the transformation of the human heart and the work of the Holy Spirit from the "fulfillment of human powers" is to deny that God made human beings with the potential to be good. The work of the Holy Spirit does not bypass the goodness of human potentiality but fulfills it. In any case, there is no reason to believe that human virtues can ever be perfected in sinful human beings apart from the grace of God.

[30]Karl Barth observes, "God always takes His stand unconditionally and passionately on this side and on this side alone: against the lofty and on behalf of the lowly" (*Church*

Dogmatics 2/1, trans. T. H. L. Parker et al. (Edinburgh: T & T Clark, 1957), p. 386.

Chapter 4: The Bible and Culture in Ethics

[1]William A. Dyrness, *Learning About Theology from the Third World* (Grand Rapids, Mich.: Zondervan, 1990), p. 28. Of course the Bible itself is culturally located, but its original text functions crossculturally for all Christians.

[2]David Kelsey, *The Uses of Scripture in Recent Theology* (Philadelphia: Fortress, 1975), p. 89. Kelsey argues for an essentially functional definition of Scripture. That is, the Bible, or at least parts of the Bible, are Scripture because they function as authoritative for the Christian community. One may accept Kelsey's functional definition without denying (as Kelsey does) that "authoritative" is a judgment about Scripture in and of itself. I would hold that the entire canon of the Bible functions as authoritative for the Christian community because Christians believe God has made it the authoritative vehicle of revelation.

[3]For the purposes of this chapter I ignore the problems raised by textual criticism. There are extensive debates about just what is the original text of Scripture. These debates are important but lie beyond the scope of this chapter and the competence of its author. I do not think they would substantially change my argument. There are also very significant differences in doctrines of the authority of Scripture, but whatever their differences, most Christians account for their beliefs and behavior in relation to Scripture.

[4]Robert McAfee Brown, *Unexpected News: Reading the Bible with Third World Eyes* (Philadelphia: Westminster Press, 1984), p. 13. "The strange new world within the Bible" is a term borrowed from Karl Barth.

[5]Unfortunately, sometimes translations of the text enshrine the interpretation of the (usually white male) translator. The text may then be narrowed in its meaning or even made to say what is not there, based on the cultural bias of the translator.

[6]Kraft writes, "The Scriptures are like the ocean and supra cultural truth like the icebergs that float in it. Many icebergs show at least a bit of themselves above the surface, some lie entirely beneath the surface. Much of God's [self] revelation . . . in the Scriptures is at least partially visible to nearly anyone who is willing to see it. . . . But much lies beneath the surface, visible only to those who search to discover what supra cultural truth lies beneath the specific cultural applications in Scripture" (Charles H. Kraft, *Christianity in Culture* [Maryknoll, N.Y.: Orbis, 1979], p. 131). Kraft's discussion of hermeneutical issues in chapter seven, "Supra Cultural Meanings via Cultural Forms," is very helpful. Still, I am not sure there are any "supracultural meanings" that exist denuded of cultural flesh. Every word of Scripture is itself a cultural form. If so, "supracultural meanings" may be more like molecules than like icebergs! Marvin Mayers, followed by Paul Hiebert, tries to improve on Eugene Nida's "relative cultural relativism" and proposes a model of ethical reflection based on "biblical absolutism and cultural relativism." While Mayers's approach has many helpful insights, it lacks the hermeneutical rigor displayed by Kraft. See chapter sixteen, "Cross-Cultural Ethics," in Marvin K. Mayers, *Christianity Confronts Culture,* 2nd ed. (Grand Rapids, Mich.: Zondervan, 1987), pp. 241-60. Also see Paul G. Hiebert, *Cultural Anthropology* (Grand Rapids, Mich.: Baker Book House, 1983), pp. 251-62.

[7]Eugene A. Nida, *Customs, Culture and Christianity* (New York: Harper & Brothers, 1954), p. 282; see also pp. 48-53. Actually even this statement is questionable, since our

understanding of the Triune God is far from absolute. But Nida's intention is to locate all that is infinite and absolute with God.

[8]George A. Lindbeck, *The Nature of Doctrine* (Philadelphia: Westminster Press, 1984), p. 35.

[9]Ibid., p. 33.

[10]Iris Murdoch, "Against Dryness: A Polemical Sketch," in *Revisions,* ed. Stanley Hauerwas and Alasdair MacIntyre (Notre Dame, Ind.: University of Notre Dame Press, 1983), p. 49.

[11]Alasdair MacIntyre, *Whose Justice? Which Rationality?* (Notre Dame, Ind.: University of Notre Dame Press, 1988), p. 393.

[12]For the sake of brevity I am simplifying MacIntyre considerably.

[13]"The Christian tradition" is in fact many different traditions, each of which describes the world differently. When I speak of "Christians" as if they were all from one tradition, I am simplifying in order to make a point. By the word *Christians* I assume a broad, central stream of the Christian tradition, including both Protestants and Catholics, which treats the Bible as Scripture.

[14]Lindbeck, *Nature of Doctrine,* p. 118.

[15]Kelsey, *Uses of Scripture,* p. 48. To approach the Bible like this is not to ignore the insights of biblical critical scholars. They may help us understand the story contained in the Bible. But the focus is not on some revelatory event that lies behind the text (as in Gerhard von Rad) nor on the experience of the community that transmitted it (as in Rudolf Bultmann), nor even on revelatory experience of the modern reader (as in Karl Barth), but on the story in the text of the canon as it now stands (see the work of Brevard Childs, such as *Introduction to the Old Testament as Scripture* [Philadelphia: Fortress, 1979]).

[16]These four "levels of moral discourse" were first distinguished by Henry David Aiken but have been adapted many times since. Henry David Aiken, *Reason and Conduct* (New York: Alfred Knopf, 1962), pp. 65-87. Compare Allen Verhey, "The Use of Scripture in Ethics," *Religious Studies Review* 4 (January 1978); James Gustafson, *Theology and Christian Ethics* (Philadelphia: United Church Press, 1974), pp. 130-33. As a *typology* of ways of relating ethics to Scripture, the four levels are far too simplistic. We learn goodness from the Bible in many more ways than this. However, the four levels still capture four questions that trouble many Christians.

[17]Gerhard von Rad, *Old Testament Theology* (San Francisco: Harper & Row, 1965), 2:204.

[18]I have no written reference for this view but have often heard it expressed by believers within Plymouth Brethren circles. The dispensationalist approach pioneered by J. N. Darby has the advantage of trying to fit the law into a narrative structure of God's work in the world. On the other hand, some of Darby's followers have propagated an extreme literalism that does violence to the original meaning of the text in its context and results in a narrow legalism. Every instruction of the Bible that is not assigned to another dispensation must be followed to the letter.

[19]The practice of cutting out any parts of Scripture that a person does not like. The prototypical example of this practice was the heretic Marcion (second century A.D.), who deleted the Old Testament and significant parts of the New which did not meet his approval.

[20]Christopher J. H. Wright, *Living as the People of God* (Leicester, U.K.: Inter-Varsity Press,

1983), pp. 151-52; also published as *An Eye for an Eye* (Downers Grove, Ill.: InterVarsity Press, 1984). Wright's classification of the law was first proposed by A. Phillips, *Ancient Israel's Criminal Law: A New Approach to the Decalogue* (London: Blackwell, 1970).

[21]Joshua 2:1-7. See John Jefferson Davis, *Evangelical Ethics* (Phillipsburg, N.J.: Presbyterian and Reformed, 1985), pp. 15-16. Norman L. Geisler is also an exponent of what he calls "ethical hierarchicalism"; see *Ethics: Alternatives and Issues* (Grand Rapids, Mich.: Zondervan, 1971).

[22]Bill Gothard's popular teaching on the principle of family hierarchy falls in this category. Gothard absolutizes the sociocultural system of patriarchy in the name of biblical principles.

[23]Geisler, *Ethics*, p. 117. Geisler makes the absurd statement concerning those with physical limitations that "a person who is physically complete has a better manifestation of humanity than one who is not." By this measure Hitler showed more humanity than Helen Keller!

[24]This observation does not apply to street people. But street people's coats are not usually worth enough to take in pawn. If they were, this rule might well be authoritative in its literal sense.

[25]See, for example, Ian T. Ramsey, ed., *Christian Ethics and Moral Philosophy* (London: SCM Press, 1966), and Gene Outka and John P. Reeder Jr., eds., *Religion and Morality* (Garden City, N.Y.: Anchor/Doubleday, 1973).

[26]This is a fundamental question of epistemology. It appears to me that the argument hinges on an evaluation of David Hume's familiar dictum "No Ought from an Is; no ethical conclusions from non-ethical premises." It is certainly possible to argue that the conception of a biblical God in itself requires some ethical conclusions. See Dewi Z. Phillips, "God and Ought," in *Christian Ethics and Moral Philosophy*, ed. Ian T. Ramsey (London: SCM Press, 1966), pp. 140-44. On the other hand, some argue that religious belief is itself dependent upon a priori moral judgments. See Kai Nielsen's article in the same volume, "Some Remarks on the Independence of Morality from Religion." Both of these positions may be argued without contradiction. A person can certainly make moral decisions about the goodness or existence of God without having belief or formal theology. But that does not imply that the person's moral ability or awareness did not come from God. If we begin with the assumptions of the biblical narrative, it is clear that God is the source of all morality. William Frankena is probably right in his assertion that a rational justification of ethics is possible without logically requiring a religious premise. See Frankena, "Is Morality Logically Dependent on Religion?" in *Religion and Morality*, ed. Gene Outka and John P. Reeder Jr. (Garden City, N.Y.: Anchor/Doubleday, 1973), p. 259. I would argue, however, that from Christian premises the ultimate meaning of both morality and reason is founded in the character of God. See C. S. Lewis, *Miracles* (New York: Macmillan, 1947).

[27]Those with painful family relationships should be reassured that God is not a parent like their parents, but rather their mother and father ought to be like their heavenly Father and Mother.

[28]Images of God as father are pervasive in both Testaments. Images of God as mother are more rare because of the patriarchal structures of Israel. Nevertheless, there are a few mother images of God. See, for example, Isaiah 66:12-13. The terms *father* and *mother* are human symbols or signs of what God is like. Since God is a spirit and has no sexual

organs, neither image should be taken as literal (see Jn 4:24).

[29]Richard J. Mouw, *The God Who Commands* (Notre Dame, Ind.: University of Notre Dame Press, 1990), p. 2. Mouw is careful not to base such surrender primarily on God's power to judge the earth, but God's absolute authority over the earth clearly entails judgment as one aspect of God's authority. Mouw's book helpfully restores obedience to a central place in ethics. Unlike Mouw, I do not think it is the central moral image of the biblical narrative.

[30]This is a pervasive theme in the writings of H. Richard Niebuhr.

[31]Perhaps the closest analogy is found in the book of Daniel, where Daniel is a student and teacher in a foreign context in which he must meet the demands of the Babylonian educational structure or face death. We are told that Daniel "responded with prudence and discretion" (Dan 2:14). But this is still a far cry from Jane's situation.

[32]In this case Jane gave Kwei-feng a stern warning and allowed her to finish the examination in a different seat. But even a year later she was unsure if she had done the right thing. One reason cheating is common in many communal cultures is that individuals often have very little sense of the private ownership of ideas. An African student once commented, "Cheating is when one person withholds that which another person has need of."

[33]Brevard Childs, *Biblical Theology in Crisis* (Philadelphia: Westminster Press, 1970), p. 126.

[34]See, for example, the results of Pharaoh's "knowledge" of God's will prior to his obedience to God's will. The result of knowledge without obedience was, "So the heart of Pharaoh was hardened" (see Ex 9:27-35).

[35]The influence of Latin American theology can be discerned in these thoughts. For example, José Míguez Bonino says, "Correct knowledge is contingent on right doing," and "faith is always a concrete obedience" (*Doing Theology in a Revolutionary Situation* [Philadelphia: Fortress, 1975], pp. 89-90). The emphasis of liberation theology is on the movement from action (praxis) to thought (biblical ethics). This emphasis is good as a corrective but must not obscure the fact that the movement is dialectical and goes both ways.

[36]Wright, *Living as the People of God.*

[37]Norman K. Gottwald, *The Tribes of Yahweh: A Sociology of the Religion of Liberated Israel 1250-1050 BCE* (London: SCM Press, 1979), p. 10.

[38]Elisabeth Schüssler Fiorenza, *In Memory of Her: A Feminist Reconstruction of Christian Origins* (New York: Crossroad, 1983).

[39]Ibid., p. 33. This short discussion only scratches the surface of the hermeneutical issues raised. Fiorenza's book includes a very helpful overview of different feminist approaches. See also Phyllis Trible, *God and the Rhetoric of Sexuality* (Philadelphia: Fortress, 1978), and Letty Russell, *Human Liberation in a Feminist Perspective* (Philadelphia: Westminster Press, 1974).

[40]Charles H. Kraft, *Christianity in Culture* (Maryknoll, N.Y.: Orbis, 1979). See pp. 280-89.

[41]I understand this as one of the major points argued persuasively in Dyrness, *Learning About Theology from the Third World.*

[42]Nelly is a graduate student at Satya Wacana Christian University. She wrote out this story in Indonesian as one of the requirements for an ethics course I taught in the spring of 1992. With her permission I have paraphrased her story in English, shortening it and emphasizing portions that suit the needs of this chapter.

[43]These are elements in the well-known "hermeneutical circle."

Chapter 5: Cultural Value Orientations in Contrast

[1]The resignation occurred a year or two later and was not necessarily related to Robert's action. Later the dean returned to a high position. Robert subsequently left the university and returned to his home country. Names and minor details in this story have been changed.

[2]Actually conflicts bearing a family resemblance to this one occur regularly in Indonesia between Indonesians from different ethnic and ideological backgrounds.

[3]Montaigne, *Essais*, Great Book of the Western World (Chicago: Encyclopaedia Britannica), p. 240.

[4]Blaise Pascal, *Pensées*, Great Books of the Western World (Chicago: Encyclopaedia Britannica), p. 225.

[5]David W. Augsburger compiles a large number of these from different authors in *Pastoral Counseling Across Cultures* (Philadelphia: Westminster Press, 1986), p. 51. Of course not all writers agree. See, for example, Erik von Kuehnelt-Leddihn: "Is there such a thing as a natural law in the sense that we all 'naturally' reject murder, lies, deceit, wanton cruelty, adultery, theft, or contempt of parents? As a world traveler and student of ethnology I deny this in the face of a certain Christian theological tradition" ("Jews, Christians, and Gentiles," *National Review* 35 [October 14, 1983]: 1282).

[6]John R. Snarey, "Cross-Cultural Universality of Social-Moral Development: A Critical Review of Kohlbergian Research," *Psychological Bulletin* 97, no. 2 (1985): 202. Compare Lawrence Kohlberg, *The Philosophy of Moral Development*, vol. 1 of *Essays in Moral Development* (New York: Harper & Row, 1981).

[7]See, for example, Carol Gilligan, *In a Different Voice* (Cambridge, Mass.: Harvard University Press, 1982). Snarey cites a large number of critics in the social sciences ("Cross-Cultural Universality"). From the perspective of ethics, see Anthony Cortese, *Ethnic Ethics: The Restructuring of Moral Theory* (New York: State University of New York Press, 1990). Cortese's whole book is an extended argument against Kohlberg's theory.

[8]Kenneth Gergen and Mary Gergen, *Social Psychology* (New York: Harcourt Brace Jovanovich, 1981), p. 229.

[9]Gilligan, *In a Different Voice*, pp. 62-63.

[10]Snarey, "Cross-Cultural Universality," pp. 202-32.

[11]Quoted in John Snarey, "A Question of Morality," *Psychology Today*, June 1987. This answer does not fit any of Kohlberg's categories.

[12]See Alasdair MacIntyre, *Whose Justice? Which Rationality?* (Notre Dame, Ind.: University of Notre Dame Press, 1988). "Not only do we have to understand each philosophy as a whole, so that the distinctive conceptions of justice and practical rationality elaborated by each thinker are understood as parts of that whole, but we have to understand each philosophy in terms of the historical context of tradition, social order, and conflict out of which it emerged" (pp. 389-90).

[13]Geert Hofstede, *Culture's Consequences: International Differences in Work Related Values* (Beverly Hills, Calif.: Sage, 1980), p. 19.

[14]D. J. Bem, *Beliefs, Attitudes and Human Affairs* (Belmont, Calif.: Brooks/Cole, 1970), p. 16.

[15]Hofstede, *Culture's Consequences*, p. 15.

[16]Clyde Kluckhohn, "Universal Categories of Culture," in *Anthropology Today*, ed. S. Tax

(Chicago: University of Chicago Press, 1962), pp. 317-18. Compare S. Ortner, "Anthropological Theory Since 1960," *Comparative Studies in Society and History* 26 (1984): 126.

[17]Clifford Geertz, *The Interpretation of Culture* (New York: Random House, 1973), p. 49.

[18]Even Adam, before the creation of Eve, was in relation to God. Abraham appears almost like a rugged individualist who sets off to find himself in isolation from community. But in fact he was already the sheik of a large clan. Abraham's real identity was found in God's promise that through his offspring all the inhabitants of the world would be blessed. Abraham believed God's promise of an enduring community and staked his identity on it. For an interesting discussion of the difference between the "traditional" and "modern" conceptions of the self, see Peter Berger, "On the Obsolescence of the Concept of Honor," in *Revisions*, ed. Stanley Hauerwas and Alasdair MacIntyre (Notre Dame, Ind.: University of Notre Dame Press, 1983), pp. 172-81.

[19]Catholic moral theologians, perhaps because of the influence of Aristotle (through Thomas Aquinas), have long stressed the primacy of the human community. It is the church or the community that stands before the judgment seat of Christ. "There is no salvation outside the Church" (Clement of Rome). In contrast, the Protestant Reformers, with their emphasis on individual election and guilt, tended to be more individualistic. The individual stands naked before God. Perhaps this is a lingering influence of Neo-Platonism with its stress on discovery of the true and the real beyond ephemeral appearances. Salvation is not found through entering into the mundane reality of a flesh-and-blood community but is an individual experience of personal rebirth.

[20]Shalom H. Schwartz and Wolfgang Bilsky, "Toward a Universal Psychological Structure of Human Values," *Journal of Personality and Social Psychology* 53, no. 3 (1987): 550-62.

[21]These are hedonism, achievement, power, self-direction, stimulation, maturity, benevolence, security, restrictive conformity, tradition and spirituality (Shalom H. Schwartz, Department of Psychology, Hebrew University, Jerusalem).

[22]Obvious examples include John 3:16-17 and Galatians 3:28.

[23]Max L. Stackhouse, *Creeds, Society and Human Rights: A Study in Three Cultures* (Grand Rapids, Mich.: Eerdmans, 1984), pp. 7-8.

[24]Other examples include Konrad Lorenz, *On Aggression* (New York: Harcourt, Brace and World, 1966) and Desmond Morris, *The Naked Ape* (New York: McGraw-Hill, 1967). As early as 1959 Dorothy Lee wrote a convincing critique of basic-need approaches to cultural values. See Dorothy Lee, *Freedom and Culture* (Englewood Cliffs, N.J.: Prentice-Hall, 1959).

[25]Florence Kluckhohn and Fred Strodtbeck, *Variations in Value Orientations* (Evanston, Ill.: Row, Peterson, 1961), p. 12.

[26]For a more complete discussion of various attempts to create models or maps of cultural value orientations, see the appendix at the back of this volume. Included in the discussion is my own chart of twelve categories of value orientations conceived as continuums. My model suggests ethical implications of different cultural value orientations.

[27]Hofstede, *Culture's Consequences*.

[28]Marvin K. Mayers, *Christianity Confronts Culture*, 2nd ed. (Grand Rapids, Mich.: Zondervan, 1987), pp. 149-54.

[29]Sherwood G. Lingenfelter and Marvin K. Mayers, *Ministering Cross-Culturally* (Grand Rapids, Mich.: Baker Book House, 1986). The usefulness of this book is multiplied by the abundant examples that show the categories lived out in practices of the Yapese

people. The book also contains biblical reflections on how biblical society tended toward the non-Western ends of the continuums. The reflections on how Jesus was fully incarnated in his culture yet also fulfilled the "Western" ideals when important values were at stake are also interesting, if sometimes a bit simplistic. Sherwood Lingenfelter's more recent book *Transforming Culture* (Grand Rapids, Mich.: Baker Book House, 1992) uses a far more sophisticated model of value orientations based on Mary Douglas's concepts of grid and group. Unfortunately the model is too complex to be helpful in the space of this chapter. See Mary Douglas, "Cultural Bias," in *The Active Voice* (London: Routledge & Kegan Paul, 1982).

30MacIntyre, *Whose Justice?* pp. 394-95.

31John Dewey, *How We Think* (New York: D. C. Heath, 1933), p. 16, as quoted in Mayers, *Christianity Confronts Culture*, p. 293.

32Crosscultural orientations toward time have been extensively studied by Edward T. Hall. See *The Silent Language* (Garden City, N.Y.: Doubleday, 1959) and *Beyond Culture* (Garden City, N.Y.: Anchor/Doubleday, 1976).

33Augsburger, *Pastoral Counseling*, pp. 111-43. Augsburger's book may be the most interesting work on crosscultural ethics from a Christian perspective that I have come across. Ironically, his chapter five, on values, is less useful than other parts of the book— perhaps because he suffers in this chapter from the counselor's value-free syndrome! For example, he has an interesting discussion of the relative merits of the Indian caste system of hierarchy and the American idea of equality. While he is helpful in pointing out that there are positive values available in the caste system that are not found in American society, I am surprised that he offers no normative conclusions on the evils of caste.

34Lucian W. Pye, *Asian Power and Politics* (Cambridge, Mass.: Harvard University Press, 1985), p. viii.

35See C. Osgood, G. Suci and P. Tannenbaum, *The Measurement of Meaning* (Urbana: University of Illinois Press, 1957). A concise summary of the findings is available in Charles Osgood, "Explorations in Semantic Space: A Personal Diary," *Journal of Social Issues* 27, no. 4 (1971): 5-64.

36Osgood, "Explorations in Semantic Space," p. 37.

37See Richard W. Brislin, *Cross-Cultural Encounters* (New York: Pergamon, 1981), p. 34.

Chapter 6: Strange Communications

1*Selected Writings of Edward Sapir*, ed. David G. Mandelbaum (Berkeley: University of California Press, 1949), p. 162; quoted in John C. Condon and Fathi S. Yousef, *An Introduction to Intercultural Communication* (Indianapolis: Bobbs Merrill, 1975), p. 171. This hypothesis has provoked vigorous debate among linguists. Linguists such as Noam Chomsky, J. J. Katz and W. L. Chafe argue that there are universal "deep structures" of language and that language is primarily interpretive. Condon and Yousef include an interesting discussion of this debate; they themselves accept a revised version of the Sapir-Whorf hypothesis as proposed by Dorothy Lee, *Freedom and Culture* (Englewood Cliffs, N.J.: Prentice-Hall, 1959).

2As quoted in E. Thomas Brewster and Elizabeth Brewster, *Language Learning Is Communication—Is Ministry!* (Pasadena, Calif.: Lingua House, 1984), p. 1. Of course language learning is often best accomplished in the midst of other tasks and should not be equated with classroom or library study.

[3]Ronald Storrs, *Orientations,* as quoted in Craig Storti, *The Art of Crossing Cultures* (Yarmouth, Maine: Intercultural, 1990), pp. 85-86.

[4]Ray L. Birdwhistell, *Kinesics and Context* (Philadelphia: University of Pennsylvania Press, 1970).

[5]Paul Theroux, *Riding the Iron Rooster* (New York: Ivy Books, 1989).

[6]A survey of attitudes to happiness throughout Asia, carried out by an organization in Hong Kong, found Indonesians to be apparently the happiest. An astonishing 94 percent of Indonesians surveyed said that they were happy. The unhappiest in Asia were the Japanese. Yet Japan is the richest nation and Indonesia is among the poorest in Asia (as measured by per capita income). It makes you wonder if there is an inverse correlation between wealth and happiness! Reported in the *Jakarta Post,* May 28, 1993, p. 1.

[7]Cited in Richard Brislin, Kenneth Cushner, Craig Cherrie and Mahealani Yong, *Intercultural Interactions* (Beverly Hills, Calif.: Sage, 1986), p. 93.

[8]William S. Condon and W. D. Ogston, "A Segmentation of Behavior," *Journal of Psychiatric Research* 5 (1967): 221-35. Cited in Condon and Yousef, *Introduction to Intercultural Communication,* pp. 127-28. Studies of unconscious eye movements give new meaning to the line from the song "You can't hide them lying eyes!"

[9]Condon and Yousef, *Introduction to Intercultural Communication,* pp. 127-28.

[10]Ibid., p. 128.

[11]Edward T. Hall, *The Silent Language* (Garden City, N.Y.: Doubleday, 1959), p. 222.

[12]Edward T. Hall, *The Hidden Dimension* (Garden City, N.Y.: Anchor/Doubleday, 1969), is a fascinating study of "proxemics," or the human use of space.

[13]Arthur Grimble, *A Pattern of the Islands,* quoted in Storti, *Art of Crossing Cultures,* pp. 23-24.

[14]Anthony J. Gittins, *Gifts and Strangers: Meeting the Challenge of Inculturation* (Mahwah, N.J.: Paulist, 1989), p. 117.

[15]Reported by David Rosenberg in the late 1970s and quoted by Miriam Adeney, " 'We Have No Sons': What You Should Know About Philippine-American Relations," in *All Things to All Men,* ed. Evelyn Miranda-Feliciano (Quezon City: New Day, 1988), p. 30. Former President Ferdinand Marcos's practice of making money in the Philippines and sending it overseas was copied from his American sponsors. While the balance of foreign ownership of Filipino property has decreased in recent years, American influence in the economy is still massively evident.

[16]See Jonathan J. Bonk, *Missions and Money: Affluence as a Western Missionary Problem* (Maryknoll, N.Y.: Orbis, 1991).

[17]Arnold van Gennep, *The Rites of Passage* (London: Routledge & Kegan Paul, 1960, rev. 1977), pp. 26-38. Cited in Gittins, *Gifts and Strangers,* pp. 124-26.

[18]Gittins, *Gifts and Strangers,* pp. 114-15.

[19]Ibid., p. 124.

[20]This was a remark during a lecture in Chicago to Lutheran and Presbyterian mission candidates on July 6, 1991.

[21]Gittins, *Gifts and Strangers,* pp. 125-26.

[22]In Hebrews 13:2 hospitality to strangers is urged for the very reason that they may turn out to be angels. Also see Genesis 18—19.

[23]Z. D. Gurevitch, "The Other Side of Dialogue: On Making the Other Strange and the Experience of Otherness," *American Journal of Sociology* 93 (March 1988): 1179-99.

[24]T. S. Eliot, "Burnt Norton," from *The Four Quartets.*

[25]Geertz, *Interpretation of Culture,* p. 13.

[26]*George MacDonald Anthology,* ed. C. S. Lewis (London: Geoffrey Bles, 1946), p. 29. I have changed the generic male language.

Chapter 7: Ethical Theory and Bribery

[1]This does not necessarily mean bribery is the most important ethical problem, but it fits the image of an ethical problem for many of the people I interviewed. Unlike poverty or injustice, it is a common problem that demands an immediate moral decision.

[2]Case study by Keith Hinton in *Case Studies in Missions,* ed. Paul G. Hiebert and Frances Hiebert (Grand Rapids, Mich.: Baker Book House, 1987), pp. 138-40. I have adjusted the money figures to reflect approximate values in 1993.

[3]*Annals of a Quiet Neighborhood,* chap. 9. Quoted in *George MacDonald: An Anthology,* ed. C. S. Lewis (London: Geoffrey Bles, 1946), p. 102.

[4]Stanley Hauerwas, *Vision and Virtue* (Notre Dame, Ind.: University of Notre Dame Press, 1981), p. 124.

[5]An interesting incidence of this principle as expressed in the Old Testament law is in Deuteronomy 25:1-3. Punishment is by flogging (possibly a more humane punishment than years of imprisonment), but a limit is placed on the punishment "lest he be degraded in your eyes." The type of punishment is cultural, but the limitation on it is theological. Other examples of laws that protect the dignity of the individual include Exodus 22:21-27; 23:4-9; Leviticus 19:9-10, 13-18, 23-25, 33-36; Deuteronomy 14:28-29; 15:12-14; 20:5-7, 19-20; 21:10-14; 22:1-4; 23:24-25; 24:5-6, 10-15, 17-22; 25:4; 27:18-19, 25. Organizations like Amnesty International work on the assumption that minimal human rights like freedom from torture are a crosscultural absolute. Of course there are widespread crosscultural differences over what constitutes a full "human." Some would functionally exclude slaves, women, twins, people with physical or mental disabilities, fetuses and so on. The Bible does not exclude any of these categories from human being.

[6]For an example of this view of bribery see Paul G. Hiebert, *Cultural Anthropology* (Philadelphia: J. B. Lippincott, 1976), pp. 260-61. Hiebert's view is also followed by Marvin K. Mayers.

[7]John T. Noonan Jr., *Bribes* (New York: Macmillan, 1984), pp. 696-98.

[8]An example of this is the way the abortion debate is defined. One tradition talks about "murdering unborn babies," and another tradition talks about eliminating unwanted fetal tissue. How the act of abortion is described determines the moral conclusions.

[9]The categories of "freedom to-freedom not to" and "fear-force" as concepts relevant to the moral evaluation of a bribe were suggested to me by Anthony J. Gittins after he read the manuscript of this chapter.

[10]Anthony J. Gittins, *Gifts and Strangers: Meeting the Challenge of Inculturation* (New York: Paulist, 1989), especially chap. 4, "Gifts, Guile and the Gospel," pp. 84-110. Gittins cites Marcel Mauss, *The Gift* (London: Cohen and West, 1970), as a major source of his ideas on gift-giving.

[11]Gittins, *Gifts and Strangers,* p. 87.

[12]This statement is greatly oversimplified. In fact the line between a gift and a bribe is less than crystal-clear, even in the United States. The legal system has attempted to make it clear, but the presence of hundreds of lobbyists with large expense accounts on Capitol Hill underlines the ambiguity in the system.

[13]Noonan, *Bribes*. In spite of the immense historical and crosscultural research displayed in Noonan's book, he shows surprisingly little interest in the cultural meaning of gifts. His legal approach to knowledge is grounded in natural law theory, which shows a strong proclivity for absolute definitions of right and wrong.

[14]William K. Frankena, *Ethics*, 2nd ed. (Englewood Cliffs, N.J.: Prentice-Hall, 1973), p. 55.

[15]See for example, Norman Geisler, *Ethics: Alternatives and Issues* (Grand Rapids, Mich.: Zondervan, 1971).

[16]This surprising conclusion was reached by both Mahatma Gandhi and Thomas Merton. This does not mean they thought killing was ever good, only that in some situations there might be something worse. In the face of horrendous injustice, if you cannot achieve nonviolent resistance, even resisting violently might be better than doing nothing at all.

[17]"If we say that we have no sin, we deceive ourselves, and the truth is not in us. If we confess our sins, he who is faithful and just will forgive us our sins and cleanse us from all unrighteousness" (1 Jn 1:8-9).

[18]E. Glenn, D. Witmeyer and K. Stevenson, "Cultural Styles of Persuasion," *International Journal of Intercultural Relations*, 1977, p. 64.

[19]Some of these ideas came out of an excellent conversation I had with Samuel Escobar at the 1989 Lausanne II Congress in Manila.

[20]Pak Nico Kana of Satya Wacana Christian University in Salatiga, Java, made this statement in a private conversation with me in November 1989.

[21]For a spirited attack on the evil power of money in missions see Jonathan J. Bonk, *Missions and Money: Affluence as a Western Missionary Problem* (Maryknoll, N.Y.: Orbis, 1991).

[22]See Noonan, *Bribes*, p. 705.

Chapter 8: The Ethical Challenge of Other Religions

[1]John Hick, Paul Knitter and others have adopted the word *pluralism* to describe their own distinctive theology of religions in contrast to *inclusivism* and *exclusivism*. While I do not accept the terms of the debate, in this chapter I generally follow the recent use of the term *pluralism*. See John Hick and Paul F. Knitter, eds., *The Myth of Christian Uniqueness* (Maryknoll, N.Y.: Orbis, 1987), and the polemical response, Gavin D'Costa, ed., *Christian Uniqueness Reconsidered* (Maryknoll, N.Y.: Orbis, 1990).

[2]This has been widely discussed by authors such as Robert Bellah, John Coleman and Roger Nesbitt.

[3]A useful summary of various Christian understandings of "the powers" is Thomas H. McAlpine, *Facing the Powers: What Are the Options?* (Monrovia, Calif.: MARC, 1991).

[4]John Hick, "The Non-absoluteness of Christianity," in *The Myth of Christian Uniqueness*, ed. John Hick and Paul F. Knitter (Maryknoll, N.Y.: Orbis, 1987), p. 30.

[5]See E. M. Forster, *A Passage to India* (New York: Harcourt, Brace and World, 1924). The book recounts the interactions of English colonial officials with their Indian subjects prior to Indian independence. See also Langdon Gilkey, "Plurality and Its Theological

Implications," in *The Myth of Christian Uniqueness,* ed. John Hick and Paul F. Knitter (Maryknoll, N.Y.: Orbis, 1987), pp. 39-40.

[6]This is a major point in John Milbank, "The End of Dialogue," in *Christian Uniqueness Reconsidered,* ed. Gavin D'Costa (Maryknoll, N.Y.: Orbis, 1990).

[7]An interesting study of the use of the exodus story in revolutionary political movements throughout history is found in Michael Walzer, *Exodus and Revolution* (New York: Basic Books, 1985).

[8]Joseph Campbell with Bill Moyers, *The Power of Myth* (New York: Doubleday, 1988), pp. 65-66.

[9]An early part of the original American dream was to be a city set on a hill, an example of peace and justice for all the world to see.

[10]This term has been widely used. See H. Richard Niebuhr, *Christ and Culture* (New York: Harper & Brothers, 1951), and Nicholas Wolterstorff, *Until Justice and Peace Embrace* (Grand Rapids, Mich.: Eerdmans, 1983). Wolterstorff helpfully engages in a crosscultural ethical dialogue between his Dutch Calvinist tradition and liberation theology, using the image of world transformation as an integration point.

[11]Two examples of a sensitive listening to other perspectives in theology are William A. Dyrness, *Learning About Theology from the Third World* (Grand Rapids, Mich.: Zondervan, 1990), and William A. Dyrness, *Invitation to Cross-Cultural Theology* (Grand Rapids, Mich.: Zondervan, 1992).

[12]Gilkey, "Plurality and Its Theological Implications," p. 44.

[13]Ibid., p. 47. From the perspective of a Christian living in a Muslim country, it is ironic that Gilkey chooses the threat of fundamentalist right-wing pretensions to theocracy as the grave threat that we need to resist at all costs from an absolute moral standpoint. The most fantastic dreams of a Jerry Falwell are child's play compared to the everyday reality of Muslim attempts to control the lives of non-Muslims. Indonesia may be the world's most benign Muslim state. But even here Islam is a weapon of domination and control far beyond the worst threat of fundamentalism in America.

[14]It must be admitted that Christian praxis was not a very likely source of the struggle for the human rights of non-Christians during much of Christian history. Jews and Muslims especially can tell many stories of periods of severe persecution. For example, in Calvinist South Africa, Muslims had to worship in secret because there was a death sentence for anyone who taught a different religion. See Taufik Ismail, "Tuan Guru di Afrika Selatan," unpublished paper quoted in *The Jakarta Post,* June 19, 1993. Nevertheless, today "Christian" countries guard the rights of non-Christians far more rigorously than Muslim countries guard the rights of non-Muslims. The rise of the Western, and increasingly worldwide, concern about human rights has complex origins. Christian commitments to essential human equality were certainly one of its sources.

[15]Kenneth Surin, "A 'Politics of Speech': Religious Pluralism in the Age of the McDonald's Hamburger," in *Christian Uniqueness Reconsidered,* ed. Gavin D'Costa (Maryknoll, N.Y.: Orbis, 1990), pp. 192-212. Surin's essay has an academic, slightly Marxist polemical flavor. The brilliance of his argument is somewhat marred by the *ad hominem* tinge. It makes it interesting for the nonpluralist but will not please his opponents.

[16]Ibid., p. 209.

[17]Arif Dirlik, "Culturalism as Hegemonic Ideology and Liberating Practice," *Cultural Critique* 6 (1987): 13-50.

[18]B. Chaturvedi and M. Sykes, *The Life of C. F. Andrews* (New York: Harper & Brothers, 1950), p. 65. Cited in A. K. Cragg, *The Christian and Other Religions* (Oxford: Mowbrays, 1977), p. 68.

[19]This perspective is clearly articulated in Robert N. Bellah, *Beyond Belief: Essays on Religion in a Post-traditional World* (New York: Harper & Row, 1970). More recently Bellah appears to have moved toward a more definitive affirmation of a Christian account of reality.

[20]See Robert N. Bellah's early article on the evolution of religion in ibid. Bellah is currently working on a book on the evolution of religion.

[21]David Brown, *A New Threshold* (London: British Council of Churches, 1976), pp. 21, 23.

[22]Raymond Panikkar, *The Unknown Christ of Hinduism* (Bangalore: Asian Trading Corporation, 1987).

[23]Clark H. Pinnock, *A Wideness in God's Mercy* (Grand Rapids, Mich.: Zondervan, 1992).

[24]John Sanders, *No Other Name* (Grand Rapids, Mich.: Eerdmans, 1992).

[25]Karl Barth, as quoted in John Hick and Brian Hebblewaite, *Christianity and Other Religions* (London: Fount, 1988), p. 42. See Karl Barth, *The Epistle to the Romans,* trans. Edwin C. Hoskyns (London: Oxford University Press, 1933).

[26]Hendrik Kraemer, *The Christian Message in a Non-Christian World* (London: Edinburgh House, 1938), p. 123.

[27]Ken Gnanakan, *The Pluralistic Predicament* (Bangalore: Theological Book Trust, 1992), pp. 45-46.

[28]Clark Pinnock in *Christian Faith and Practice in the Modern World,* ed. Mark A. Noll and David F. Wells (Grand Rapids, Mich.: Eerdmans, 1988), p. 166.

[29]David L. Edwards and John R. W. Stott, *Essentials* (London: Hodder & Stoughton, 1988), p. 327; also published as *Evangelical Essentials: A Liberal-Evangelical Dialogue* (Downers Grove, Ill.: InterVarsity Press, 1988).

[30]Since Lynn White's famous essay "The Historic Roots of Our Ecologic Crisis," *Science* 155 (1957), this has become a commonplace accusation in the environmental movement. Some feminists also see in Judeo-Christian religion the roots of the worldwide oppression of women.

[31]"Not many of you were wise by human standards. . . . But God chose what is foolish in the world to shame the wise" (1 Cor 1:26-27).

[32]Quoted by Jürgen Moltmann in *Christian Uniqueness Reconsidered,* ed. Gavin D'Costa (Maryknoll, N.Y.: Orbis, 1990), p. 154.

[33]Pascal suggested that in the absence of certainty it is better to believe than not, because if Christianity turns out to be true you gain eternal life. If it is false you still win, since the personal and social effects of faith are preferable to those of unbelief.

[34]Such an evaluation of truth is itself based on a Christian worldview. Then again, it may also stem from an ambivalent view of the social benefits of institutional Christianity.

Chapter 9: Women and Men as Strangers

[1]For a discussion of the role of categories in crosscultural interactions, see Richard W. Brislin, *Cross-Cultural Encounters* (New York: Pergamon, 1981), pp. 52-108.

[2]Brislin calls this "salient information." Ibid., p. 78.

[3]Stereotypes may be derived from personal contacts with one or two Australians or Dutch, distant observation of the strange behavior of tourists, history lessons in school about

Dutch colonialism and of course dozens of American movies, mostly of the *Rambo* or *Basic Instinct* type. It is remarkable how all the worst American movies seem to be shown all over the world.

[4]In an Australian documentary on the effect of American TV (1993), one commentator suggested that Australian youth now think that *Beverly Hills 90210* (also shown on Indonesian TV) is the way to live. Another person on the same show commented that America is the first empire in history that has succeeded in conquering the whole world and imposing its culture without sending any armies. Fortunately that is an overstatement, but it makes a good point. In the space of just a few years, Indonesians who formerly had very little contact with Western culture have become exposed to nightly American television programs.

[5]There are of course exceptions and anomalies. Women in many cultures routinely uncover their breasts in the context of breastfeeding. Dress codes are usually more "modern" (Western) in cities and at tourist attractions.

[6]This story is related in Gary Althen, *American Ways* (Yarmouth, Maine: Intercultural, 1988), p. 89.

[7]Different notions of privacy are well illustrated by the story of a conservative woman missionary who was on a remote island where the only bathing place was a pool in the river. In desperation for privacy to take a bath, she waited till the middle of the day when everyone took a rest. Then she crept down to the river and took off her clothes. When she looked up she found that the entire village had come down to watch. They wanted to see what a white woman looked like under all her funny clothes!

[8]In some heavily touristed locations it hardly seems to matter because there are so many foreigners following the trends of their own cultures.

[9]Clothing relative to status is a tricky area, depending on the culture. In one city where I was advised not to wear shorts, I noticed that many local men wore shorts. On questioning the advice, I was told that they were lower-class men. To be more respectable I should wear "trousers." Since I was unconcerned about perceptions of my status in that situation, I felt quite free to wear shorts. If my role there had required me to interact as a professional, I would have worn trousers. Farmers wear short shorts while working in the muddy paddy fields in Indonesia. But if I wore shorts to class, my students would be scandalized (or at least highly amused)!

[10]Theories of prehistoric "matriarchal" societies have a long history but lack any clear confirmation and are generally discounted by anthropologists today. See Michelle Zimbalist Rosaldo and Louise Lamphere, eds., *Woman, Culture and Society* (Stanford, Calif.: Stanford University Press, 1974), pp. 2-4.

[11]This is a real example drawn from field work in West Africa done by Mary Stewart Van Leeuwen, *Gender and Grace* (Downers Grove, Ill.: InterVarsity Press, 1990), pp. 113-14.

[12]Paul Starr, *The Social Transformation of American Medicine* (New York: Basic Books, 1984).

[13]Even warfare is not an invariably male activity. Myths of women warriors abound, and there are clear historical exceptions to the rule, as in the case of St. Joan of Arc. Twentieth-century revolutionary struggles such as in China, Indonesia and Israel have included prominent participation by women. Modern Western military forces are now undergoing rapid structural change to bring about equal opportunity for participation in warfare. But it is safe to say that in all "traditional" societies, warfare was an exclusively male domain.

[14]Cited from a United Nations report in Francesca Fearon, "The Slow March of Asian Women," *World Press Review,* August 1987, p. 56. For many more alarming statistics see Ruth Leger Sivard, *Women: A World Survey* (Washington, D.C.: World Priorities, 1985).

[15]Cited in David W. Augsburger, *Pastoral Counseling Across Cultures* (Philadelphia: Westminster Press, 1986), p. 214. The vivid imagery of this quote gives us a hint why so many millions of people followed Mao in his revolution for liberation.

[16]Simone de Beauvoir, *The Second Sex,* as cited in Rosaldo and Lamphere, eds., *Woman, Culture and Society,* p. xiii.

[17]Betty Friedan, *The Feminine Mystique* (New York: Norton, 1963).

[18]See Stanley Hauerwas, *A Community of Character* (Notre Dame, Ind.: University of Notre Dame Press, 1981), pp. 155-95.

[19]For an interesting review of the theories from a Christian perspective, see Van Leeuwen, *Gender and Grace,* especially chaps. 4—6.

[20]John C. Condon and Fathi S. Yousef, *An Introduction to Intercultural Communication* (Indianapolis: Bobbs Merrill, 1975), pp. 73-74. See also Florence R. Kluckhohn and Fred L. Strodtbeck, *Variations in Value Orientations* (Westport, Conn.: Greenwood, 1973), pp. 17-19.

[21]This complexity is well illustrated by the torturous debate surrounding the issues of "date rape" and "sexual harassment."

[22]In the Himalayan Mountains of north Pakistan we found a different culture. Women moved around freely without veils and modestly interacted with foreigners in spite of a language barrier. One evening we had dinner with a village family and were amazed to see all the members of the family eating together and serving each other regardless of sex. Having been only in public places, we had never seen men and women even sitting together in the same room, let alone eating together.

[23]There is no statistical support for this hypothesis. It was suggested in a confidential interview with a Western male who has lived for many years in various Middle Eastern countries. His estimate applied to what he referred to as "tentmaker missionaries."

[24]The event occurred many years ago in a small town. This story calls to mind the account of Jesus in conversation with the Samaritan woman at the well (Jn 4:4-42). The disciples were astonished not that he was talking to a Samaritan but that he was talking to a woman. Jesus repeatedly broke conventional taboos that marginalized women.

[25]Quoted in Augsburger, *Pastoral Counseling,* p. 215.

[26]Laws of Manu, 328 and 330, as cited in Linda Gupta, "Kali the Savior," in *After Patriarchy: Feminist Transformations of the World Religions,* ed. Paula M. Cooey, William R. Eakin and Jay B. McDaniel (Maryknoll, N.Y.: Orbis, 1991), pp. 18-19.

[27]E. Lord in *Examples of Cross-Cultural Problems Encountered by Americans Working Overseas: An Instructor's Handbook* (Alexandria, Va.: HumRRO, 1965), pp. 2-27. Cited in Pierre Casse, *Training for the Cross-Cultural Mind* (Washington, D.C.: Society for Intercultural Education, Training and Research, 1980), p. 54.

[28]College-educated women in America make about 55 percent as much as men with the same level of education, and women managers average only 50 percent of the income earned by men in the same types of jobs. See "Where Are Women Working?" unsigned editorial in *New Ministries* (Richmond, Calif.), March 1985. The "glass ceiling" that prevents women from rising above the levels of middle management has been widely discussed in the American media.

[29]See Nancy Tanner, "Matrifocality in Indonesia and Africa and Among Black Americans," in *Woman, Culture and Society,* ed. Michelle Zimbalist Rosaldo and Louise Lamphere (Stanford, Calif.: Stanford University Press, 1974), pp. 129-56.

[30]Hildred Geertz, *The Javanese Family: A Study of Kinship and Socialization* (New York: Free Press of Glencoe, 1961), pp. 78-79. Cited in Tanner, "Matrifocality," p. 135.

[31]The prevalence of this problem was evident in an international conference on "Role Conflicts of Women in Asia" held at Hanchow University in China in November 1993, as reported by Frances Adeney. See her paper "Ideology and Role Conflicts of Women in Indonesia," available from the author.

[32]Reported by Fearon, "Slow March of Asian Women," p. 56.

[33]Tanner, "Matrifocality," p. 151.

[34]See Carlien Patricia Woodcroft-Lee, "Separate but Equal: Indonesian Muslim Perceptions of the Roles of Women," in *Women's Work and Women's Roles: Economics and Everyday life in Indonesia, Malaysia and Singapore,* ed. Lenore Manderson (Canberra: Australian National University, 1983), p. 179.

[35]Sivard, *Women,* p. 22.

[36]Woodcroft-Lee, "Separate but Equal," p. 177.

[37]Women's life expectancy at birth in both Indonesia and Pakistan is fifty-four years. Sivard, *Women,* p. 6. The primary cause of this low rate is poverty. The life expectancy of men is not much better. Life expectancy of women in Western countries is about seventy-eight years.

[38]For a fuller explanation of this interpretation, see Van Leeuwen, *Gender and Grace,* pp. 33-51.

[39]I use the word *lead* very broadly to include lecture, head a committee, attend a prestigeous conference, preach, make an important report, take an important client, represent the organization, etc.

[40]See her autobiography: Pauline Hamilton, *To a Different Drum* (Singapore: Overseas Missionary Fellowship Books, 1984). My own conversion was deeply influenced by her example and personal care.

[41]Paulo Freire, *Pedagogy of the Oppressed* (New York: Herder & Herder, 1970), p. 40.

[42]Augustine, *The City of God,* trans. Marcus Dods, Great Books of the Western World (Chicago: Encyclopaedia Britannica, 1957), p. 519 (19.11).

Chapter 10: The Unity of Personal and Social Ethics

[1]Linda Adams (not her real name) wrote this case study for a graduate course I taught on crosscultural ethics at New College Berkeley, fall 1990. Names and minor details have been changed. "Mabuk" is a pseudonym for a very real African country.

[2]This emphasis has been a hallmark of the ministry of John Perkins in Pasadena, California. Perkins urges black and white middle-class Christians to move back into the inner city and by their presence demonstrate the reconciling truth of the gospel

[3]Joe Holland and Peter Henriot, *Social Analysis* (Washington, D.C.: Center of Concern/ Maryknoll, N.Y.: Orbis, 1983), p. 14.

[4]This is necessarily oversimplified. On the injustice of the prison system see Daniel W. Van Ness, *Crime and Its Victims* (Downers Grove, Ill.: InterVarsity Press, 1986), and Bernard T. Adeney, "Living on the Edge: Ethics Inside San Quentin," *Journal of Law and Religion* 6, no. 2 (1988). The Rodney King case showed that when evil is exposed, whites

and blacks can be mobilized to protest police repression.

⁵In this limited sense Karl Marx was right: "Religion is the opiate of the masses." Prayer is far too complex to reduce to the terms of this short discussion. I do not mean that only prayer that is linked to the struggle for justice is valid. Every form of honest communication with God is good. There are as many kinds of prayer as there are purposes for relating to God. My point in this section is only that prayer as a substitute for obedience is sin.

⁶In ethics and biblical studies there is an interesting discussion about whether Paul's use of these terms applies to personal spiritual beings (demons or evil spirits), social and political structures or some combination. See Thomas H. McAlpine, *Facing the Powers* (Monrovia, Calif.: MARC, 1991), for a nuanced discussion of various options. I am not sure the two poles are mutually exclusive. They may be two different ways of conceptualizing the same spiritual reality. I am unhappy with the current missiological preoccupation with demons. It is sensationalist and tends to objectify evil outside human volition. On the other hand, those who reject the possibility of personal evil beings and limit "the powers" to impersonal sociopolitical forces seem reductionist. Without evidence, they discount both the personal language of the Bible and the conviction of most of the non-Western world that evil spirits exist. Nonbelief in the world of spirits is a relatively recent Western faith.

⁷This idea is used by Michael Walzer as part of his argument for "just war theory" in *Just and Unjust Wars* (New York: Basic Books, 1977). The deontological element in ethics indicates that there are some evils that *must* be resisted no matter what the outcome or the odds of success.

⁸Reinhold Niebuhr, *Moral Man and Immoral Society* (New York: Scribner's, 1932), p. 81. In a personal conversation I had with John C. Bennett, who was a close friend and colleague of Niebuhr, Bennett recounted that "Reinie" regretted this statement later in his life. After seeing the idealism of first Hitler and then Stalin, he came to emphasize the importance of rational, planned action for justice. "Ultra-rational hopes and passions" were too dangerous. But I still like the quote. Passions and hopes are necessary, provided they are grounded in the values of the kingdom of God, are submissive to the spirit of Christ and do not involve a "teleological suspension of the ethical" to reach some ideal goal.

⁹Comment by Daniel Berrigan in a conversation.

¹⁰A few people did hear. One nuclear engineer from Lockheed quit his job and joined the group. How much little groups like ours influenced the major national nuclear debate of the 1980s that culminated in dramatic disarmament is impossible to know. We never dreamed of such success, and in any case disarmament came at the initiative of the Soviets.

¹¹For an interesting analysis of how Third World Christians view their Western associates, see Tim Stafford, *The Friendship Gap* (Downers Grove, Ill.: InterVarsity Press, 1984), chap. 7.

¹²I believe I heard this statement from the late Paul Ramsey or read it in one of his books.

¹³The idea is from Francis Schaeffer.

¹⁴See Max Weber, *The Protestant Ethic and the Spirit of Capitalism* (New York: Scribner's, 1958).

¹⁵The farmers won but the environment lost. The land they were given was meant to be

a green belt to protect the lake. This case was reported to me by Nico Kana of Satya Wacana Christian University. Satya Wacana faculty protested to the World Bank against the injustice done to the farmers.

[16]In biblical Hebrew and Greek, the words for "righteousness" and "justice" are the same words. The personal and the social were not separated. We may assume that Jesus had both concepts in mind in Matthew 5.

[17]Augustine, *The City of God,* trans. Marcus Dods, Great Books of the Western World (Chicago: Encyclopaedia Britannica, 1957), p. 515 (19.7).

Appendix: Maps or Models of Cultural Value Differences

[1]Ruth Benedict, *Patterns of Culture* (New York: Penguin, 1934). Benedict elaborated this typology in relation to Japan and the West in *The Chrysanthemum and the Sword* (New York: Meridian, 1946).

[2]See David W. Augsburger, *Pastoral Counseling Across Cultures* (Philadelphia: Westminster Press, 1986), pp. 111-43, for a good discussion of shame and guilt from a Christian perspective.

[3]Ibid., pp. 79-110.

[4]Talcott Parsons and Edward Shils, *Toward a General Theory of Action* (Cambridge, Mass.: Harvard University Press, 1951), p. 77.

[5]Florence Kluckhohn and Fred Strodtbeck, *Variations in Value Orientations* (Evanston, Ill.: Row, Peterson, 1961), p. 12. An interesting study that begins with Kluckhohn and Strodtbeck is John C. Condon and Fathi Yousef, *An Introduction to Intercultural Communication* (Indianapolis: Bobbs-Merrill, 1975). Condon and Yousef expand Kluckhohn and Strodtbeck's categories from five sets of three options to twenty-five sets.

[6]A. Inkeles and D. J. Levinson, "National Character : The Study of Modal Personality and Sociocultural Systems," in *The Handbook of Social Psychology,* ed. G. Linzey and E. Aronson (Reading, Mass.: Addison-Wesley, 1969), 4:447.

[7]Geert Hofstede, *Culture's Consequences: International Differences in Work Related Values* (Beverly Hills, Calif.: Sage, 1980).

[8]Ibid., p. 323.

Index